A History of the Lewis and Clark Journals

A History of the
Lewis and Clark Journals

by Paul Russell Cutright

University of Oklahoma Press
Norman

A PLAINS REPRINT

By Paul Russell Cutright

The Great Naturalists Explore South America (New York, 1943)
Theodore Roosevelt the Naturalist (New York, 1956)
Meriwether Lewis: Naturalist (Portland, Oregon, 1968)
Lewis and Clark: Pioneering Naturalists (Urbana, 1969)
A History of the Lewis and Clark Journals (Norman, 1976)

Library of Congress Cataloging in Publication Data

Cutright, Paul Russell, 1897–
A history of the Lewis and Clark journals.

Bibliography: p.
Includes index.
1. Lewis, Meriwether, 1774–1809. Original journals of the Lewis and Clark expedition, 1804–1806. 2. Historians—United States—Biography.
I. Title.
F592.4.C87   917.8'04'2   74–28244
ISBN 0–8061–1246–8 (hardcover)
ISBN 0–8061–3247–7 (paperback)

2 3 4 5 6 7 8 9 10 11

For
MARJORIE
and
JACKY

Preface

A well-known historian, writing in 1904, provided this intuitive comment: "The story of the records of the transcontinental exploration of Meriwether Lewis and William Clark (1803–1806) is almost as romantic as that of the great discovery itself."[1]

Looked at today, almost three-quarters of a century later, the story presents even more romance, for it has been greatly enlarged, livened, and illuminated, due to the accession of many new elements, including unexpected discoveries that have fired the imagination.

Many individuals, in addition to Lewis and Clark themselves, constitute the dramatis personae: Thomas Jefferson, third president of the United States, whose mind conceived the daring concept of exploring unmapped lands beyond the Mississippi; Sergeants John Ordway, Charles Floyd, and Patrick Gass, and Privates Joseph Whitehouse and Robert Frazer, all members—and journalists—of the party who accompanied Lewis and Clark; David M'Keehan, obscure schoolteacher and bookseller, who wormed himself into history by publishing, without credentials, Sergeant Gass's *Journal*, the first of the accounts to come from the press; Nicholas Biddle, Philadelphia lawyer, legislator, and man of letters, whose talents produced the first approved history of the Expedition; Charles Willson Peale, artist and museum proprietor, who painted portraits of west-

---

[1] Reuben Gold Thwaites, "The Story of Lewis and Clark's Journals," American Historical Association *Annual Report for Year 1903*, 58 Cong., 2 sess., *House Doc. 109*, Doc. No. 745, 107.

ern animals that Lewis and Clark had given him for display in his museum; Dr. Elliott Coues, surgeon, ornithologist, and consummate annotator, who in 1893 stimulated a rebirth of interest in the Expedition with his highly documented reissue of Biddle's edition; Reuben Gold Thwaites, author, historian, and editor, whose indefatigable labors resulted in the multivolumed work, *Original Journals of the Lewis and Clark Expedition,* which serves today as the basic, indispensable source for all Lewis and Clark scholars; Milo M. Quaife, writer and editor, who brought to press *The Journals of Captain Meriwether Lewis and Sergeant John Ordway*; Ernest Staples Osgood, historian, author, and editor, whose innate abilities in transcription, collation, and interpretation resulted in the publication of *The Field Notes of Captain William Clark, 1803–1805*; and Donald Jackson, writer, editor, and distinguished scholar, whose inspired industry presented historians with *Letters of the Lewis and Clark Expedition with Related Documents, 1783–1854.*

Indeed, the list of participants does not end here, for there were others—men like Dr. Benjamin Smith Barton, Alexander Wilson, Paul Allen, and Francis P. Harper, and such women as Julia Clark Voorhis and Lucile M. Kane. Though perhaps less important to the element of romance than those mentioned above, each played a consequential role, as will become obvious hereinafter.

Prominent learned institutions had substantial parts in the story, among them the American Philosophical Society, Academy of Natural Sciences of Philadelphia, State Historical Society of Wisconsin, Minnesota Historical Society, Historical Society of Pennsylvania, National Archives, Yale University Library, and Newberry Library.

Contributing, too, in some measure, were such one-time and current publishers as Bradford and Inskeep of Philadelphia; Zadok Cramer, Pittsburgh; Mathew Carey, Philadelphia; Longman, Hurst, Rees, Orme, and Brown of London; Francis P. Harper and Dodd, Mead and Company, both of New York City; Yale University Press, New Haven; and University of Illinois Press, Urbana.

Settings? Some of the world's leading cities: Philadelphia, Washington, New York, Pittsburgh, St. Louis, St. Paul, London, Paris, and Dublin; and some lesser ones, such as Weimar, Germany (now East Germany); Dordrecht, the Netherlands; Frederick, Maryland; and Lebanon (Libanon), Pennsylvania.

—2—

Portions of the story have previously been told, but generally piecemeal. They need to be brought together, tied into one coherent literary package, and this I have attempted to do.

But other portions of the story remain to be told. For instance, I am privileged herein to report on facts surrounding the discovery in 1966 in a Philadelphia bookstore of a new and heretofore unknown manuscript of Private Joseph Whitehouse—actually a paraphrase of his original journal—and to describe and evaluate its content.

I break new ground, too, as the result of my discovery in the archives of the American Philosophical Society of a significant collection of letters, more than one hundred of them, written during the period when the *Original Journals of Lewis and Clark* were being prepared for publication (1902–06). Reuben Gold Thwaites wrote the majority of them, with I. Minis Hays, secretary of the society, and Robert Dodd, of Dodd, Mead and Company, contributing others. Collectively, these reveal many facts heretofore unknown about this most important work, including invaluable commentary on Thwaites's discovery of Whitehouse's original journal and his finding in New York City of a mass of letters, journals, maps, and other documents, originally the property of William Clark, all previously unknown.

I have had available to me, also, another large collection of letters, the property of Yale University Library. These were written by Elliott Coues to Francis P. Harper in 1892–93, while Coues was editing and annotating Harper's reissue of Biddle's 1814 edition of Lewis and Clark. This correspondence, like that of Thwaites, constitutes another rich lode for the historian to mine. It heightens our admiration for Coues as editor, and also brings to light new information, such as his rediscovery of the original journals at the American Philosophical Society and his subsequent use of them.

I turn new earth in other ways. No one until now has attempted to appraise the writings *about* Lewis and Clark: the flood of books (retellings, fiction, juveniles, biographies) and the mountainous mass of periodical matter. In a chapter devoted entirely to this assay, I try to separate the wheat from the chaff, to underline errors and misrepresentations that, through perennial repetition, have tended to become accepted as facts, and to salute those authors who, in our opinion, have best exhibited objectivity, factual reporting, and sound scholarship.

In still another chapter I continue to disturb virgin soil by recognizing the contributions of illustrators to Lewis and Clark writings, among them Charles Willson Peale, Charles B. J. F. de St. Mémin, Karl Bodmer, George Catlin, and Charles M. Russell, whose engravings, water colors, paintings, crayons, and pencil sketches have added so much color to pages of books and articles, especially within recent years. In this same chapter, I do not overlook, too, the outstanding work of photographers, such as Albert and Jane Salisbury and Ingvard Henry Eide, in illustrating Lewis and Clark.

Additionally, being convinced that many Lewis and Clark enthusiasts are inadequately informed about the lives of such acknowledged scholarly contributors as Biddle, Coues, Thwaites, Quaife, Osgood, and Jackson, I have tried to do something about that by providing biographical data. If one wishes to evaluate the work of a man like Elliott Coues, for example, he is certainly in a far better position to do so if he knows that Coues in his day was probably the foremost ornithologist in the United States, that he spent many of his earlier years in the West, traveled in that time much of the Lewis and Clark trail, and subsequently worked as one of the editors of *The Century Dictionary*. He was thus well equipped—as were the others mentioned above—to undertake the task of editing Lewis and Clark. Since all students of the Expedition owe much to these men, I think it appropriate, and important, to bring their lives more closely into focus.

Finally, I have compiled a bibliography of the writings *about* Lewis and Clark. It runs to some two hundred and fifty titles and, though incomplete (to find and list each and every title would obviously be a near-to-impossible chore), it is a compilation that this writer would have liked to have available to him in the beginning of his studies about the Expedition.

—3—

World literature abounds in graphic, highly personal accounts of adventure, exploration, and discovery. We cite, for example, the classics of such men as Alexander von Humboldt and Henry Walter Bates about South America; Marco Polo and Sir Richard F. Burton about Asia; Alfred Russel Wallace about the Malay Archipelago; R. Gordon Cumming and John H. Speke about Africa; Coronado, Alexander Mackenzie, and Lewis and Clark about North America; Vilhjalmur Stefansson and Admiral Richard Byrd about polar ice-caps; and, of course, the accounts of Columbus and Darwin, which, because of the lustrous geographical and biological reports they contain, are regarded by many historians as transcending all others.

It has been my pleasure to read all of the above, as well as many other accounts which rival them in interest, provocative narration, or reportings of exceptional attainment. Yet none has so captured my fancy, and so fired my enthusiasm, as has the account by Lewis and Clark. And I am not alone in my enthusiasm. Donald Jackson, for example, has written, "No other story in our national experience is like this one."[2] Bernard DeVoto has extolled it as "the most important original narrative of North American exploration."[3] And Elliott Coues, waxing even more enthusiastic, has declared, "The story of this adventure [by Lewis and Clark] stands easily first and alone."[4]

But what is it about this story of Lewis and Clark that, for so many people, puts it above others? The only explanation satisfying this writer—and that which might conceivably satisfy others—is that it contains a greater number of allied components that agreeably and compellingly stir the mind. (1) From first to last it reflects the elaborate—we might better say the inspired—preparation Jefferson gave to the Expedition, as is evidenced by his discerning choice of leaders, his insistence on multiple journals, and his clear-cut statement of objectives. (2) It is a story simply told, written with an evident sense of purpose. (3) It reveals human character at its best: the magnanimity of Lewis, the official leader, in sharing the command with Clark, the sympathy and understanding exhibited by both com-

[2] Donald Jackson, in foreword to Ralph K. Andrist's *To the Pacific with Lewis and Clark*, 7.
[3] Bernard DeVoto (ed.), *The Journals of Lewis and Clark* (Boston, Houghton Mifflin Co., 1953), v.
[4] Elliott Coues (ed.), *History of the Expedition Under the Command of Lewis and Clark*, 4 vols. (New York, Francis P. Harper, 1893), I, v–vi.

manders toward the Indians, and the dogged persistence of rank and file—John Ordway, George Drouillard, John Shields, and all the rest—when faced with seemingly insurmountable odds. (4) It exposes to view, far more than ever before, that territorial immensity west of the Mississippi lying between Canada on the north and Spanish lands on the south, with its diversity of heretofore relatively unknown and unmapped plains, deserts, badlands, mountains, and forests. (5) It is replete with instances of triumph over, or escape from, unfriendly Indians, dangerous animals, disease, extremes of temperature, sleep-dispelling insects, hunger, and almost every form of hardship known to man. (6) It is surcharged with the excitement of discovery of unknown animals, plants, rivers, waterfalls, and Indians. (7) It contains moments of great exultation: escape from the hostile, tribute-demanding Teton Sioux; finding the elusive Shoshonis, whose horses were so vitally necessary for crossing the Rockies; conquering the snow-covered, redoubtable Bitterroots; attaining the Pacific Ocean; and, finally, that extreme moment of exultation, the beaching of dugouts at St. Louis on the completion of the twenty-eight-month, adventure-filled odyssey. Any way one looks at it, the story is one of universal appeal, a bountiful chronicle that, as evidence proves, achieves added stature with each passing year.

Not surprisingly, therefore, my pursuit of Lewis and Clark, begun almost twenty years ago, took on from the start semblances of an ardent, purposeful, sustained love affair. Few events in my life have been attended with more pleasure than the thousands of miles I have traveled on several trips along the Lewis and Clark route, with stops at such historic points as the site of Fort Mandan, where the Expedition passed the winter of 1804–05; the White Rocks region of the Upper Missouri; Three Forks, where the Gallatin, Madison, and Jefferson merge to form the Missouri; the "most distant fountain" at Lemhi Pass; the Lolo Trail, which winds at high elevation through the wild magnificence of the Bitterroots; the site of Fort Clatsop on present-day Lewis and Clark River; and that remote spot on Two Medicine River where Lewis, in defense of life, killed two Blackfoot Indians.

Additional travel has taken this writer to museums and libraries where the rewards, in their own way, proved equally enjoyable.

Time will not erase recollection of that day at the Academy of Natural Sciences of Philadelphia when I first set eyes on, and was allowed to examine, that remarkable collection of more than two hundred dried, preserved plants that Meriwether Lewis had brought back from western habitats, or of another day, at the American Philosophical Society, when for the first time I was privileged to see and hold in hand those several priceless, morocco-bound notebooks which constitute the original journals of the Lewis and Clark Expedition.

I cherish many other experiences and rewards deriving from my perennial pursuit of Lewis and Clark: the discovery of previously unknown and unpublished letters and other documents which have further illuminated aspects of the Expedition; the establishing of friendships among Lewis and Clark students; and the profitable hours spent in interview with recognized scholars of the Expedition.

It is hoped that this present work will reflect in some measure the enthusiasm which prompted its beginning and insured its completion.

PAUL RUSSELL CUTRIGHT

Acknowledgments

For advice and information I am indebted to many persons, and to the several institutions they represent:

ACADEMY OF NATURAL SCIENCES OF PHILADELPHIA
Ruth E. Brown, head librarian
Lillian C. Jones, assistant librarian
Alfred E. Schuyler, curator of botany

AMERICAN PHILOSOPHICAL SOCIETY LIBRARY, Philadelphia
Gertrude D. Hess, former associate librarian
Murphy Smith, manuscripts librarian

BEAVER COLLEGE LIBRARY, Glenside, Pennsylvania
Josephine Charles, assistant librarian

DETROIT PUBLIC LIBRARY
Bernice S. Sprenger, chief, Burton Historical Collection
Alice C. Dalligan, curator of manuscripts

GRINNELL COLLEGE LIBRARY, Grinnell, Iowa
Mary E. Klausner, archivist

HENRY E. HUNTINGTON LIBRARY, San Marino, California
Ray E. Billington

HISTORICAL SOCIETY OF PENNSYLVANIA, Philadelphia

Nicholas Biddle Wainwright, editor, *The Pennsylvania Magazine of History and Biography*
Conrad Wilson, archivist

LIBRARY COMPANY OF PHILADELPHIA
Edwin Wolf, II, head librarian
Lillian Tomkin, archivist

McGILL UNIVERSITY LIBRARY, Montreal
Alison Thomas, archivist

MARYLAND HISTORICAL SOCIETY LIBRARY, Baltimore
F. William Filby, librarian and assistant director

MINNESOTA HISTORICAL SOCIETY, St. Paul
Lucile M. Kane, curator of manuscripts

MISSOURI HISTORICAL SOCIETY, St. Louis
George R. Brooks, director

NEW YORK HISTORICAL SOCIETY, New York City
James J. Heslin, director
Sue Gillies, reference librarian

NEW YORK PUBLIC LIBRARY, New York City
John P. Baker, executive assistant

STATE HISTORICAL SOCIETY OF WISCONSIN, Madison
Josephine L. Harper, manuscripts curator

YALE UNIVERSITY LIBRARY, New Haven
Archibald Hanna, curator
Rutherford D. Rogers, university librarian

I wish to thank the American Philosophical Society and the State Historical Society of Wisconsin for permission to publish letters in their files written by Reuben Gold Thwaites while Thwaites was engaged in editing *Original Journals of the Lewis and Clark Expedition, 1804–1806*; Yale University Library for permission to publish the Elliott Coues-Francis P. Harper correspondence (Western Americana MSS, S-99); the Newberry Library for allowing me to use the recently discovered paraphrase of Private Joseph Whitehouse's journal; and the Missouri Historical Society *Bulletin* for permission to reprint "A Journal of Private Joseph Whitehouse: a Soldier with Lewis and Clark."

I owe expressions of gratitude to the following: William Clark Adreon, great-great-great-grandson of William Clark and member of the Lewis and Clark Trail Committee of Missouri; Roy E. Appleman, historian, National Park Service, Washington, D.C.; Dr. E. G. Chuinard, past president of the Lewis and Clark Trail Heritage Foundation, Portland, Oregon; Larry Gill, manager, Northwest Farm Magazine Unit, Spokane, Washington; Robert E. Lange, member of the Governor's Lewis and Clark Trail Heritage Foundation Committee for Oregon; Henry S. Miller, of the Pennsylvania Bar, Jenkintown, Pennsylvania; Wilmoth Peairs, University of North Carolina Library, Chapel Hill; Ralph S. Space, forest supervisor (1954–63), Clearwater National Forest, Orofino, Idaho; Mrs. Dorothy Martin (daughter of Milo M. Quaife); and George W. White, geologist, University of Illinois.

I am greatly indebted to Dr. Roy M. Chatters, former head of the Radioisotopes and Radiations Laboratory, Washington State University, Pullman, and member of the State of Washington's Lewis and Clark Trail Advisory Committee, for helping me locate living descendants of Milo M. Quaife and for providing essential information about air guns; to Donald Jackson, editor of *The Papers of George Washington*, University of Virginia, Charlottesville, for reading critically portions of this manuscript and for supplying valuable data about the recently discovered paraphrase of Private Joseph Whitehouse's journal (see Appendix A); to Ernest S. Osgood, professor emeritus of history and editor of *The Field Notes of Captain William Clark, 1803–1805*, Wooster, Ohio, for material aid in the preparation of Chapter IX; and to C. A. Peairs, Jr., of the Massachusetts Bar and author of *Massachusetts Practice: Business Corporations*, Westboro, for commentary on the case of *Minnesota Historical Society* vs. *United States of America in re Lewis and Clark Expedition Papers* (see Appendix B).

Additionally, I wish to express my profound gratitude to Mary S. Sturgeon, associate professor emeritus of English, and to Marjorie Darling, dean of admissions emeritus, Beaver College, Glenside, Pennsylvania, for their expenditure of time and effort in reading painstakingly my entire manuscript, and for reaffirming the thesis that words, like flowers, have evident color and fragrance.

Contents

Illustrations

ILLUSTRATIONS

Sage Grouse (*Centrocercus urophasianus*) by William Clark
Lewis' Wild Flax (*Linum lewisii*)—specimen collected by M. Lewis

MAP

A History of the Lewis and Clark Journals

CHAPTER I

Thomas Jefferson

The seeds which ultimately burst their casings to grow into the Lewis and Clark Expedition—and by extension into the publications which ensued—were planted by Thomas Jefferson (1743–1826). As early as 1783, while in Congress as a representative from Virginia, he wrote to General George Rogers Clark, older brother of William Clark, inquiring if he would be interested in "exploring the country from the Mississippi to California."[1]

Jefferson failed in this attempt to have the West explored, and in three other attempts during the decade which followed: in 1785 with John Ledyard, in 1792 with Dr. Moses Marshall, and again later that same year with André Michaux. Details of these abortive efforts have been told and retold, are familiar to all Lewis and Clark students, and need not be repeated.

The climate for exploring the trans-Mississippi country by a party of Americans improved appreciably, however, when Jefferson in 1801 was sworn in as president of the United States. As such he could exercise the powers of that office to advance earlier unrealized aspirations, and with chances of success greatly enhanced. Testing his strength, on January 18, 1803, he sent a secret message to Congress requesting that it authorize a group of men to "explore the whole line, even to the Western ocean."[2]

[1] Reuben Gold Thwaites (ed.), *Original Journals of the Lewis and Clark Expedition, 1804–1806*, 8 vols. (New York, Dodd, Mead & Co., 1904–05), VII, 193.
[2] *Ibid.*, 208–209.

When Congress acceded to Jefferson's request and appropriated a sum of $2,500 to support the venture, he acted at once, as is well known, by designating Captain Meriwether Lewis (1774–1809) as leader of the projected party and Lieutenant William Clark (1770–1838) as second in command. At that moment Lewis was serving as personal secretary to the president, and Clark, recently retired from army life, was residing near Louisville, Kentucky, in the home which the Clark family had built and occupied since moving from Caroline County, Virginia, in 1785. The two were quite as jubilant, it would seem, as Columbus must have been after Ferdinand and Isabella named him commander of the Niña, Pinta, and Santa Maria. Wrote Clark to Lewis, on receipt of the news, "I will cheerfully join you . . . and partake of all the Dangers Difficulties & fatigues, and I anticipate the honors & rewards of the result of such an enterprise should we be successful in accomplishing it."[3]

Reports to the contrary, Lewis and Clark, it would appear, first met, and became close friends, while serving under General Anthony Wayne in the Ohio campaign against the Indians and British which terminated with Wayne's victory in 1794 at the battle of Fallen Timbers.

—2—

Throughout his adult life Jefferson was a stickler for keeping records. For instance, he began his *Garden Book* on March 30, 1766, just two weeks short of his twenty-third birthday, and did not conclude it until the fall of 1824, fifty-eight years later.[4] Thus, when it seemed likely that André Michaux would lead a party to the West, Jefferson prepared instructions for him, a portion of which reads:

> The method of preserving your observations is left to yourself, according to the means which shall be in your power. It is only suggested that the noting of them on the skin (the hide of some animal?) might be best for such as are most important, and that further details may be committed to the bark of the paper birch, a

[3] *Ibid.*, 259.

[4] Edwin Morris Betts (annotator), *Thomas Jefferson's Garden Book, 1766–1824* (Philadelphia, American Philosophical Society, 1944).

substance which may not excite suspicions among the Indians, & little liable to injury from wet and other common accidents.[5]

As the time drew near for Lewis and Clark to set out for the land of High Plains and "Shining Mountains," Jefferson fashioned an even more elaborate and refined set of instructions. A comparison with that inscribed to Michaux leaves little doubt that Jefferson by now attached even greater importance to the keeping and preservation of records. As evidence, he wrote:

> Your observations are to be taken with great pains & accuracy, to be entered distinctly & intelligibly for others as well as for yourself, to comprehend all the elements necessary, with the aid of the usual tables, to fix the latitude and longitude of the places at which they are taken, and are to be rendered to the war-office, for the purpose of having the calculations made concurrently by proper persons within the U.S.[6] Several copies of these as well as of your other notes should be made at leisure times, & put into the care of the most trustworthy of your attendants, to guard, by multiplying them, against the accidental losses to which they will be exposed. A further guard would be that one of these copies be on the paper of the birch, as less liable to injury from damp than common paper.[7]

Elsewhere in his instructions Jefferson explained that "other notes" should include observations on climate, geography, Indians, minerals, animals, and plants—"especially those [forms of life] not known in the U.S."[8] "It is truly remarkable," Jefferson once declared, that so few public figures take notes, without which "history becomes fable instead of facts."[9]

---

[5] Donald Jackson (ed.), *Letters of the Lewis and Clark Expedition with Related Documents, 1783–1854* (Urbana, University of Illinois Press, 1962), 671.

[6] This reference to the war office points up the fact, not always understood, that the Lewis and Clark Expedition was a military one and, therefore, all records, at least in Jefferson's mind, would automatically, at the conclusion of the journey, revert to the United States government. In light of later developments, we should not lose sight of this point.

[7] Thwaites, *Original Journals*, VII, 248.

[8] *Ibid.*

[9] Edward T. Martin, *Thomas Jefferson: Scientist* (New York, Henry Schuman, 1952), 19.

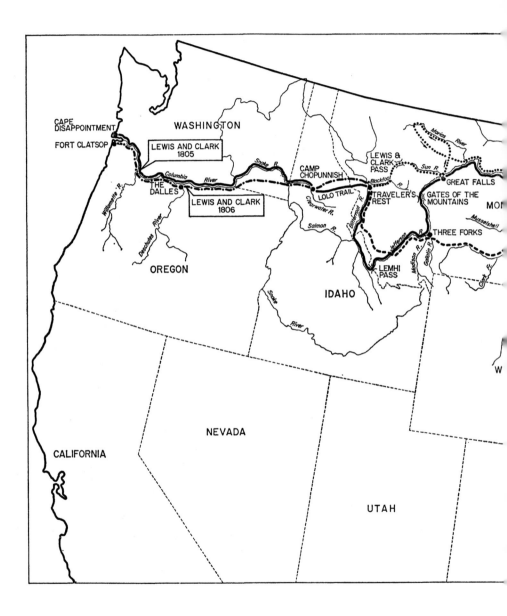

CAPE DISAPPOINTMENT

FORT CLATSOP

WASHINGTON

LEWIS AND CLARK 1805

Columbia River

Snake R.

CAMP CHOPUNNISH

LEWIS & CLARK PASS

Marias River

Sun R.

GREAT FALLS

THE DALLES

Willamette R.

Deschutes River

LEWIS AND CLARK 1806

OREGON

Clearwater R.

LOLO TRAIL

Bitterroot R.

Salmon R.

Blackfoot R.

TRAVELER'S REST

GATES OF THE MOUNTAINS

Jefferson R.

THREE FORKS

Musselshell

MOI

Madison R.

Gallatin R.

Clark Fk.

LEMHI PASS

IDAHO

Snake River

NEVADA

CALIFORNIA

W

UTAH

6

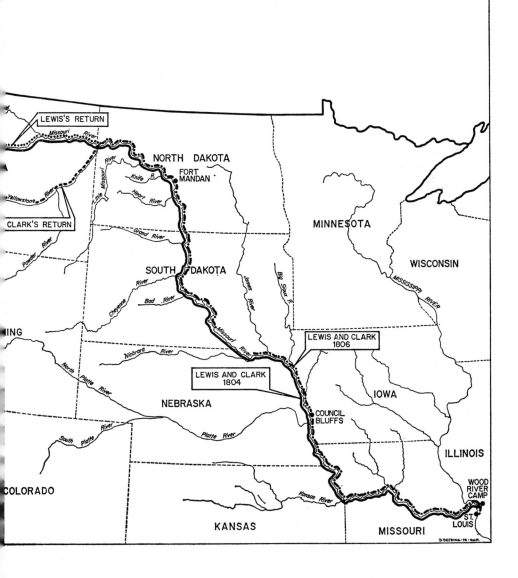

LEWIS'S RETURN

Missouri River

NORTH DAKOTA

FORT MANDAN

Yellowstone River

Little Missouri River

Knife R.

Heart River

CLARK'S RETURN

Powder River

Grand River

SOUTH DAKOTA

MINNESOTA

WISCONSIN

MISSISSIPPI RIVER

Cheyenne River

Bad River

James River

Big Sioux R.

ING

Niobrara River

Missouri River

LEWIS AND CLARK 1806

North Platte River

LEWIS AND CLARK 1804

NEBRASKA

IOWA

COUNCIL BLUFFS

South Platte River

Platte River

ILLINOIS

COLORADO

Kansas River

WOOD RIVER CAMP

KANSAS

MISSOURI

ST. LOUIS

D. DEERING-76-OWP.

7

It was July 5, 1803, when Meriwether Lewis, after speaking his farewells to Jefferson, left the nation's capital and began his journey to the West. He traveled by way of Charlestown, Frankfort (now Fort Ashby, West Virginia), Uniontown, and "Redstone old fort" (today's Brownsville, Pennsylvania) to Pittsburgh, negotiating the distance in ten days.[10]

Because of delays beyond his control, Lewis did not leave Pittsburgh and begin his descent of the Ohio River until late August. He traveled by keelboat, and in all likelihood he was on the deck of that boat when, on August 30, he wrote the first lines of the official record of the Lewis and Clark Expedition: "Left Pittsburgh this day at 11ock with a party of 11 hands 7 of which are soldiers, a pilot and three young men on trial they having proposed to go with us throughout the voyage."[11] With additional journalistic contributions from Clark and others, this record would continue, without significant break, until September 23, 1806 (three years less twenty days later), when the durable band of explorers, having completed the traverse of the continent, tied up their boats at St. Louis.

In writing his journal, Lewis employed pen and ink, as did the other diarists of the party; and the ink was of excellent quality, for the handwriting of the men as seen in their journals is even today, almost one hundred and seventy years later, distinct and legible. Among the many items Lewis listed as having purchased before leaving the East were "6 papers of Ink powder" and "4 Metal Pens brass or silver." [12] On occasion, at least some of the chroniclers employed old-fashioned quill pens. For instance, after one of the hunters shot a bald eagle at the mouth of the Yellowstone River in the spring of 1805, Sergeant Ordway reported, "I took the quills to write."[13]

It has often been said that the Lewis and Clark party was the

[10] Thwaites, *Original Journals*, VII, 256.

[11] Milo M. Quaife (ed.), *The Journals of Captain Meriwether Lewis and Sergeant John Ordway* (Madison, State Historical Society of Wisconsin, 1916), 31. Hereinafter cited as *Ordway*. Two of the "young men on trial" may have been John Colter, who would later discover what is now Yellowstone National Park, and George Shannon, who played a special role later, as we shall see, in helping Nicholas Biddle with his paraphrase of the Lewis and Clark journals.

[12] Thwaites, *Original Journals*, VII, 232.

[13] Quaife, *Ordway*, 193.

writingest crew on record, for most historians of the Expedition concede that at least eight of that group did pen day-to-day accounts: the two captains themselves; Sergeants Charles Floyd, John Ordway, Patrick Gass, and Nathaniel Pryor; and Privates Joseph Whitehouse and Robert Frazer. All of these journals are extant today, excepting those by Pryor and Frazer, and have been published. Since we have Lewis' word for it that he had directed each of the sergeants to "keep a separate journal from day to day,"[14] we must assume that Pryor obeyed orders. Evidence of Frazer's journal is in the form of a prospectus that he released soon after the party had returned to St. Louis.[15]

The continued day-to-day task of penning observations and happenings must at times have bordered on the impossible, especially so on those days when such burdens as numbing cold, enervating heat, and the distractions of hordes of blood-siphoning mosquitoes were added to illnesses and debilitating fatigue. There was, for instance, that bitterly cold, snowy day on the Lolo Trail when Clark declared, "I have been wet and as cold in every part as I ever was in my life."[16] Yet Clark, on that occasion, managed to contribute an entry of some four hundred and fifty words.

Sergeant Ordway was the most faithful of all the reporters. Not once during the entire journey, 863 days all told, did he fail to make his entry. Clark was almost as conscientious. He recorded events every day except while on a hunting trip away from Fort Mandan, February 3–12, 1805. However, he did summarize happenings of those days on his return, so that, for all practical purposes, his journal, too, is complete.

As to the other journalists, Sergeant Floyd persisted in his entries, missing not one, until two days before his death on August 20, 1804. Positive proof of Sergeant Gass's fidelity with pen eludes us, since his original journal has not come to light. In M'Keehan's paraphrase of it, however, we find a number of gaps. Private Whitehouse's original likewise contains several hiatuses, and it terminates abruptly with his entry for November 6, 1805.

Inexplicably, Lewis' journal, as we know it, has three lengthy

---

[14] Thwaites, *Original Journals*, I, 33.
[15] Jackson, *Letters*, 345–46.
[16] Thwaites, *Original Journals*, III, 69.

missing sections, each of several weeks' duration.[17] Some historians insist that Lewis faithfully discharged his duties as a reporter, that these missing parts have been lost and may yet be found. Thwaites, for one, stated confidently, "There appears to be no doubt that he regularly kept his diary. It is possible that the missing notes, in whole or in part, were with him when he met his death in Tennessee, and were either accidentally or purposely destroyed by others."[18]

Other historians of the Expedition have grave doubts about Lewis' reportorial consistency. They raise the question as to why Lewis sent Clark's journal to Jefferson from Fort Mandan instead of his own—if he had one. They are cognizant of the fact, too, that the two captains were separated just three times for anything like an extended period as they traveled toward the Pacific, yet during each of these intervals Lewis *did keep a journal*, but left no entries (at least none has been found) for days immediately preceding or following.[19] If Lewis did record events and observations on a daily basis, then the anomalies just mentioned are difficult to explain.

All students of the Expedition regret exceedingly the omissions in Lewis' journal, being tremendously impressed—when Lewis' pen was active—with his extraordinary output of valuable data. His sum of *technical* information, for example, far exceeded that found in all the other journals combined.

The value of the multiple journals rests primarily on the circumstance that each diarist saw with different eyes, reported what others overlooked. For example, only Sergeant Ordway reported the loss of manuscript material that occurred on July 14, 1804: "Capt. Clarks notes & remarks of 2 days blew overboard this morning in the Storm, and he was much put to it to Recolect the courses &.C."[20]

[17] The first of these hiatuses extended from May 14, 1804, to April 7, 1805 (with exceptions such as February 3 to 12), the second from August 27 through December 31, 1805 (again with exceptions, notably September 18 to 22 and November 29 to December 1), and the third from August 13 through September 24, 1806.

[18] Thwaites, *Original Journals*, I, xxxv.

[19] We should not overlook still another hiatus by Lewis, one of fifty-four days in his "Ohio Journal" of 1803 (the diary of his journey from Pittsburgh to Camp Dubois, published in Quaife's *Ordway*). For more about Lewis' apparent journalistic lapses, see Paul R. Cutrife's *Lewis and Clark: Pioneering Naturalists*, 48, 119–20, 207, 263.

[20] Quaife, *Ordway*, 97.

Jefferson's foresight in urging that Lewis and Clark maintain written records takes on added significance when we realize that the history of the Expedition available to us today consists not only of the diaries,[21] but also of the rough "Field Notes" of Clark, the several documents containing scientific data on such subjects as geography, ethnology, zoology, botany, mineralogy, and meteorology, and the numerous maps which are the product of Clark's industry and innate talent. It goes without saying, of course, that if Lewis and Clark had returned without any manuscript record whatever—without journals, maps, and other documentation—then the history of the Expedition would today be essentially "fable instead of facts." Many persons recall the reception given to John Colter's oral, unsupported story of his discovery of what is now Yellowstone National Park, with its geysers, mud pots, and other phenomena, and of how, for years afterwards, this region was referred to deprecatingly by some disbelieving individuals as "Colter's Hell."

We should note, before concluding this section about existing documentary material, that not one of the journalists responded to Jefferson's suggestion of committing notes to the paper of the birch. This lovely birch (*Betula papyrifera*), known by such common names as white, canoe, and paper, is a common sight along streams and lakes of northern woodlands, but Lewis and Clark, traveling in lower latitudes, apparently did not encounter it. Jefferson, if not Lewis and Clark, knew that the tough, resinous bark of this birch is easily separated into thin orange-colored sheets, providing the "paper" on which in earlier years people occasionally wrote letters. It is too bad that no paper birch documents were returned by the explorers. If one had been, and it now reposed in the vault of some library, what a prized possession it would be!

—4—

With the advent of spring at Fort Mandan in 1805, Lewis and

21 Existing manuscript journals by members of the Lewis and Clark party may be found today in four different repositories: Sergeant Floyd's in the State Historical Society of Wisconsin, Madison; Private Whitehouse's in Newberry Library, Chicago; Sergeant Ordway's in the American Philosophical Society, Philadelphia; and those of Lewis and Clark in the American Philosophical Society and Missouri Historical Society, St. Louis.

Clark readied a large shipment of letters, maps, reports, journals, and specimens to be carried downstream by the keelboat, almost all of it consigned to Jefferson. Two items of this special cargo demand our attention, since they will shortly preface this history of the Lewis and Clark publications. One was a letter from Lewis to Jefferson, and the other, a significant ethnological document. The former, dated April 7, 1805, summarized for the president events from the start of the journey in May, 1804, through the waning days of winter at Fort Mandan in 1805. The latter provided a huge mass of statistical data about Indian tribes inhabiting both sides of the Missouri as far west and north as the Knife River, a tributary of the Missouri which entered about sixty miles north of present-day Bismarck, North Dakota.

The consignment from Fort Mandan arrived in Washington in mid-summer, at which time Jefferson was in Monticello. After learning specific details about it, he at once wrote to various correspondents expressing his delight and gratification that it contained "an accurate map of the Missouri to the Mandan towns," a "minute account of the country, it's soil, productions, animals, waters, climate &c.,"[22] a box of minerals, horns, dressed skins, Indian utensils, and two live animals, a magpie (*Pica pica hudsonia*) and a prairie dog (*Cynomys ludovicianus*).[23]

Early in the following year Jefferson publicly made known the importance he attached to Lewis' letter from Fort Mandan and the accompanying statistical data on Indians of the Missouri. He did so by preparing and sending to Congress a message, which was read to that body on February 19, 1806. His initial lines read:

> In pursuance of a measure proposed to congress by a measure of January 18th, one thousand eight hundred and three, and sanctioned by their appropriation for carrying it into execution, Captain Merriwether Lewis, of the first regiment of infantry, was appointed, with a party of men, to explore the river Missouri, from its mouth to its source, and, crossing the highlands by the shortest portage, to seek the best water communication thence to the Pacific ocean; and

[22] Jackson, *Letters*, 258.
[23] In his shipment of live animals from Fort Mandan, Lewis included four magpies, a prairie dog, and a prairie sharp-tailed grouse (*Pedioecetes phasianellus campestris*), but all died in transit except the prairie dog and one of the magpies.

Lieutenant Clarke was appointed second in command. They were to enter into conference with the Indian nations on their route, with a view to establishment of commerce with them.

Continuing, the president informed senators and representatives of Lewis and Clark's successful ascent of the Missouri as far as the Mandan villages, of the subsequent semiarctic winter among the Indians, and of preparations for their continuance of the journey. He advised, too, of his receipt of Lewis' letter, a general map of the country between the Mississippi and the Pacific, and the document providing statistical data about the Missouri nations, and that he was hereby presenting copies of these to each member of the Congress.

Jefferson concluded his message by saying that "to render the statement as complete as may be, of the Indians inhabiting the country west of the Mississippi," he was giving each member additionally: (1) "Historical Sketches of the Several Indian tribes in Louisiana, south of the Arkansas River," by Dr. John Sibley;[24] (2) an account of the Red River of the South by Dr. Sibley; (3) "Distances up Red River by the course of the river;" (4) observations of Mr. William C. Dunbar[25] and Dr. George Hunter[26] while exploring the Red and Washita Rivers; and (5) "Meteorological Observations by Dunbar and Hunter."

Later that same year Jefferson's message, and the various documents alluded to above (excepting the map),[27] received wide circulation and increased publicity when they appeared in book form. Like many publications of that day it bore a multiworded title: *Message of the President of the United States communicating Discoveries made in exploring the Missouri, Red River and Washita, by Cap-*

---

[24] Dr. John Sibley (1757–1837), physician, Indian agent, and Louisiana planter, was born in Massachusetts, studied medicine, and in 1802 moved to Louisiana. The following year Jefferson put him in charge of a party to explore the Red River of the South.

[25] William Dunbar (1749–1810), scientist, was born in Scotland and came to the United States about 1770. In 1804 Jefferson appointed him and Dr. George Hunter to explore the Washita River and the region bordering on the Red.

[26] Dr. George Hunter (1775–1823), chemist, apothecary, and physician, came to Philadelphia from Scotland in 1774. In 1804–05, under directives from Jefferson, he and Dunbar, as mentioned, explored the Washita.

[27] For further particulars regarding this map, see Jackson, *Letters*, 237, 238n.

tains Lewis and Clark,[28] *Doctor Sibley, and Mr. Dunbar; with a Statistical Account of the Countries Adjacent.*

This volume (printed in Washington, D.C.) apparently attracted considerable attention, for, still later that year, two other nearly identical editions appeared, one in New York and the other in Natchez, Mississippi, and in 1807 still another, in London. The current bibliophile interested in adding any of these to his collection may find them hard to obtain. When Victor Hugo Paltsits, of the New York Public Library, prepared bibliographic data in 1904–05 for Thwaites's *Original Journals,* he reported finding only fifteen copies of the Washington edition, five of the New York, two of the Natchez, and six of the London.[29]

The text of the Washington edition runs to one hundred and seventy-five pages, with only one third of them devoted to actual Lewis and Clark history. Yet, for two reasons at least, we must recognize the importance of this work. It contains the first writings of Lewis and Clark about the Expedition to be published in book form, and it became the prime source for much of the copy that later went into what are known today as the Apocrypha or counterfeit editions— about which more later.[30]

— 5 —

As earlier remarked, Meriwether Lewis, on leaving Pittsburgh in late August, 1803, wrote the first words of the official day-to-day record of the Expedition. William Clark concluded that manuscript record in St. Louis on September 26, 1806, three years and one month later. In his final entry Clark said simply, "a fine morning we commenced wrighting &c."[31]

[28] In early writings the spelling is more often Clarke than Clark. Jefferson's *Message* has it both ways, with "Clark," correctly, on title page and "Clarke," incorrectly, in the text. Misspellings continued until 1892, when Elliott Coues determined that William Clark and immediate family never added a terminal *e.*

[29] For additional bibliographic data on these editions, see Thwaites, *Original Journals,* I, lxiii–lxv, and Coues, *History,* I, cix–cxi.

[30] The very earliest published manuscript material by Lewis and Clark seems to have been a letter from Clark to William Henry Harrison dated April 2, 1805, which appeared in the Baltimore *Telegraph and Daily Advertising* of July 25, 1805. For this letter, see Thwaites, *Original Journals,* VII, 314–16.

[31] *Ibid.,* V, 395.

Historians have disagreed, and doubtless will continue to do so, about what Clark had in mind when he alluded to "wrighting." Reuben Gold Thwaites, for instance, interpreted the word as meaning that Lewis and Clark on this date engaged themselves in transcribing their "individual journals . . . into neat blank books—bound in red morocco and gilt-edged—with the thought of preparing them for publication."[32] If so, they must have been *concluding* their transcription, for, as we see it, it would have been impossible for them during the short period of about four weeks spent in St. Louis to have copied all their rough notes, running to hundreds of pages, and, at the same time, to have contended successfully with other demands, such as the preparing of reports for the secretary of war, writing discharge papers and testimonials, arranging to transport a delegation of High Plains Indians to Washington, caring for numerous animal and plant specimens, and attending many social events.

More importantly, Lewis and Clark while in St. Louis each wrote a letter. Lewis addressed himself to Jefferson, and Clark to his brother (whether George Rogers or Jonathan is uncertain). Both captains were well aware that these communications would at once, after reaching their destinations, be headlined in newspapers. It was important, therefore, that they be worded carefully. To Lewis, whose pen moved rapidly in sentence structure, this was no problem; but to Clark, acutely aware of his limitations as a grammarian, it was a matter of considerable concern. However, Lewis quickly, as becomes an intimate friend, resolved the matter by writing Clark's letter for him, after which Clark copied it.[33]

Both men knew, too, that Clark's letter would be published first, for it had to travel only as far as Kentucky, while Lewis', addressed to Washington, would require much more time in transit. Thus Clark's first appeared October 9, in a Frankfort, Kentucky, paper, the *Palladium*, but Lewis' not until November 3, in the *National Intelligencer* of Washington. Before long, as other papers printed the letters, the entire country was apprised of the safe return of Lewis and Clark and their party.

[32] *Ibid.*, I, xxxv.
[33] Both of these letters, the one Lewis wrote for Clark and Clark's copy of it, are extant, the former in the Missouri Historical Society, St. Louis, and the latter in the Filson Club, Louisville, Kentucky.

Lewis' communication to Jefferson read in part as follows:

St. Louis September 23rd 1806

Sir:

It is with pleasure that I announce to you the safe arrival of myself and party at this place . . . no accedent has deprived us of a single member of our party since I last wrote from the Mandans in April 1805. In obedience to your orders we have penetrated the Continent of North America to the Pacific Ocean and sufficiently explored the interior of the country to affirm that we have discovered the most practicable communication which dose exist across the continent by means of the navigable branches of the Missouri and Columbia Rivers. . . . we v[i]ew this passage across the continent as affording immence advantages to the fur trade. . . . That portion of the Continent watered by the Missouri and all it's branches from the Cheyenne upwards is richer in beaver and Otter than any country on earth particularly that portion of it's subsiduary streams lying within the Rocky mountains; the furs of all this immence tract of country including such as may be collected on the upper portion of the river St. Peters, the Assiniboin & Red rivers may be conveyed to the mouth of the Columbia by the 1st of August in each year and from thence be shiped to and arrive at Canton earlier than the furs which are annually shiped from Montreal arrive in England. . . .

The British N. West company of Canaday have for several years past carried on a partial trade with the Mandans Minnetares and Avahaways on the Missouri from their establishments on the Assiniboin near the entrance of Mouse R. at present I have every reason to believe that they intend forming an establishment very shortly on the Missouri near those nations with a view to ingroce the fur trade of that River. . . . if we are to regard the trade of the Missouri as an object of importance to the U. States the strides of this company toward that river cannot be too vigelently watched nor too firmly and speedily opposed by our government. . . . I have brought with me several skins of the Sea Otter 2 skins of the native Sheep of N. America. 5 skins and skelitons complete of the Bighorn or mountain ram, and a skin of the mule deer besides the skins of several other quadrupeds and birds natives of the country through which we have passed; I have also preserved a pretty extensive collection of pla[n]ts in Horteo have obtained 10 [Indian] vocabularies. have also prevailed on the principal Chief of the Mandans

16

[Big White] to accompany me to Washington. . . . With rispect to the exertions and services rendered by this estimable man Capt. Wm. Clark on this expedition I cannot say too much, if sir, any credit be due to the success of the arduous enterprize in which we have been engaged he is equally with myself entitled to the consideration of yourself and that of our common Country. . . . I am very anxious to learn the state of my friends in Albemarle particular[l]y whether my mother is yet living. I am with every sentiment of esteem your most Obt. Servt.

MERIWETHER LEWIS
Capt. 1st U. S. Regt. Infty.[34]

Jefferson's delight in receiving this letter may be imagined, particularly so since he had had no word from Lewis since the latter's letter from Fort Mandan had reached him on July 13, 1805, more than a year before. At that date he was disposed to believe, as did many others, that the Expedition would arrive at the Pacific by midsummer and be back in St. Louis before the onset of winter. When the year ended without word from Lewis and Clark, and the winter, spring, and summer months of the ensuing year went by with still no report, Jefferson, as well as relatives and friends of members of the party, began to despair of seeing them again. And Jefferson may have been more acutely despondent, for he had it on his conscience that he had sired the Expedition and then committed it to a journey of uncommon peril. He exposed some of his emotion when he replied to Lewis' letter: "I received, my dear Sir, with unspeakable joy your letter of Sep. 23 announcing the return of yourself, Capt. Clarke & your party in good health to St. Louis. The unknown scenes in which you were engaged, & the length of time without hearing of you had begun to be felt awfully."[35]

Historians have not overlooked the prime import of the two letters dispatched by Lewis and Clark from St. Louis at this time. When published, they established the base upon which the prestige of the Expedition initially rested. It was a puny base, since the letters actually disclosed so little that the Expedition accomplished, but Lewis had in mind enlarging it substantially in the near future. To that end, after visiting his family in Charlottesville and reporting

[34] Thwaites, *Original Journals*, VII, 334–37.
[35] Jackson, *Letters*, 350–51.

17

to Jefferson in Washington, he went to Philadelphia. Here he soon encountered a printer, John Conrad, whom he engaged to publish the history of the Expedition.

Almost concurrently Lewis released a prospectus announcing the forthcoming publication of *Lewis and Clark's Tour to the Pacific Ocean through the Interior of the Continent of North America.* This work, the prospectus further stated, would be prepared by Lewis himself and "divided into two parts, the whole comprised in three volumes octavo, containing from four to five hundred pages, each," and would be "put to press at as early periods as the avocations of the author will permit him to prepare them for publication." Volume one would contain "a narrative of the voyage"; volume two, "the geography of the region traversed and a view of the Indian Nations"; and volume three, "the scientific results . . . which may properly be distributed under the heads of Botany, Mineralogy and Zoology." The prospectus concluded by announcing that, "Detached from this work, there will be published on a large scale, as soon as a sufficient number of subscribers be obtained to defray the expense, LEWIS & CLARK'S MAP OF NORTH AMERICA."[36]

A few weeks later, when Lewis left Philadelphia to return to Washington, he had good reason to believe that at least the first of the three volumes would come from the press before the year (1807) ended. No one then could have foreseen that seven years would elapse, that it would be 1814 before the history appeared, that it would then be in an abbreviated, emasculated form, and that Lewis himself would have nothing to do with its final preparation.

[36] *Ibid.,* 394–95. Different versions of this prospectus appeared. One, to be found in Thwaites, *Original Journals,* VII, 363–66, carried the information that the first part of the work would sell for ten dollars, the second for eleven dollars, and the map for ten dollars. See also Jackson, *Letters,* 397n.

CHAPTER II

Patrick Gass and David M'Keehan

Having no supernatural powers of divination, Jefferson could not have foreseen that his instruction to Lewis and Clark to keep multiple journals might later lead to trouble. The president had in mind, of course, that Lewis, on his return, would prepare the history of the Expedition. But what was there to prevent one of the other journalists from publishing his account ahead of Lewis'? Nothing at all, as both Jefferson and Lewis soon learned.

Even before Lewis left Washington for Philadelphia, where he issued his prospectus and signed a contract with John Conrad, he had received the unwelcome intelligence that "there were several unauthorized and probably some spurious publications . . . preparing for the press, on the subject of my late tour to the Pacific Ocean by individuals entirely unknown to me."[1] As a consequence, on March 18, he released to the public, through the *National Intelligencer* and other newspapers, a letter bearing his signature. It read in part:

> I have considered it a duty which I owe the public, as well as myself to put them on their guard with respect to such publications, lest from the practice of such impositions they may be taught to depreciate the worth of the work which I am myself preparing for publication before it can possibly appear, as much time, labor, and expense are absolutely necessary in order to do justice to the several

[1] Jackson, *Letters*, 385.

subjects which it will embrace. . . . To Robert Frazier only has permission been given either by Gen. William Clark or myself, to publish any thing in relation to our last voyage. . . . I think it my duty to declare that Robert Frazier, who was only a private on this expedition, is entirely unacquainted with celestial observations, mineralogy, botany, or zoology, and therefore cannot possibly give any accurate information on those subjects, nor on that of geography, and that the whole which can be expected from his journal is merely a limited detail of our daily transactions. With respect to all unauthorized publications relative to this voyage, I presume that they cannot have stronger pretensions to accuracy of information than that of Robert Frazier.[2]

In light of events quickly upcoming, Lewis made a mistake in belittling Frazer's scientific capabilities, though what he said about them was true enough. For one thing, David M'Keehan would soon take advantage of the mistake. For another, Frazer's journal seemingly had more meat in it than Lewis had knowledge of. According to one writer, it "was in many respects more interesting than that of his commanders,"[3] and to another, Frazer was an articulate man, and "his journal might have been a major contribution to our knowledge of the expedition."[4]

Even though Lewis declared that the unauthorized publications of which he had reports were "by individuals entirely unknown" to him, we have some doubts as to the truth of the statement, for just six days after papers carried his caveat, the Pittsburgh *Gazette* printed a prospectus written by David M'Keehan announcing the forthcoming publication of Sergeant Patrick Gass's journal. Portions of the prospectus most pertinent to our study read as follows:

> PROPOSALS for publishing by subscription, By David M'Keehan, Bookseller, a Journal of the Voyages & Travels of a Corps of Discovery, under the command of Captain Lewis and Captain Clarke.

[2] *Ibid.*, 385–86.

[3] John R. McBride, "Pioneer Days in the Mountains," *Tullidge's Quarterly Magazine of Utah*, Vol. III (July, 1884), 316.

[4] Jackson, *Letters*, 346n. Sometime late in 1806 Frazer released a prospectus, thus declaring his intention to publish; but the only surviving evidence of that intent is a manuscript map in the Library of Congress. A copy of Frazer's prospectus exists in the library of the State Historical Society of Wisconsin. For additional detail about both map and prospectus, see Jackson, *Letters*, 346n.

. . . An authentic relation of the most interesting transactions during the expedition;—A description of the country, and an account of its inhabitants, soil, climate, curiosities, & vegetable and animal productions. By Patrick Gass, one of the persons employed in the expedition: with geographical & explanatory notes. . . .

. . . To recommend the correctness of this work, the publisher [M'Keehan] begs leave to state, that at the different resting places during the expedition, the several journals were brought together, compared, corrected, and the blanks, which had been unavoidably left, filled up. . . . To this he will add, the following extract from a certificate delivered by Captain Lewis to Mr. Gass, dated St. Louis, 10th Oct. 1806.

"As a tribute justly due to the merits of the said *Patrick Gass*, I with cheerfulness declare, that the ample support, which he gave me, under every difficulty; the manly firmness, which he evinced on every occasion; and the fortitude with which he bore the fatigues and painful sufferings incident to that long voyage, intitles him to my highest confidence and sincere thanks, while it eminently recommends him to the consideration and respect of his fellow citizens."

M'Keehan concluded his prospectus by saying that the work would be published in one volume, that it would be ready for delivery in two months from that date, and that, in spite of heavy expenses, "including the original purchase money," it would sell for just one dollar.[5]

A few points about this prospectus need comment. For one, it excludes any reference to Gass's rank as sergeant, and for another, it provides the first published affirmation of the fact that the journalists of the Expedition often compared and corrected, and even copied, each other's accounts. Though thus early stated, and later confirmed by historians who collated Clark's entries with Lewis' (and Whitehouse's with Gass's and Ordway's), it is surprising that an occasional writer even today asserts that the journals were done separately, without conference or comparison. We should not overlook, too, M'Keehan's mention of "original purchase money." About this, we reserve comment until later.

But what of this man M'Keehan? The picture we get of him is like a daguerreotype dimmed by age. We know little beyond the

---

[5] *Ibid.*, 390–91.

fact that he had obtained a better than average education, had taught school for a time in or near Wellsburg, Virginia (now West Virginia), and in 1807 operated a book and stationery store in Pittsburgh in front of the court house. He may have been the David McKeehan who graduated from Dickinson College in Carlisle, Pennsylvania, in 1787 and was admitted to the Pennsylvania bar in 1792.[6] In ensuing pages of this chapter, where we quote from a letter by M'Keehan, we learn something of his character.

—2—

Excepting Lewis and Clark and the Indian girl, Sacagawea, Patrick Gass (1771–1870) is better known to Americans than any other member of the Corps of Discovery. The reasons are several. By virtue of his sergeantcy, his name crops up with greater frequency in the journals of Lewis and Clark than that of most others. He was the first of the journalists to publish his account, so that he early came to the attention of readers.[7] He was the first member of the party to be immortalized biographically.[8] And, in the matter of longevity, he far outstripped all others.

Gass was born June 12, 1771, in Falling Springs, a village near present-day Chambersburg, Pennsylvania. In 1775 his father moved the family to Maryland, near old Fort Frederick, situated some fifty miles south of Fort Cumberland. In the early eighties he moved again, this time to Catfish Camp, now Washington, Pennsylvania.

Young Patrick early developed an irresistible impulse to see other parts of his country. It is said that, even before he had attained his majority, he "had made several trips across the mountains to Hagerstown, Maryland, and Mercersburg, Penn.; and had travelled the dangerous emptiness of what is now West Virginia and Ohio."[9]

In his twenty-first year (1792), Gass joined Captain Caton's Rangers and was stationed at Yellow Creek, near Wheeling, where

---

[6] *Ibid.*, 391 n.

[7] Patrick Gass, *A Journal of the Voyages and Travels of a Corps of Discovery*, ed. by David M'Keehan (1807; reprint ed., Minneapolis, Ross and Haines, 1958), xii.

[8] John G. Jacob, *The Life and Times of Patrick Gass.*

[9] Gass, *Journal*, ix–x.

a small fort had been built for the protection of the frontiersmen against Indian attack. While there, he seems to have escaped any actual Indian fighting. Two years later, having terminated his army stint under Caton, Gass decided to become a carpenter—perhaps, as we shall see, one of the more important decisions of his young manhood—and seems to have developed into a competent one. At one time, for instance, he helped construct a home for James Buchanan, father of the James Buchanan who later took up residence in the White House.[10]

In 1799, when war with France threatened, Gass laid down his hammer and saw and enlisted in the Tenth U.S. Infantry. He was sent from Carlisle to Harper's Ferry, but was discharged soon afterwards as war clouds dissipated. However, he soon reenlisted, and in 1803 we find him at Kaskaskia, Illinois, attached to an infantry company commanded by Captain Russell Bissell.

When, in late November of that year, Lewis and Clark arrived at Kaskaskia, they carried a letter to Captain Bissell from Henry Dearborn, secretary of war, which read in part, "You will be pleased to furnish one Sergeant & Eight good Men . . . to go with Capt. Lewis. . . ."[11] On learning of Lewis and Clark's plans to explore the trans-Mississippi West, Gass immediately requested a transfer in order to accompany them. However, needing a good carpenter, Bissell refused. Thereupon, according to one source, "the resolute Patrick persisted, and having found out Captain Lewis's whereabouts hunted the latter up and put the case plump. The result was his enlistment as a private under Captain Lewis, his own commanding officer's objections notwithstanding."[12] At that time, we are informed, Patrick Gass was "five feet seven . . . compactly built, broadchested and strong-limbed, lean and wiry."[13]

Lewis' "Ohio journal," though it alluded to the stop at Kaskaskia, made no mention of Gass. The earliest reference to him was made

---

[10] Coues, *History*, I, ci. At some point in his youth Gass made a trip aboard a keelboat to New Orleans, and the experience thus gained must have proved of value to him, as he later ascended the Missouri with Lewis and Clark aboard another keelboat. For mention of this New Orleans trip, see Gass, *Journal*, x.

[11] Jackson, *Letters*, 103.

[12] Coues, *History*, I, cii.

[13] *Ibid.*, xcix. His discharge papers described him "as about five feet seven inches tall, dark complexion, gray eyes, dark hair" (Jackson, *Letters*, 648n.).

by Clark in his "Field Notes," kept during the winter at Camp Dubois. Therein, under date of January 3, 1804, we find two lists of the men constituting the party, with Gass's name on both.[14] Clark did not say so, but we may presume that Gass, an experienced carpenter, played an important role in the construction of winter quarters on Wood River.

After the Expedition began the ascent of the Missouri, Gass came in for no particular journalistic comment until August 22, 1804, two days after the death of Sergeant Charles Floyd. On that date Clark wrote, "ordered a Vote for a Sergeant to chuse one of three which may be the highest number, the highest numbers are P. Gass had 19 votes, Bratten & Gibson."[15] Gass may have been a modest man; he included no mention of his election in his own journal. Obviously he was popular with the other enlisted men, otherwise they would not have chosen him to this position of leadership.

Thereafter, because of his elevation in rank, Gass figured more prominently in affairs of the Expedition. He probably supervised the construction of Fort Mandan, since he was the only journalist to describe the manner in which it was built, and the following spring Lewis and Clark definitely named him to head a detail which had the responsibility of building several dugout canoes. His commanders, too, often attached him to special parties. For example, Lewis chose him, with Drouillard and Charbonneau, to form the group that, on August 1, 1805, forged ahead with Lewis to look for the Shoshonis, whose horses were so desperately needed in the crossing of the Rockies. And I think we may correctly assume that Lewis and Clark relied on Gass's experiences as a carpenter when it came time to design and construct Fort Clatsop. On the return trip, when Lewis left Great Falls to explore the headwaters of the Marias River, he put Gass in charge of the contingent of men left behind that would make the portage around the falls.

Following demobilization of the party in St. Louis, Gass was one of the men who accompanied Lewis to Washington. He remained there briefly, and then went to Wellsburg, at that time a small town on the Ohio above Wheeling and some forty miles southwest of

[14] Ernest Staples Osgood (ed.), *The Field Notes of Captain William Clark, 1803–1805* (New Haven, Yale University Press, 1964), 12.
[15] Thwaites, *Original Journals*, I, 117.

Pittsburgh. It was there (or in Pittsburgh) that, soon afterward, he made the acquaintance of David M'Keehan.

In ensuing years Gass participated in the War of 1812, lost an eye in the battle of Lundy's Lane, and somewhat later, at the age of sixty, married a twenty-year-old girl who bore him six children. He lived on until 1870, dying in his ninety-ninth year. He thus survived all others of the Corps of Discovery—Clark by thirty-two years, and Lewis by sixty-one.

—3—

With this brief account of Gass's life open to us, we are in a better position to approach, follow, and appraise the publication of his journal. At what date M'Keehan first saw Lewis' open letter to the public warning against unauthorized editions we will never know, but on April 14, 1807, the Pittsburgh *Gazette* carried a long letter by M'Keehan addressed: "To his Excellency Meriwether Lewis, Esquire, Governor of Upper Louisiana."[16] The opening paragraph went:

> Your publication in the National Intelligencer, dated the 14th of last month, has forced into notice an obscure individual, who, of course, has had the misfortune of being "entirely unknown to you," to defend his character and his rights. However unpleasant it may be to his feelings to appear before the public in his own defense; and however he may regret the necessity of drawing their attention to the remarks he may offer, it is some consolation that the conduct of his antagonist claims of him no scrupulous adherence to the rules of formality, or of punctilious delicacy; and that to meet Your Excellency on the subject of your publication requires to *you* no apology. Your rapid advancement to power and wealth seems to have changed the humble and respectful language of a *Sir Clement* into that of him who commands and dispenses favours; even your subscription lists, when you offer your learned works for publication must be "promulgated."[17]

M'Keehan's wording of this initial paragraph sets the tone for

---

[16] Some weeks earlier Jefferson had appointed Lewis governor of the Territory of Louisiana and Clark brigadier general of militia to the territory.

[17] Jackson, *Letters*, 399–407.

those which follow. He depicts himself throughout as a David attacked by a Goliath, caustically and consistently addresses Lewis as "Your Excellency," and derides his use of such polysyllabics as "promulgated." Parenthetically, we think it likely that Jefferson helped structure Lewis' open letter; it contains other uncommon words—"depreciate," "subjoined," and "expunged" among them—that don't square with our knowledge of Lewis' vocabulary, and it bears other marks of erudition suggesting the president's hand.

Farther along M'Keehan quotes excerpts from Lewis' letter and then asserts:

> . . . it may perhaps be agreeable to Your Excellency to know the reasons of my interfering in this affair of the journals of what you modestly call *your* late tour. You will therefore please to understand, that, without soliciting either your permission or authority, I have purchased the journal of one of the persons [obviously Gass] engaged in the late expedition . . . that I have arranged and transcribed it for the press, supplying such geographical notes and other observations, as I supposed would render it more useful and satisfactory to the reader.[18]

As to M'Keehan's purchase, one writer has said, "Gass received as his share of the work the copyright and 100 copies of the book; M'Keehan had the balance of the edition, which he sold at some profit."[19] To the contrary, we have M'Keehan's own statement, earlier quoted, that his expenses included "the original purchase money." As to his geographical notes, they number precisely thirty and contribute next to nothing in rendering the work more valuable.

From here on M'Keehan's letter boils down to "some short observations" which he declared he was forced to make. Actually they are anything but short, for they constitute approximately two-thirds of his entire homily. In one of them he attempted to discredit Lewis' technical knowledge by suggesting that he lacked wisdom in not emulating Alexander Mackenzie's candor, that British explorer on one occasion having said, "I do not possess the science of the naturalist." In another, he accused him of duplicity, insisting that Lewis was

---

[18] *Ibid.*

[19] Coues, *History*, I, cxviii. Earle R. Forrest, who wrote the introduction for the 1958 Ross and Haines edition of Gass, said that Gass "received only 100 copies as his share of the venture" (Gass, *Journal*, xii).

guilty of such by extending to Frazer permission to publish with one hand and deprecating with the other the worth of Frazer's diary.

In yet another "observation," M'Keehan broadly implied that Cruzatte's shooting of Lewis, an unfortunate event of the return journey, had been no accident. Also, quite falsely, he charged Lewis with having continued to draw pay as Jefferson's secretary at the same time he was receiving compensation as an army officer.

M'Keehan's most indictable charge, however, was that Lewis, after having received princely monetary rewards from the government, high praise from the president, and appointment to the governorship of Louisiana, was now "contending with the poor fellows, who for their small pittance were equally exposed with yourself to the toils and dangers attending the expedition, about the publication of their journals, which cost them so much trouble and anxiety to keep and preserve."[20]

From beginning to end, and looked at from any angle, M'Keehan's letter was injudicious, intemperate, even vicious. And it was made even worse by the circumstance that, by openly exposing it in the Pittsburgh *Gazette*, he was obviously addressing it to the public, though ostensibly to Lewis.

To his credit, Lewis made no reply. At an early age, while still residing on his Albemarle County farm in Virginia, he doubtless had learned that if you fool around with a jackass you are likely to get kicked.

—4—

The original manuscript journal of Sergeant Gass has long since vanished. Since this colorful Irishman later admitted that he "never learned to read, write, and cipher till he had come of age,"[21] his diary was probably on the order of those written by Sergeant Floyd and Private Whitehouse, namely, replete with examples of nonadherence to prescribed rules governing spelling, punctuation, and syntax. M'Keehan's reworded version, entitled *A Journal of the Voyages and Travels of a Corps of Discovery*, was published in Pittsburgh in July, 1807. By and large, it was grammatically sound, and what he pro-

[20] Jackson, *Letters*, 402.
[21] Coues, *History*, I, xcix.

fessed it to be, namely, an authentic account of the Lewis and Clark Expedition. Also, and more significantly, it was the first detailed account to reach the public.

No two individuals think alike about M'Keehan's paraphrase. An early appraiser declared, "No man shall exceed Mr. Patrick [Gass] in the faculty of keeping close to the direct business of the story, and carrying it right on without ever digressing into a paragraph of reflection, or admiration, or wonder, or extended description, or triumph, or piety, or theorizing, or even explanation."[22] Another reviewer of that day deplored the "most provoking dryness of our good friend Mr. Patrick Gass."[23] Some fifty years later Gass's biographer, John G. Jacob, extolled the work: "All is plain unpretending matter of fact, just such notings as a mathematician might make in a scientific traverse of the land."[24] Still later, Elliott Coues regarded it as "a valuable check upon the narrative of Lewis and Clark itself, in the minutiae of dates, places, etc., and on this account may not inaptly be termed the *Concordance*."[25] Much to the contrary, Donald Jackson viewed it as ". . . in many ways . . . a miserable piece of work, for upon Patrick Gass's sketchy notes, the editor [*i.e.*, M'Keehan] had placed the burden of an elegant prose style."[26]

Our chief complaint is that M'Keehan did not reproduce Gass's original *verbatim ac litteratim*, or, if he felt himself duty bound to make alterations, did not limit his changes to nothing more than correcting spelling, punctuation, capitalization, and the like. Instead, he manipulated the language of the tough, untutored, tobacco-chewing army sergeant into the resolutely correct, preceptorial prose of the early-nineteenth-century schoolmaster. For example, imagine if you can the sergeant in real life employing the words M'Keehan provided for him on April 5, 1805, when he described the sexual promiscuity and consequent venereal disease among the Mandan and Hidatsa Indians:

If this brief journal should happen to be preserved, and be ever

---

[22] *Eclectic Review* (London), Vol. V. Pt. 1 (February, 1809), 106–107.

[23] *Ibid.*, Pt. 2 (November, 1809), 1053.

[24] Jacob, *The Life and Times of Patrick Gass*, 107.

[25] Coues, *History*, I, cxvii.

[26] Donald Jackson, "The Race to Publish Lewis and Clark," *Pennsylvania Magazine of History and Biography*, Vol. LXXXV, No. 2 (April, 1961), 174.

thought worthy of appearing in print; some readers will perhaps expect, that, after one long friendly intercourse with these Indians, among whom we have spent the winter . . . we ought to be prepared now, when we are about to renew our voyage, to give some account of the *fair sex* of the Missouri; and entertain them with narratives of feats of love as well as of arms. . . . It may be observed generally that chastity is not very highly esteemed by these people, and that the severe and loathsome effects of *certain French principles* are not uncommon among them.[27]

Although M'Keehan took exceptional liberties with the wording of Gass's journal, he did not, we think, alter truth in any significant respect. For that we may be grateful, since Gass proved his worth as an observer, on many occasions reporting matters completely overlooked or disregarded by the other journalists of the party. For example, he was the only one to describe the manner in which the Arikara and Mandan Indians constructed their conical earth lodges.[28]

How did Gass and M'Keehan fare financially in this publication venture? If, as alleged, Gass received only the copyright and one hundred printed volumes, he must have been disenchanted. Unquestionably M'Keehan fared better. He had several things going for him: (1) Gass's journal, as we know, was the first of those kept by members of the Expedition to come from the press; (2) the names Lewis and Clark were on the tongues of most everyone and could not yet have lost their magic; (3) prospective purchasers abounded; and (4) the price of one dollar set by M'Keehan was within the reach of even those of modest means.

During the next seven years (1808–14), six additional editions of Gass's journal appeared. One was published in London, one in Paris, one in Weimar (now East Germany), and the remaining three in Philadelphia. The Paris edition—"*par Patrice Gass*"—had the distinction of being the first translation of an authentic Lewis and Clark journal. By considerable, however, the most interesting of these six Gass editions were those published in Philadelphia. They appeared in consecutive years (1810, 1811, and 1812) and were all by the same publisher, Mathew Carey. It seems reasonable to believe that

---

[27] Gass, *Journal*, 87.
[28] *Ibid.*, 61.

Carey would not have risked his money on these editions without assurance from Pittsburgh that M'Keehan had done well with his.

The primary interest attaching to the Carey editions of Gass is due, as every student of Lewis and Clark knows, to the complement of remarkably unconventional illustrations Carey introduced, and to the additional fact that in recent years these have decorated pages of so many books and magazine articles about Lewis and Clark.

Mathew Carey (1760–1839), about whom historians of the Expedition up to now have been rather conspicuously silent, deserves more attention than he has received. He was born January 28, 1760, in Dublin, Ireland, where, at the age of nineteen, he wrote an article regarded by authorities as seditious. To escape imprisonment, he fled to France. Here he had the good fortune to meet men of influence, among them Lafayette. A year or two later he returned to Ireland, was jailed for more seditious writing, and, on his release, took passage for the United States. He arrived in Philadelphia in November, 1785, with only a few dollars in his pockets and, to his knowledge, no friends in the city except those he had made on board ship. Luckily for him, however, Lafayette had preceded him to Philadelphia and, learning of his plight, introduced him to important residents of the city and gave him four $100 notes on the Bank of North America. According to one writer, "This was the beginning of Carey's fortune."[29]

Early in the next year Carey started the *Pennsylvania Herald* and *American Monitor* and, subsequently, still other publications. As he became more affluent, he opened and operated a bookstore, published many books (among them some by James Fenimore Cooper), wrote still others, and, extracurricularly, involved himself in numerous charitable, economic, political, and religious activities of the city. In short, as one historian has said, he "passed a life of great industry and achievement, which at times was eventful as any found in fiction."[30] But neither Carey nor anyone else of his day would have dreamed that a measure of his fame would subsequently hinge upon

[29] J. Thomas Scharf and Thompson Westcott, *History of Philadelphia*, 3 vols. (Philadelphia, L. H. Everts & Co., 1884), III, 1796.

[30] Joseph Jackson, *Encyclopedia of Philadelphia*, 4 vols. (Harrisburg, National Historical Association, 1931), II, 370.

the illustrations he provided for his editions of Sergeant Gass's journal.

Whether Carey observed expected amenities by purchasing the copyright of the journal from M'Keehan we cannot say. One source has stated that it was pirated.[31] In any event, Carey in 1810 brought out the first of his three editions. As to pagination, paragraphing, and wording, it was near identical with M'Keehan's. However, as indicated above, it differed in one obvious, significant particular. To enhance its appearance, and thereby its salability, Carey inserted six full-page engravings. In so doing, he was probably unaware of the fact that he was making graphic history of sorts by giving to the world the first illustrated Lewis and Clark journal.

Each engraving was a masterpiece exemplifying what a draftsman may accomplish if allowed to employ unrestrained imagination in portraying subjects about which he knows next to nothing. Carey did not identify his engraver, nor did the latter leave any clue as to his own identity.

Interest in these pictures, which are delightfully preposterous, has advanced perceptibly during the last few years as writers of Lewis and Clark literature seeking novel illustrative material have reproduced them increasingly. For instance, a recent biography of Lewis displays all six.[32] They have to be seen to be believed; and they strike us as even more preposterous when we compare those of the first edition with those of the third, which have been altered. For example, the engraving of the first entitled "Captain Clark & his men shooting Bears" depicts three anatomically incredible grizzlies, with the one on the right presumably dead, since it is on its back with legs pointing stiffly toward the heavens. But in the counterpart of the third edition it is the bear *on the left* that is in much the same fixed state of *rigor mortis*. Also, in the 1810 picture captioned "An American having struck a Bear but not killed him, escapes into a Tree," the bear (another inconceivable grizzly) has many of the features of an English sheep dog of mild demeanor, while that in

---

[31] James and Kathryn Smith, "Sedulous Sergeant, Patrick Gass," *Montana, the Magazine of Western History*, Vol. V. No. 3 (Summer, 1955), 22.

[32] Richard Dillon, *Meriwether Lewis: a Biography*, following 108 and 204.

the 1812 engraving looks more like a vicious overfed razorback with mind attuned to manslaughter.[33]

During the autumn of his life Sergeant Gass expressed pride in the recognition accorded his published diary. Writing in 1829 to John E. Eaton, secretary of war under Andrew Jackson, he said, "I accompanied Captains Lewis and Clarke to the Pacific Ocean, and on our return had published my dailey Journal, which book I am informed is honored with a place in the library of Congress."[34] He was proud, too, of *The Life and Times of Patrick Gass*, written and published by John G. Jacob in 1859, the first biography about any member of the Expedition. The durable sergeant, however, may never have been apprised of the fact that the translator of the German (Weimar) edition dubbed him prefatorially, "Sir Patrick Gass."[35]

[33] Existing Carey editions are probably scarcer than the 1807 M'Keehan, but not as scarce as Paltsits' census of 1904–05 would indicate. He was able to locate just seven copies of the 1810 edition and four each of the 1811 and 1812 (Thwaites, *Original Journals*, I, lxxiii–lxxiv). Peter Decker, New York bookseller, has provided this writer with his estimates of current prices for the above if in excellent condition: $175 to $250 for the 1807 M'Keehan, and $250 to $300 for each of the Careys.

[34] Jackson, *Letters*, 647.

[35] Thwaites, *Original Journals*, I, lxxv. In years since 1814 publishers have printed reissues of Gass's *Journal* in 1847 (Dayton, Ells, Claflin & Co.), 1904 (Chicago, A. C. McClurg & Co.), and 1958 (Minneapolis, Ross and Haines).

CHAPTER III

Apocrypha

And then came the counterfeit editions, or Apocrypha, at least eight
or nine of them. One by one, over a period covering almost half a
century, they appeared, each a dark and uncomely smudge on the
well-favored countenance of the fourth estate, and another illustration of what Sophocles had on his mind earlier than 400 B.C. when
he wrote in *Antigone*, "For money you would sell your soul."

These apocryphal editions began to come from presses almost at
once following publication of Jefferson's 1806 *Message to Congress*
and the M'Keehan-Gass Journal of 1807—and indeed were inspired by them. The first (two of them) appeared in 1809, one in
Philadelphia and the other in London, with the former probably
the prototype.[1] It staggered under a title longer than a prophet's
beard: *The Travels of Capts. Lewis & Clarke, by order of the Government of the United States, performed in the years 1804, 1805, &
1806, being upwards of three thousand miles, from St. Louis, by
way of the Missouri, and Columbia Rivers, to the Pacifick Ocean:
Containing an Account of the Indian Tribes, who inhabit the Western part of the Continent unexplored, and unknown before. With
copious delineations of the manners, customs, religion, &c., of the
Indians. Compiled from various authentic sources, and Documents.
To which is subjoined, A Summary of the Statistical View of the*

---

[1] The copyright date (April 17) of the Philadelphia edition suggests the later
publication of the London one.

Indian Nations, from the Official Communication of Meriwether Lewis. Embellished with a Map of the Country inhabited by the Western Tribes of Indians, and Five Engravings of Indian Chiefs.

We cite the title in full for two reasons: one, because it remains relatively unchanged in succeeding editions, and, two, because on first reading, at least, it looks innocent enough, being simply an unequivocal declaration that the volume contains an authentic account of the travels of Lewis and Clark. The reader of that day who picked up the book and noted such parts of the title as "The Travels of Capts. Lewis & Clarke" and "Official Communication of Meriwether Lewis" could have had no cause to question their legitimacy. The title page seems faultless, too, unless one chances to look for the name of the compiler and finds none—only that of the publisher, Hubbard Lester. Even major headings of the text bear the marks of verisimilitude: "Recommendation from the President," "Message from the President," "Travels to the Pacifick Ocean," "Statistical View," and "Historical Sketches of the Several Tribes in Louisiana."

The magnitude of the hoax foisted upon the public by the compiler of this volume (and the others) is revealed only through making a scrupulous examination of the text. By so doing one learns that the fabricator skillfully interwove fact and fiction, plagiarized barefacedly, and, from first to last, left the precise impression intended, namely, that the work was genuine Lewis and Clark. As one reviewer commented after studying it, "If our simplicity is not greater than that of other persons, this book . . . will be sent for, and somewhat eagerly too, as Capt. Lewis's own account . . . of the late adventurous journey across the western part of the American continent."[2]

In examination of the text, to prove the point, we may logically begin with a look at "Recommendation from the President." The very first words betray the compiler's intent: "The following REC- OMMENDATION from the President of the United States to Congress explains the Nature, and bears ample testimony of the value of this novel and arduous undertaking." The design of the writer seems inescapable; he wished to lull the public into believing that Thomas Jefferson was actually recommending the work to them.

But it is in the section titled "Travels to the Pacifick Ocean" that

[2] *Eclectic Review* (London), Vol. V, Pt. 2 (November, 1809), 1052.

we find the false heart, lungs, and other visceral parts of this shoddy composite. It constitutes 140 of the total of 300 pages, and is the portion which the compiler leans on most heavily to justify his title, which, as we know, begins with the words, "The Travels of Capts. Lewis & Clarke." Herein, from the very beginning, he utilizes the pronoun "I" so cleverly that the reader is easily persuaded into believing that the words have come straight from the pen of Meriwether Lewis. In one place, for example, Lewis purportedly says, "Captain Clark kept an account of the distances of places from one to another; which were not kept by myself, for which reason I hope it will be sufficient apology for subjoining two of his statements." At no time, needless to say, did Lewis write these words. In fact, the only authentic parts of the entire section are two letters, one by Lewis to the president and the other by Clark to William Henry Harrison, both reprinted from Jefferson's *Message*.

The perpetrator of this section began it with a short description of Lewis and Clark's ascent of the Missouri to the Mandan villages. He then continued with what one writer has aptly called, "the great theft from Jonathan Carver,"[3] that is, a calculated plagiarism from Carver's *Travels Through the Interior Parts of North America in the Years 1766, 1767 and 1768*.[4] That it was a brazen theft is obvious, for the compiler not only palmed off the material as genuine Lewis and Clark, but also, in no place, extended credit to Carver. Elliott Coues put it this way:

> It is really a notable literary forgery, in constructing which the operator even went so far as to cut out of Carver's narration names which would serve to identify tribes of which Carver treated, in order that what was said of them might be misapplied to other tribes met by Lewis and Clark. This miserable trick, by which Carver was robbed and ethnology travestied, has misled every bibliographer.[5]

The concluding pages of this spurious section were devoted to a summary account of the Knisteneaux (Cree) and Chipewyan Indians of Canada lifted from Alexander Mackenzie's journal and,

[3] Coues, *History*, I, cxiii.
[4] Specifically, 115–39 of Chapter I, "Of the Origin, Manners, Customs, Religions, and Languages of the Indians," as found in the Philadelphia edition of 1796.
[5] Coues, *History*, I, cxii.

surprisingly, credited to him.[6] However, here again, the compiler contrived to make it appear that Lewis and Clark had associated on intimate terms with these tribes, whereas that was not the case.

The only authentic Lewis and Clark matter in the entire volume is that found in the sections titled "Message from the President" and "Statistical View," and in the two letters earlier mentioned. This material takes up precisely thirty-seven pages—little more than 10 per cent of the total.

We have examined two copies of this original 1809 American counterfeit edition, one in the Library Company of Philadelphia and the other in the New York Historical Society. Both are small in size (12mo), bound in brown leather, and printed on cheap paper that today is yellowed and crumbly. Both, too, are illustrated with five engravings of Indians[7] and a chart titled "Map of the Country Inhabited by the Western Tribes of Indians." William Clark's cartographical genius had nothing to do with the fashioning of this chart, though its creator, whoever he may have been, clearly intended to leave that impression, since he located Forts Mandan and Clatsop on it. Disproving any handiwork by Clark, we find topographical inaccuracies and omissions at every latitude. For example, the Jefferson River is depicted as originating in Canada just below a large body of water denominated "Lake Assiniboin," and the Cascade Range is conspicuous by its absence.

One could buy this miserable miscellany for $1.62½, a reasonable price even in those days, and the best possible argument for believing that many persons did buy it, and that the compiler profited, is the fact that so many other similar editions soon followed.

—2—

What of the known apocryphal editions that ensued? Two of them were translations, both into German, and both greatly abridged. The title page of one designated "Libanon" as its place of publication,

[6] *Voyages from Montreal, on the River St. Lawrence, through the Continent of North America, to the Frozen and Pacific Oceans, in the Years 1789 and 1793* (London, 1801).

[7] The engravings bear the captions "Sioux Queen," "Sioux Warrior," "Mahas [Omaha] Chief," "Ottoes [Oto] Chief," and "Serpentine [Snake] Chief."

while the other stipulated "Friedrichstadt." Since these had been printed in German, one might easily assume that they came from German presses, as this writer did at first. However, both editions were printed in the United States, the former in Lebanon, Pennsylvania, in 1811, and the latter in Frederick, Maryland, in 1812.

The current crop of Lewis and Clark students, if interested at all in these counterfeits, is probably more familiar with three editions that followed close on the heels of the German translations. One was conceived and born in Philadelphia (1812) and the other two in Baltimore (1812 and 1813), and, unlike the previous illegitimate offspring, all three had a parent. At least, the title page of each carried the name of William Fisher, Esq., as compiler. Struck by this deviation from the norm, one writer commented:

> William Fisher, Esq. must have been a bold man, and he may not have been a bad man too. Whereas the compiler, editor, thief or whatever he may have been, of the London and Philadelphia editions of 1809, retired behind an anonym, William Fisher not only stole his production bodily . . . but also formally announced himself as the author of the same.[8]

This commentator, however, seems not to have questioned the authenticity of William Fisher. Did such a man exist? We think not, for city directories of both Philadelphia and Baltimore for 1812 and 1813, and for years immediately before and after, do not list him, and neither do other standard reference sources. And, after all, is it reasonable to believe that any man of sound mind, knowing that he was trafficking in bogus material, would voluntarily expose a flank or any other part of his vulnerable anatomy?

The prime interest attaching to the Fisher editions, however, is that two of them, those of 1812, carry the first known published likenesses of Lewis and Clark. In the 1812 Baltimore they are captioned, "Lewis and Clark, Returned." The Philadelphia edition of the same year has no caption whatever for them, so that the viewer is faced with the problem of determining which is Lewis and which is Clark, a sticky problem indeed, since neither likeness bears the slightest resemblance to existing, authentic portraits of the two men. Quite obviously, the artist had never set eyes on either Lewis or

[8] Coues, *History*, I, cxvi.

Clark and had depicted them as fancy dictated, so that his portraits are just as spurious as the texts they illustrate. Nevertheless, in recent years authors and publishers have accorded them a semblance of respectability by reproducing them in books and magazine articles dealing with the Expedition. In these published works, they have attracted interest and speculation much as representations of basilisks, centaurs, gryphons, and other mythological creatures have done in centuries past.

With the publication in 1814 of *The History of the Expedition Under the Commands of Captains Lewis and Clark,* which was the first authorized and authentic account, one might have thought that the era of counterfeit editions would end, for what compiler would now be so foolhardy as to risk dollars on the specious when the genuine was at hand?[9] Yet one individual at least did so, in 1840; and he, too, like his predecessors, hid behind an anonym. His publisher was B. F. Ells, Dayton, Ohio.

On the verso of the title page of this Dayton counterfeit we find an advertisement in which the anonymous compiler attempted to explain why he produced it: "The great demand for the Journal of Lewis and Clark has induced the republication of the work, with the addition of extensive and interesting notes, and numerous illustrations on wood." The notes are neither extensive nor interesting, and the text is substantially a replay of earlier counterfeits.

The only feature setting this edition apart from the others is the illustrations, fifteen in all: one of Lewis, one of Clark, and the remainder of Indians, animals, and landscapes.[10] The sketches of Lewis and Clark, like those in the Fisher editions, provide another instance of lively imagination at work. Captions identify them, but, if these were reversed, viewers would be no worse off than before.

[9] The first account, published in Philadelphia in two volumes, was edited by Nicholas Biddle and today is often referred to as the Biddle edition.

[10] Joseph Sabin, *Dictionary of Books Relating to America* (New York, 1868), mentions still another counterfeit, one published in 1851 by Ells, Claflin & Co., Dayton, Ohio. Paltsits, however, could not authenticate this (Thwaites, *Original Journals,* I, lxx). Also spurious, but quite different, was a book published in Dublin in 1822 titled *Travels in North America.* This purports to narrate the experiences of one George Philips, an Irishman who left home for an extended tour in America. After visiting the West Indies and Mexico, he arrived in St. Louis, where he attached himself to Lewis and Clark for the traverse of the continent. On the return he left the party at Fort Mandan to travel in Canada.

—3—

The apocryphal editions are today collectors' items only and, even though they bring fancy prices at auctions, are of no value whatever to historians. Appearing when they did, however, they influenced adversely the reception accorded the 1814 authentic account.

Words from *Much Ado About Nothing* perhaps explain the successes enjoyed by the counterfeits. Therein Shakespeare has Claudio saying to Leonato, "Bait the hook well, this fish will bite." And that, of course, is precisely what compilers of these editions did—and in turn so did the buying public.

CHAPTER IV

Meriwether Lewis

Early in 1807 Thomas Jefferson appointed three men to important posts in the recently acquired Territory of Louisiana: Meriwether Lewis to that of governor,[1] William Clark to those of agent of the United States for Indian affairs and brigadier general of militia, and Frederick Bates to that of secretary, a position equivalent to that of lieutenant governor. Each appointment proved to be of greater consequence than Jefferson could have foreseen.

No one seems to have quarreled with Clark's credentials for either of the jobs the president gave to him, even though, looked at from a military standpoint, it was quite a jump from lieutenant in the Corps of Artillerists[2] to brigadier general of militia. Some people, however, did express disapproval of Lewis' qualifications for the office of governor—and with justice. He was completely inexperienced in the mercurial realm of politics and, as time proved, lacked the temperament and other correlative prerequisites vital to coping with executive problems routinely resolved by a more practiced official. Jefferson made the appointment, jubilant at the successes of

[1] Jefferson nominated Lewis as governor on February 28, 1807, and the United States Senate confirmed that nomination on March 2.

[2] Jefferson had promised Clark a captaincy. It was almost time for the Expedition to start up the Missouri when Lewis received a letter from the secretary of war informing him that the best he could do for Clark was a lieutenancy in the Corps of Artillerists.

the Expedition and desirous of honoring its young leader. It was an illusory reward, and an egregious error, as the president would soon discover. If, instead, he had insisted that Lewis sit down forthwith and devote all of his energy and talent to putting the journals into shape for publication, then our history books of today would unquestionably record an entirely different ending to the life of Meriwether Lewis.

As to Frederick Bates, he soon emerged as Lewis' bitterest critic and enemy, a persistent, deceitful gadfly, and at a most inopportune time for Lewis.

To assume the responsibilities of their new offices, both Clark and Bates left the East soon after receiving their appointments and arrived in St. Louis in April.[3] Lewis did not accompany them. Even though the United States Senate confirmed Jefferson's nomination of him as governor on March 3, 1807, he did not join Clark and Bates in the territorial capital until March 8, 1808, more than a year later.

The year was crucial to Lewis, and we shall examine it as fully, and critically, as available information allows. Certain aspects of it, as we assess them, cast light on the cause of Lewis' early death, and thus on his failure to prepare the journals of the Expedition for publication.

Lewis spent most of the first third of the year in Philadelphia, where he seems to have arrived in mid-April. As already reported, his first actions there were to engage John Conrad to publish the journals and to release the prospectus. In weeks ahead he accomplished much more, as he met and interviewed other men, primarily botanists, ornithologists, gardeners, and artists, whom he persuaded to make drawings of plants, animals, and Indians and to describe formally his botanical and zoological specimens.

We are unable to establish a definite chronology for these meetings, though one of the first men he called on was Bernard McMahon (c.1775–1816), florist and prominent seed merchant of the city at that time. Before Lewis left Washington for Philadelphia, he had received a letter from McMahon which said in part:

---

[3] Clark received his appointment and Senate confirmation on the same dates as Lewis. In late March Clark wrote Lewis from Fincastle, Virginia, "I shall proceed without delay to St. Louis" (Jackson, *Letters*, 388).

I would wish you to be here before the 20th inst. [April] as there is at present a young man boarding in my house, who, in my opinion, is better acquainted with plants, in general, than any man I ever conversed with on the subject . . . he is to depart, to the northward . . . about the 20th inst. He is a very intelligent Botanist, would be well inclined to render you any service in his power, and I am confident would defer his intended journey, to the first of May to oblige you.[4]

The young man in question was Frederick Pursh (1774–1820), a German-born and German-trained botanist. He had come to the United States in 1799, at the age of twenty-five, and was presently employed collecting plants for Dr. Benjamin Smith Barton (1766–1815), distinguished professor of botany at the University of Pennsylvania, hence his plan to "depart to the northward" in the near future.

McMahon's introduction of Pursh to Lewis turned out to be an event of considerable import to both men. Lewis, on his part, was immediately satisfied that McMahon had not overrated Pursh's botanical capabilities. As evidence, on May 10 he gave him thirty dollars to assist him "in preparing drawings and arranging specemines of plants" for his work, and two weeks later advanced an additional forty dollars.[5] Pursh, on his part, expressed delight, for, of Lewis' plants entrusted to him, all were "either entirely new or but little known" excepting no more than a dozen.[6]

Lewis had sound reasons for engaging Pursh. He himself possessed no facility with crayon or brush, and he regarded his botanical knowledge as inadequate to the task of describing plants in the Linnaean manner. Pursh had competence in both skills.

In 1803, when Lewis had visited Philadelphia to prepare for the Expedition, he had carried with him letters of introduction from Jefferson to important scientists of the city. One of these was to Dr. Barton, who instructed Lewis in methods then current of preserving plant specimens and, on the eve of Lewis' departure from the city, loaned him a copy of Antoine du Pratz's *History of Louisiana* to

[4] *Ibid.*, 398.
[5] *Ibid.*, 462, 463n.
[6] Frederick Pursh, *Flora Americae Septentrionalis*, 2 vols. (London, White, Cochrane & Co., 1814), I, xi.

carry with him on his western travels. This book is still extant,[7] and in it we find an inscription by Lewis which is the only evidence available that Lewis visited Dr. Barton in 1807. This inscription reads:

> Dr. Benjamin Smith Barton was so obliging as to lend me this copy of Monsr. Du Pratz's history of Louisiana in June 1803. It has since been conveyed by me to the Pacific Ocean through the interior of North America on my late tour thither and is now returned to it's proprietor by his Friend and Obt. Servt. Meriwether Lewis, Philadelphia, May 9, 1807.[8]

Lewis had other reasons for calling on Dr. Barton. For one thing, two years earlier, after Jefferson had received Lewis' shipment of plants from Fort Mandan, he had given the specimens to Barton to describe. Because of ill health, Barton had been unable to perform this taxonomic assignment, so that it was now up to Lewis to reclaim his specimens. For another reason, Lewis would have been eager to discuss with Dr. Barton the plans for publishing the botanical section of the journals.

Beyond reasonable doubt Lewis visited the well-known Philadelphia gardener, William Hamilton (1745–1813). Hamilton owned an estate near Bartram's Gardens known as "Woodlands." Because of its greenhouses and gardens with their generous display of both exotic and native plants, this estate was once characterized by Jefferson as "the only rival which I have known in America to what may be seen in England."[9] Hamilton had been favored in 1805 with a packet of seeds Lewis had sent from Fort Mandan. Two years later, shortly before Lewis arrived in Philadelphia, Jefferson advised Hamilton by letter, "It is with great pleasure that, at the request of Governor Lewis, I send you the seeds now inclosed, being part of the Botanical fruits of his journey across the continent. . . . He will be with you shortly. . . ."[10] Lewis would have wanted to

---

[7] In the Library Company, Philadelphia; it is the second edition, published in London in 1774.

[8] For more about this copy of Du Pratz's book, see Paul R. Cutright, "Lewis and Clark and Du Pratz," Missouri Historical Society *Bulletin*, Vol. XXI, No. 1 (October, 1964), 31–35.

[9] Sarah P. Stetson, "William Hamilton and His 'Woodlands'," *Pennsylvania Magazine of History and Biography*, Vol. LXXIII (1949), 26–33.

[10] Jackson, *Letters*, 389.

meet Hamilton, if for no other reason than to check on his successes in growing the Fort Mandan seeds.

If Lewis saw more of one man than another on this stay, that man was Charles Willson Peale (1741–1827), noted artist and hyper-kinetic proprietor of the Philadelphia Museum, better known as Peale's Museum. This institution at that time was the foremost of its kind in the United States, and Lewis and Jefferson were of one mind in acknowledging it to be the most logical repository for the con-siderable number of zoological and ethnological specimens the Ex-pedition had returned from the West. As a consequence, all of these items, excepting a few retained by Jefferson for his private museum at Monticello and a similar moiety fancied by Lewis and Clark themselves, were given outright to Peale.

Being the recipient of such a windfall, which enhanced the pres-tige of his museum enormously, Peale was easily persuaded by Lewis to make portraits of particular animals of the collection. Ac-tually, he seemed delighted, for on May 5 he wrote to a friend, "The drawings for Governor Lewis's Journal I mean to draw my-self."[11] Two of these drawings have survived, one of Lewis' wood-pecker (*Asyndesmus lewis*) and another of mountain quail (*Oreor-tyx pictus pictus*). Interested persons may see them today in the library of the American Philosophical Society.[12] That Peale made portraits of other animals for Lewis is proved by a letter written by Clark at later date. In it he said, ". . . Mr. Peal has drawn three of the berds, the Braroe [*i.e.*, the badger, *Taxidea taxus*] & Antelope, and an engraving has been made of the Big Horn."[13] Unfortunately, none of these portraits has survived, except, of course, those of the woodpecker and quail mentioned above.

A special feature of Peale's Museum was a gallery of portraits he had painted of the more celebrated Americans of his time. A month or so before Lewis came to Philadelphia, Peale wrote Jefferson, "Mr. Lewis is richly entitled to a place amongst the Portraits of the Museum, and I hope he will do me the favor of sitting as soon

[11] *Ibid.*, 411.

[12] At the American Philosophical Society is a drawing of a horned toad (*Phry-nosoma cornutum*) bearing the legend, "Drawn by C. W. Peale." Evidence un-earthed by Donald Jackson suggests that it was drawn by another artist, Pietro Ancora.

[13] Jackson, *Letters*, 490.

as he arrives here."[14] Lewis did sit for Peale (and so did Clark, but not until three years later). Of course, the thought did not even enter the mind of either of the explorers that these portraits of them would one day be regarded as the most skillfully executed and truest-to-life of all the several likenesses made in their lifetimes; that they would be reproduced countless times by future historians of the Expedition; and that ultimately they would find a permanent home among other treasures now carefully preserved by the Independence National Historical Park, Philadelphia.

Peale was not a man to pass up opportunities. He not only persuaded Lewis to sit for a portrait, but also induced him to consent to having his figure perpetuated in wax. The finished likeness showed him dressed in an elegant Indian robe that the Shoshoni chief, Cameahwait, had presented to him. Peale wrote Jefferson that his object in preparing this wax figure was "to give a lesson to the Indians who may visit the Museum, and also to shew my sentiments respecting wars."[15] Regrettably, this unique representation of Lewis disappeared long ago, its fate unknown.

Lewis did not rely entirely on Peale for animal portraits. He turned also to Alexander Wilson (1766–1813), the Scottish-born artist-naturalist who is best remembered for his illustrated, multi-volumed *American Ornithology*. In this work Wilson wrote, "It was the request and particular wish of Captain Lewis made to me in person that I make drawings of each of the feathered tribe as had been preserved, and were new."[16] Therein, too, as evidence of good faith, we find four bird portraits by Wilson: Lewis' woodpecker, Clark's nutcracker (*Nucifraga columbiana*), western tanager (*Piranga ludoviciana*), and black-billed magpie (*Pica pica hudsonia*).

To illustrate further the journals, Lewis desired drawings of some of the Indians in a delegation he had brought back with him from the High Plains and who were then visiting such cities as Washington and Philadelphia. To obtain these portraits, he sought out Charles de St. Mémin (1770–1852), a French artist who had fled to the United States in the 1790's as a refugee from the French

---

[14] *Ibid.*, 374n.

[15] *Ibid.*, 439.

[16] Alexander Wilson, *American Ornithology*, 9 vols. (Philadelphia, Bradford & Inskeep, 1808–14), III, 31–32.

Revolution. An entry in Lewis' account book reads in part, ". . . paid St. Memin for likenesses of the indians &c. necessary to my publication . . . $83.50."[17] Several of these, both crayons and watercolors, are extant today in various museums and private collections.[18]

Still another person Lewis approached for illustrations was John James Barralet (c.1747–1815), an Irish-born engraver. To him he paid the sum of forty dollars "for two drawings [of] water falls."[19] In a letter to one of Lewis' kin, Clark later stated that Barralet had made the two drawings and that they were of "the falls of the Missouri & Columbia."[20] The fate of these is unknown.

In his prospectus, it will be recalled, Lewis had declared that a map, on a large scale, would accompany the three volumes of his account. Presumably, he had in mind that Clark would make this chart, if he had not already done so. Conscious, however, that their determinations of longitude en route to the Pacific, due to a fickle chronometer, could not be depended on, Lewis induced Ferdinand Rudolph Hassler (1770–1843), a Swiss mathematician then teaching at West Point Military Academy, to make corrections and, for that task, paid him $100.[21]

Some three years earlier, Lewis had been honored by election to membership in the American Philosophical Society, then the most prestigious scientific organization in the United States. News of his election had reached him in St. Louis just before the Expedition started up the Missouri. Minutes of the society record that Lewis attended three of its stated meetings during his 1807 visit: April 17, June 19, and July 17.

As to how else Lewis spent his time in Philadelphia, we know

---

[17] Jackson, *Letters*, 411 n.

[18] For reproduction of fourteen of St. Mémin's drawings of Indians, see Dorothy Wollon and Margaret Kinard, "Sir Augustus J. Foster and 'The Wild Natives of the Woods,' 1805–1807," *William and Mary Quarterly*, Ser. 3, Vol. II, No. 2 (April, 1952), 191–214. St. Mémin also made at least three portraits of Lewis and one of Clark. For more about these and other known likenesses of Lewis and Clark, see Paul R. Cutright, "Lewis and Clark: Portraits and Portraitists," *Montana, the Magazine of Western History*, Vol. XIX, No. 2 (Spring, 1969), 37–53.

[19] Jackson, *Letters*, 463n.

[20] *Ibid.*, 490.

[21] When Clark came to Philadelphia in 1810 following Lewis' death, he was unable to find Hassler's "Calculations" among Lewis' papers (Jackson, *Letters*, 491).

very little. His account book tells us that he stayed at a boarding-house run by a Mrs. Wood, and that, on April 20, he gave her five dollars to purchase "a douzen of porter" and, on May 5, ten dollars for a dozen of ale. The same source reveals, too, that he paid a man named Varnum ten dollars for distributing the prospectus of his work.[22] During this period Lewis wrote one letter to Jefferson (and it may have been the only one, since the president was most diligent about filing his correspondence). Dated June 27, it was brief and limited its content mainly to reporting on errands Jefferson had asked him to run for him, such as having two watches repaired and a ring reset by Henry Voight, Philadelphia watchmaker, and having the head and horns of a bighorn sheep prepared by Peale. The only other information Lewis provided was that he anticipated returning to Washington about the fifteenth of July.[23]

All we can do about Lewis' other activities is to speculate. Presumably, he busied himself trying to enlarge the number of his subscribers. He must have made courtesy calls on Robert Patterson, Benjamin Rush, and Caspar Wistar, each of whom in 1803 had welcomed him warmly and provided much gratuitous help and advice. It would be surprising, too, if he made no effort to become acquainted with at least some of the men who constituted that dedicated coterie of naturalists then active in the city, men such as George Ord,[24] Constantine Rafinesque,[25] Thomas Say,[26] Charles

[22] *Ibid.*, 393, 463n.

[23] *Ibid.*, 418.

[24] George Ord (1781–1866), a ship's chandler by vocation, early became associated with the small group of more advanced naturalists who, in 1812, founded the Academy of Natural Sciences of Philadelphia. He is perhaps best known for his *Sketch of the Life of Alexander Wilson* (Philadelphia, 1828).

[25] Constantine Samuel Rafinesque (1783–1840) was born in Turkey and came to Philadelphia in 1802. He was a merchant by training. After a period as professor of botany at Transylvania University, Lexington, Kentucky, and travel west of the Alleghenies, he returned to Philadelphia, where he wrote many books and pamphlets.

[26] Thomas Say (1787–1834) was born in Philadelphia, became one of the founders of the Academy of Natural Sciences and an important contributor to its *Journal*. He was geologist on Major Stephen Long's expedition to the West in 1819–20 and in 1825 accompanied Robert Owen to New Harmony, Indiana. His principal scientific work was *American Entomology*, 3 vols. (Philadelphia, 1824–28).

Lesueur,[27] and John Godman.[28] Beyond question, he accepted numerous invitations to banquets and other affairs held in his honor. If he did not receive the key to the city, he must have been given its equivalent.

Lewis' known successes in furthering the publication of his work may be summed up in the shortness of a sentence. He obtained a publisher, released a prospectus, engaged artists and naturalists to figure and describe his animal and plant specimens, persuaded still other draftsmen to make drawings of Indians and waterfalls, and induced a mathematician to correct navigational determinations.

Since Lewis did not live to experience the satisfaction of turning the pages of his completed work, and none of the illustrations made for him appeared in the first authorized published account,[29] it would be easy to conclude that his industry in Philadelphia availed nothing. But such a conclusion would be false, for that industry ultimately led to collateral increments both consequential and far-reaching. For instance, many of the portraits made by Peale, Wilson, Pursh, and St. Mémin have survived, and today they decorate increasingly the pages of books and articles devoted to America's most celebrated team of explorers. Then, too, because Lewis entrusted his herbarium to Pursh, current botanists have Pursh's descriptions of more than one hundred western plants new to science when discovered by Lewis, each credited to Lewis with Pursh's abbreviated legend, "*v.s. in Herb. Lewis.*" And, without Pursh's attention, botanical nomenclature would have been deprived of such binomials as *Lewisia rediviva* (bitterroot), *Clarkia pulchella* (ragged robin), *Linum lewisii* (Lewis' wild flax) and *Philadelphus lewisii* (Lewis' syringa). Not to be overlooked, too, were the zoological contributions of Ord, Rafinesque, Say, Lesueur, and Godman. Because of Lewis' presence in Philadelphia and his consignment of specimens to Peale's Museum, Ord, in years immediately ahead, formally de-

---

[27] Charles A. Lesueur (1778–1846) was a French artist-naturalist who came to the United States in 1816. He wrote widely on ichthyological topics, and furnished many of the plates which lent distinction to early volumes of the *Journal* of the Academy of Natural Sciences.

[28] John D. Godman (1794–1830) was born in Maryland, studied medicine in Baltimore, and practiced in various places, including Philadelphia. He wrote *American Natural History*, 3 vols. (Philadelphia, 1826).

[29] The Biddle edition, 1814.

scribed more animals discovered by Lewis than any other individual, Rafinesque and Say described still others, and Lesueur made drawings of such western animals as antelope and coyote that illustrated John Godman's *American Natural History*.

What more should we say about this visit by Lewis to Philadelphia? Perhaps nothing at all, if we did not know of the sequel, a tragic one that may have had its beginning in Philadelphia. Viewed in that light, we are led to wonder why Lewis lingered so long in Philadelphia (could he not have accomplished what he did in less time?); why, especially in his letter to Jefferson, did he express no concern about his delay in reporting for duty in St. Louis; and why, during the three months, did he prepare no copy at all for John Conrad? For it is known that he did not.

—2—

Lewis left Philadelphia for Washington in the latter part of July. By then he had been governor of Louisiana *in absentia* for more than four months. A period of eight months ensued in which he continued as governor *in absentia*. The question comes to mind immediately: why did Lewis delay so long in reporting to St. Louis? In his earlier years, and throughout the months of exploring the West, he was a man who took his responsibilities seriously. But at some unfortunate moment after Lewis left Philadelphia something happened that turned his life around, and not for the better. If we knew what happened, we would most likely no longer be in doubt as to the cause of the delay. Since we do not, we can only conjecture.

Is it conceivable that Lewis, conscious of difficulties inherent in the job of governor and regarding his own powers inadequate to handling them, developed a bad case of nerves?

Did he become despondent when unsuccessful in love? There were romantic episodes in this period, with Lewis at one point declaring that he was determined to get a wife.[30] He, of course, never married.

Or did he fall a victim to alcohol, perhaps as a result of an ungovernable depression of mind when his offer of love was rejected?

In an attempt to arrive at a satisfactory answer, we have weighed every fact available to us, constructed alternate theories, balanced

[30] Dillon, *Meriwether Lewis*, 285.

one against another, and have discussed all aspects with historians whose opinions we value. In the end, we lean to the belief that alcoholism was the answer, and cite as strong supporting evidence a portion of a letter Jefferson subsequently wrote: "He [Lewis] was much afflicted & habitually so with hypochondria. This was probably increased by the habit into which he had fallen & the painfull reflections that would necessarily produce in a mind like his."[31]

But whatever the cause of Lewis' delay in reporting to St. Louis may have been, we are convinced that it was emotionally inspired, and that it contributed to his early, self-inflicted death, at the age of thirty-five.

—3—

Black robes, as someone has said, do not make a God of man. Neither do military insignia insure success in political life. Lewis found that out soon after he finally arrived in St. Louis. The troubles he experienced have been told again and again and need no retelling, except to emphasize that he encountered bitter opposition from Bates, fancied himself on the border of bankruptcy when a new administration in Washington refused to honor legitimate expenses he had incurred, and, intermittently, suffered mental torment because he had failed to further the publication of the journals.[32] The combination of these worries weighed heavily on Lewis' mind, already scarred by earlier ones.

Perhaps the soundest proof of a troubled mind was the near collapse of communication between Lewis and Jefferson, and the resultant deterioration of what had been an intimate friendship. The president had cause for reproving Lewis, as he did in a letter written to him ten months after they had last met: "Since I parted with you in Albemarle [County, Virginia] in Sep. last I have never had a line from you, nor I believe has the Secretary of War. . . ."[33]

[31] Jackson, *Letters*, 575n.

[32] In a letter to Jefferson dated November 13, 1809, Conrad said, "Govr. Lewis never furnished us with a line of the M.S. nor indeed could we ever hear any thing from him respecting it tho frequent applications to that effect were made to him (Jackson, *Letters*, 469).

[33] In a letter from Jefferson to Lewis dated July 17, 1808 (Jackson, *Letters*, 444).

As the summer of 1809 neared an end, Lewis decided to travel to Washington, where he hoped in consultation with federal officials to resolve his worrisome financial problems. He left St. Louis on September 4 and eleven days later arrived at Chickasaw Bluffs, the present site of Memphis, Tennessee, and then the location of Fort Pickering. The fort's commanding officer, Captain Gilbert C. Russell, met him and subsequently reported, ". . . the Boat in which he was a passenger landed him at Fort Pickering in a state of mental derangement . . . he had made [en route] two attempts to kill himself, in one of which he had nearly succeeded."[34]

Captain Russell personally took charge of Lewis. At the end of two weeks he could detect in Lewis no remaining symptoms of derangement and considered him sufficiently recovered to resume his journey. Presumably Lewis thought so himself, though he did alter his route of travel. He indicated this change when writing at Fort Pickering on September 22 to his friend Captain Amos Stoddard: "I am now on my way to the city of Washington and contemplated taking . . . Orlianes [New Orleans] in my rout, but my indisposition has induced me to change my route and shall now pass through Tennessee and Virginia."[35]

Lewis left Fort Pickering on September 29. He followed the Natchez Trace and had as his companion Major James Neelly. Late in the afternoon of October 10 he arrived at a remote roadhouse called Grinder's Inn. According to Major Neelly, Lewis, earlier on that same day, had "appeared at times deranged in mind."[36] That night Lewis died a victim, in our opinion, of his own hand.

We have dwelt at some length on the final months of Lewis' life, for to the events of those months we must turn for explanation of his tragic death and consequent much-delayed publication of the authentic history of the Expedition.

The tragedy of Grinder's Inn mounts when we reflect that Lewis carried with him on this ill-fated journey the maps, notebooks, and other holographic documents constituting what would one day, when published, become *Original Journals of the Lewis and Clark Expedition*, and that these would now of necessity pass to other hands.

[34] *Ibid.*, 573.
[35] Thwaites, *Original Journals*, VII, 368.
[36] Jackson, *Letters*, 467.

Jefferson, more conscious than others of the immediate detriment to publication created by Lewis' death, expressed himself in these words: ". . . no pen can ever give us so faithful & lively an account of the countries & nations which he saw, as his own would have done, under the guidance of impressions made by the objects themselves."[37]

[37] *Ibid.*, 474n.

CHAPTER V
Nicholas Biddle

How paradoxical that the role of preparing for publication the Lewis and Clark journals should fall to a man who had never traveled farther west than the Susquehanna River, had never heard the eerie wail of a coyote, had never seen the vast herds of bellowing bison in the days of their abundance, had never scented the pungency of sagebrush—in short, had never experienced any of the sights and sounds and odors common to the High Plains or other parts of the great land expanse west of the Mississippi so familiar to Meriwether Lewis, who, but for insensate destiny, would himself have prepared the journals.

Happily for future historians of the Expedition, the man who succeeded to Lewis' intended role was Nicholas Biddle (1786–1844), a young Philadelphia lawyer possessed of rare literary ability.

However, before detailing Biddle's contributions to Lewis and Clark history, we should report pertinent events which occurred in the interval between Lewis' death and Biddle's involvement. Perhaps the first of these was a message received by Jefferson from the Philadelphia publishers, C. and A. Conrad and Company. Dated November 13, 1809, just one month after the tragedy at Grinder's Inn, the message reminded the former president of the contract they had signed in 1807 with Lewis, of expenses they had since incurred, and of an obvious fact, that publication of the journals was "already much too long delayed."[1]

[1] Jackson, *Letters*, 468–69.

To this letter Jefferson, then at Monticello, replied:

> Govr. Lewis had in his lifetime apprised me that he had contracted with you for the publication of his account of the expedition. I had written to him some time ago to know when he would have it ready & was expecting an answer when I received the news of his unfortunate end. James Neelly, the U.S. agent to the Chickasaws, writes me that "he has two trunks of papers . . . amongst which is said to be his travels to the Pacific ocean; that some days previous to his death he requested of him (Neelly) in case any accident happened to him, to send his trunk, with the papers therein *to the President,* but he thinks it very probable he meant, *to me* [not James Madison]." . . . I am waiting the arrival of Genl. Clarke, expected here in a few days, to consult with him on the subject. His aid & his interest in the publication of the work may render him the proper depository to have it prepared & delivered over to you. But my present idea is (if he concurs) to order it on to the President, according to his literal desire, and the rather because it is said that there are in his trunks vouchers for his public accounts, and when it may be within my sphere to take any definite step respecting it, you shall be informed of it.[2]

Clark seems to have arrived at Monticello about two weeks later, for on December 11 Jefferson wrote to "Messrs. Conrad & Co." that "Genl. Clarke called on me a few days ago. . . . He is himself now gone on to Washington, where the papers [of Lewis] may be immediately expected, & he will proceed thence to Philadelphia to do whatever is necessary to the publication."[3]

Two pieces of paper preserved today at the Missouri Historical Society bear witness that Clark had prepared in advance for this trip to the East and that he had well in mind his primary objectives. On one of the pieces he had jotted down the names and addresses of such prominent Philadelphians as John Conrad, Charles Willson Peale, Bernard McMahon, Benjamin Rush, Caspar Wistar, and Benjamin Smith Barton, all of whom, presumably, he wished to consult.[4] On the other he had scribbled reminders, such as, "If a man can be got to go to St. Louis with me to write the journal &

---

[2] *Ibid.,* 474–75.
[3] *Ibid.,* 479.
[4] *Ibid.,* 397.

price," and "get some one to write the scientific part & natural history—Botany, Mineralogy & Zoology."[5]

The success of Clark's trip, one necessitating many weeks of travel and consultation, hinged on whether or not he could find someone "to write the journal." From some source, possibly Jefferson, he learned that William Wirt, a Richmond attorney and biographer of Patrick Henry, would be a good man for the job if he could be induced to take it on. To find out, Clark, early in January, 1810, wrote to William Meriwether, a cousin of Meriwether Lewis then in Richmond, and asked him to see Wirt. A few days later Meriwether replied, saying in part, "I presented your favor of the 11th instant to Mr. Wirt . . . but if it was necessary [for him] to copy the journal, that it would take more time than he could spare . . . and it was understood between us, that it should be first ascertained, that Mr. Jefferson, would not undertake the work."[6]

Whether Clark, while at Monticello, discussed with Jefferson the possibility of his assuming the editorship of the journals will probably never be known. Certainly no man then alive could have submitted credentials for this task equal to those held by Jefferson. Attesting to uncommon literary talent, he had written the Declaration of Independence and a widely applauded book, *Notes on the State of Virginia*. His large personal library contained adequate reference material.[7] He was a versatile and accomplished naturalist, as is proved by Dr. Barton's deposition: ". . . in the various departments of . . . botany and zoology, the information of this gentleman is equalled by that of few persons in the United States."[8] He had familiarized himself with maps then available purporting to delineate trans-Mississippi geography and had schooled himself in the use of such navigational instruments as sextant and theodolite. He was a most inquisitive student of the American Indian. And, as persistent advocate and promoter of the Expedition, he understood, far more than anyone else, the importance of publishing all data brought back by Lewis and Clark. Otherwise, in his opinion, as we know, the

[5] *Ibid.*, 486.

[6] *Ibid.*, 489.

[7] This was the second of three libraries amassed by Jefferson in his lifetime, and the one subsequently presented to Congress which served to launch the Library of Congress. His first had been destroyed by fire.

[8] Betts (annotator), *Thomas Jefferson's Garden Book*, 172.

history of this extraordinary exploration would become fable instead of fact.

Of course, Jefferson did not undertake the task of preparing the Lewis and Clark journals for publication. Even if urged by Clark to do so, he probably demurred on the grounds of advanced age (he was then sixty-five) and an overweening desire to spend his remaining years at Monticello as a gentleman farmer, unhampered, in so far as possible, by weighty responsibilities akin to those which had burdened him through so much of his earlier lifetime.

—2—

After a brief stop with Jefferson at Monticello, Clark went on to Washington. Here he and President Madison's private secretary examined Lewis' effects, which had meanwhile arrived from Grinder's Inn, and Clark was given custody of all documentary material pertaining to the Expedition. He then left Washington for Philadelphia, arriving early in January, 1810. At one time or another while there, he called upon all of the men whose names he had jotted down on paper before leaving St. Louis. John Conrad assured him of his readiness to proceed with publication of the journals once he had the manuscript in his hands. McMahon produced Lewis' herbarium which, three years earlier, Lewis had left with Pursh.[9] Dr. Barton agreed to write the volume of the history limited to descriptions of plants, animals, and other natural-history specimens. And Charles Willson Peale showed Clark the portraits of western animals he had drawn at Lewis' request. Peale, too, urged Clark to write the narrative portion of the journal himself. But, as the artist told his son Rembrandt soon afterward, "I found that the General was too diffident of his abilities."[10]

The odds are prohibitive that we shall ever learn who suggested to Clark that Nicholas Biddle would be a good man to edit the journals. Unfortunately, the suggestion was made just as Clark was

[9] But not all of the specimens. McMahon did not know that Pursh, without leave, had lifted a number from Lewis' collection and had added them to his own.

[10] Jackson, *Letters*, 493. At some time during his stay in Philadelphia, Clark sat for a portrait by Peale (as Lewis had done in 1807). Conrad planned to use the two likenesses as illustrations in the projected history (*Ibid.*, 492), but, unfortunately, his intention went askew.

concluding his visit to Philadelphia, and by then Biddle was absent from the city. However, Clark left a note for him in which he described the nature of the work to be done and requested a reply. With that done, Clark set out for Fincastle, Virginia, home of his father-in-law, Colonel George Hancock.

By the width of an eyelash Biddle almost missed joining that select fraternity of men today recognized as constituting the flower of Lewis and Clark scholars. On March 3, 1810, having returned to the city and examined his mail, he wrote Clark that he had neither the health nor the leisure necessary "to do sufficient justice to the fruits of your enterprise and ingenuity."[11] But Biddle, responsive to the ever-whirling wheel of change, soon entertained second thoughts. Just two weeks later he addressed himself to Clark again:

> I had the pleasure of writing to you on the 3rd inst. upon the subject of your intended publication. Being unwilling to disappoint you I was afraid of undertaking a work which I feared I might not be able to execute to my own or your satisfaction. Having since then seen Mr. Conrad & Dr. Barton, what I learned from them, joined with a prospect of better health & more time than I had originally expected induced me to consent provided you had not in the meantime, as I thought probable, made a better choice. Mr. Conrad mentioned to me today that your last letter of the 9th inst. represents you as under no engagement of that sort. I will therefore very readily agree to do all that is in my power for the advancement of the work; and I think I can promise with some confidence that it shall be ready as soon as the publisher is prepared to print it. Having made up my mind today, I am desirous that no delay should occur on my work. As therefore you express a wish that I should see you, I am arranging my business so as to leave on Wednesday next, and take the route by Hagerstown, Winchester & c. In this way I hope to make you a short visit very soon after the receipt of my letter. In the meantime I remain with high respect Yrs. & c.[12]

Nicholas Biddle was then just twenty-six years old. As evidence of unusually early development of mental aptitudes, he had been granted admission to the University of Pennsylvania at the age of ten. During the next three years he satisfied all requirements for

[11] *Ibid.*, 495.
[12] *Ibid.*, 496.

graduation, but the university, citing his extreme youth, denied to him his diploma. He then entered Princeton, from which he graduated in 1801, at the age of fifteen, the youngest person up to that time to graduate from that college. In years immediately ahead Biddle studied law and, from time to time, contributed letters and essays to *Port Folio*, a popular contemporary magazine. In 1804 he went to Europe, where he remained for three years, first as secretary to the United States minister to France and then as temporary secretary to James Monroe, American minister to Great Britain. As occasion permitted, Biddle traveled through other European countries, particularly those bordering on the Mediterranean.

On his return to the United States, in July, 1807, Biddle opened a law office and resumed his contributions to *Port Folio*, at times adopting the pseudonym of Oliver Oldschool. Extremely successful in both endeavors, he was soon torn between a strong desire to give most of his time to writing and an equally impelling one to concentrate on law. He was in this uncertain state of mind when he received Clark's note inquiring whether he would be interested in editing the journals of Lewis and Clark.

Clark, having yet to meet this paragon of precocity, was, of course, unable to size him up until Biddle joined him in Fincastle. He may well have questioned whether one so young possessed the maturity and serious turn of mind equal to the task ahead. Biddle's passport, obtained before he left for Europe, described him as five feet seven in height, with "chestnut eyes, middling mouth, high forehead, round chin, fair complexion, chestnut hair and eyebrows, and oval face."[13] But, as Clark soon determined, there was nothing "middling" about Biddle's intellect, energy, or perseverance.

In a letter to Henry Dearborn dated April 15, Clark revealed something of what he and Biddle had been able to accomplish during their days together in Fincastle:

> Since my return from Washington, I have been closely employed making such arrangements of my journal, and Memorandoms, as are necessary for the edition. Mr. Nicholas Biddle (the gentleman who writes the Naritive) left us yesterday. He has been with me

[13] Thomas Payne Govan, *Nicholas Biddle, Nationalist and Public Banker, 1786–1844* (Chicago, University of Chicago Press, 1959), 12.

nearly three weeks takeing such Notes as will enable him with the explanations made on such parts of the journal as required it, to proceed without dificulty. Such parts as relate to science only, have been selected and sent on by Mr. Biddle to Doctr. Barton, and shall place in his hands the specimens of plants.[14]

While at Fincastle, Biddle read the journals and, while so doing, jotted down numerous questions to put to Clark. By great good fortune, these questions and Clark's answers, in Biddle's own handwriting, are extant today, carefully preserved in the library of the American Philosophical Society. These queries exceed three hundred in number, with the great majority of them inquiring about the customs, dress, languages, religion, and so forth of Sioux, Mandans, Nez Percés, Chinooks, and other Indian tribes. Biddle's absorption in ethnological matters reflected not only his own personal interest in the American Indian, but also a strong belief that readers of the history would share his interest. In support of this, we find him saying to Clark in one of his letters, ". . . in our towns, and in Europe too where we know nothing of Indians every little matter is a subject that excites curiosity."[15] Thus Biddle's own curiosity resulted in a considerable fund of information about western Indians not found in the original journals of Lewis and Clark.[16]

Returned to Philadelphia, Biddle lost no time in getting to work in earnest on the job he had agreed to undertake. One of his first acts was to release a prospectus (almost precisely three years after Lewis had issued the original). It announced that the much-delayed history of the Expedition would be published in the near future by C. and A. Conrad and Company, that the account would consist of two parts (one, narrative of the journey, and two, description of scientific discoveries) and that the price of the first part (in two octavo volumes) would be ten dollars, and of the second (one volume) eleven dollars.[17] He had hastened to publish the prospectus, Biddle in-

[14] Jackson, *Letters*, 546.

[15] *Ibid.*, 552.

[16] Biddle's "Notes" were presented to the American Philosophical Society by Charles J. Biddle in June, 1949, and are in two parts. The first is a marble-backed notebook of some thirty pages obscurely titled, "Garden Book." The second part, surprisingly, is actually an addendum to Lewis' "Ohio Journal," Biddle having taken advantage of blank pages he found therein.

[17] Jackson, *Letters*, 546–48.

formed Clark, because of rumors that "a second edition of Gass's journal" would soon appear and he wished to forestall it if possible.[18]

With the prospectus released, Biddle began writing. His enthusiasm seems to have been unbounded, for he soon wrote Clark that he habitually rose each morning at five and gave "seven or eight and even more hours a day" to the work, actually transcribing and paraphrasing.[19] With no difficulty at all, we can understand, and share, Biddle's enthusiasm, for he was spending hours daily reading and rereading the original handwritten entries of Lewis and Clark which collectively constitute one of the most exciting and valuable accounts of discovery and exploration ever written.[20]

Biddle found the task far from easy. Testifying to that fact, he soon confided to a friend, "I find it exceedingly troublesome, for not a word was prepared for the press by Captain Lewis & the papers are very voluminous."[21] Before long he received a modicum of assistance. Writing from Louisville in late May of that year, Clark advised Biddle that he was sending to him George Shannon, one of the party who had accompanied Lewis and Clark. Somewhat later Biddle told Clark that he had derived much help from Shannon, who was "very intelligent and sensible & whom it was worth your while to send here."[22]

In spite of the problems Biddle had to endure, on July 7, just three months after beginning his writing, he was able to inform Clark, "I have sent you & ten men up into a bottom to look for wood to make canoes after the unhappy failure of your iron boat; so that you see how far I am."[23] Biddle was here alluding, of course, to

[18] *Ibid.*, 551. This would appear to have been the edition published by Mathew Carey in 1810.

[19] *Ibid.*, 550–51.

[20] Biddle had at hand, too, the journals of Sergeants Ordway and Gass, though, in his opinion, the former was much better than the latter (*Ibid.*, 551).

[21] *Ibid.*, 555.

[22] *Ibid.*, 568. Private George Shannon is best known to students of the Expedition as that member of the party who got lost on two occasions and who, in 1807, while with a group attempting to return the Mandan chief, Big White, to his home, was shot in the leg by an Arikara and later lost that limb. After he had concluded his stay in Philadelphia helping Biddle, he studied law at Transylvania University, became a member of the Kentucky House of Representatives (1820), and still later a Missouri state senator.

[23] *Ibid.*, 550.

events of July 10, 1805, when Clark, with a number of axmen, left the White Bear Islands campsite (just above Great Falls, Montana) and proceeded upstream to look for cottonwood trees large enough for dugout canoes. By that date the party had consumed fourteen months since starting the ascent of the Missouri, exactly one-half of the time expended during the entire journey.

In weeks and months ahead, Biddle's work became even more onerous. To one correspondent he said, "Dr. Barton & myself have undertaken to publish the papers of Capts. Lewis & Clarke, but as the chief labor falls upon myself, I find it exceedingly troublesome, & for some months past have been obliged to devote to it a most persevering & undivided attention."[24]

At the root of some of Biddle's complaint was the fact that he set extremely high standards for himself. For instance, in order to do justice to his remarks about the American Indian, he read books available to him on the subject and directed additional questions to Clark about Mandans and other aboriginals. In one letter to Clark he inquired about the precise meaning of the French term *bois roulé* (literally "rolled wood"—a mixture of tobacco with particles of various woods), and said in conclusion, "It is of some consequence to be accurate."[25]

Nevertheless, on June 28, 1811, slightly more than one year after Biddle began his "troublesome" literary adventures with Lewis and Clark, he was in a position to write Clark, ". . . by diligence [I] have at length been able to get completely thru the manuscripts and am now ready to put the work to the press as soon as Mr. Conrad wishes it."[26]

---

[24] *Ibid.,* 555n.

[25] *Ibid.,* 552.

[26] *Ibid.,* 568. It was in this same letter that Biddle asked Clark to explain his military rank while with the Expedition. Clark replied, "You express a desire to know the exact relation which I stood in Point of Rank, and Command with Captain Lewis—*equal in every point of view*—(I did not think myself very well treated as I did not get the appointment which was promised me. As I was not disposed to make any noise about the business have never mentioned the particulars to any one, and must request you not to mention my disappointment & the cause to any one)" (*Ibid.,* 571). As is well known, Jefferson had told Lewis that he would obtain a captaincy for Clark, but when his recommendation reached the War Department, the best they could do for him was "Lieutenant of Artillerists." But for Biddle's inquiry, we would have no specific knowledge of Clark's feelings on this matter.

No blame attaches to Biddle that major obstacles soon arose to shatter his optimism about early publication of the journals. There were several. For one thing, the War of 1812 intruded, thwarting endeavors in every walk of life. For another, Dr. Barton, because of deteriorating health, failed to produce the extremely important volume on the scientific results of the Expedition. Then, without forewarning, came the most devastating blow of all, the collapse of the publishing firm of C. and A. Conrad and Company.[27]

Faced with this series of disheartening setbacks, Biddle displayed mettle heretofore unrevealed. Reluctantly, he discontinued further thought of a technical volume and bent all his efforts toward finding another publisher, a task made far more difficult because of conditions arising out of the war with Britain. More than a year passed before he was successful, a period most distressing to him, and to such other concerned parties as Clark and Jefferson, because "the work would lose some of its interest by so much delay."[28] It was February 23, 1813, before Biddle advised Clark that he had come to terms with the Philadelphia publishing house of Bradford and Inskeep. The terms were stiff, but he had been obliged to accept them "owing to the nature of the times."[29]

At a somewhat earlier date, Biddle had been elected to the state legislature of Pennsylvania. Because of his commitments to Clark, he had neglected his duties as a legislator, and also as a practicing lawyer. Now that he had obtained Bradford and Inskeep as publisher, he felt free to ask another man to complete what little remained undone with the history. For that job, he chose Paul Allen, a fellow contributor to *Port Folio*. To Jefferson, by way of explanation, he wrote:

> I had written off roughly nearly the whole [of the history] when other occupations intervened, & on Genl. Clark's visit here last spring I gave up the manuscripts to Mr. Allen who was to take the rude outline as I had left it, add from the original journals whatever

[27] When Clark heard of Conrad's failure, he expressed indignation: "He has disappointed me in a way I had not the smallest suspicion of. I think we might have expected from him some intimation of his situation which would have prevented a delay of the work" (*Ibid.*, 580).

[28] *Ibid.*, 577.

[29] *Ibid.*, 582.

had been omitted in the first rapid sketch—mould the whole as he thought best and superintend the publication.[30]

Paul Allen (1775–1826), a graduate of Brown University, had obtained employment with *Port Folio* after coming from Providence, Rhode Island, the city of his birth, to Philadelphia about 1800. A contemporary described him as "rather below the middle size . . . an ordinary looking man . . . with a character of sluggishness, slovenly inaptitude and moroseness. . . . Yet there is not a better natured fellow on the earth."[31]

Whatever Biddle's opinion of Allen, he obviously regarded him as capable of doing what little remained to be done with the work, for which he paid him $500. Allen made one notable contribution, and for that all students of the Expedition are beholden to him. He persuaded Jefferson to write a memoir of Lewis; though, when we read his letter to the former president, we may wonder that the latter acquiesced. Allen wrote in part, "I wish very much to enliven the dulness of the Narrative by something more popular splendid & attractive. The publick taste has from a variety of adventious causes been gorged to repletion on fanciful viands & the most nutritive & invigorating aliments will not be relished unless seasoned with Something of that character."[32]

Elliott Coues, who could come up with the incisive phrase as well as the next one, said that this letter by Allen "exhibited an achievement in impudence that deserves to become historical."[33] Jefferson possibly entertained similar thoughts about it, for after completing the memoir, he sent it to Biddle—not to Allen—and with it a note which read:

> The part you have been so good as to take in digesting the work entitles you to decide on whatever may be proposed to go out under it's auspices; and on this ground I take the liberty of putting under cover to you, and for your perusal, my letter to Mr. Allen, which I will request you to seal & hand on to him. I am happy in this occasion of expressing my portion of the thanks all will owe you for

[30] *Ibid.*, 595.
[31] *Dictionary of American Biography* (1928), I, 202–203.
[32] Jackson, *Letters*, 586.
[33] *History*, I, xvn.

the trouble you have taken with the interesting narrative, and the assurance of my sentiments of high esteem and respect.[34]

—3—

The History of the Expedition Under the Commands of Captains Lewis and Clark (presumably Biddle's title) came from the press early in 1814. It was March 23 of that year when Biddle wrote Clark, "I have at last the pleasure of informing you that the Travels are published—that they have sold very well I understand, and have been well thought of by the readers."[35]

Biddle was premature in saying that they sold very well. The opposite was true, the primary reasons being the lapse of time—almost seven years—between conclusion of the continental traverse and the publication, and the appearance in that interval of the several editions of Gass's *Journal* and of an equally large number of counterfeits. As a result, the great bulk of those persons who, in 1807, would have been eager to obtain copies, had long since lost interest in them.

Bradford and Inskeep published some two thousand sets, each (of two volumes) priced at six dollars. Elliott Coues, source of these figures, also revealed that, of the two thousand sets, 583 were either defective or missing, so, apparently, "no more than 1,417 perfect copies of Lewis and Clark ever existed."[36] Thus, the size of this printing (further reduced by loss and ordinary wear and tear) explains why the book is so rare today, and why copies in near perfect condition bring fantastic prices when offered at auction.[37]

The book as published was, of course, not all that Biddle's pros-

[34] Jackson, *Letters*, 594.
[35] *Ibid.*, 598.
[36] Coues, *History*, I, xci.
[37] Paltsits located fourteen copies. Peter Decker, New York bookseller, in a letter to me dated October 15, 1970, states, "A friend of mine has just concluded a census of the Allen [*i.e.*, Biddle] ed. of the L & C Expedition in printed boards and has come up with 21 copies. I think there are still more unaccounted." Recently (1967) a copy, described as in near perfect condition, was sold at auction by Parke-Bernet Galleries, New York City, for $35,000. Writing in 1893, Elliott Coues said, ". . . the price of a perfect copy has of late years settled somewhere about $50—more or less, according to the respective tempers of buyers and sellers" (*History*, I, xci).

pectus had announced it would be; there was no accompanying scientific volume. Looked at from any angle, this exclusion was most regrettable, for thereby the world learned but little of the vast number of plant and animal species new to science discovered during the progress of the Expedition, and Lewis was literally robbed of the recognition he deserved, and should have received, as one of our foremost pioneering naturalists.

Regrettable also was the anomaly that this 1814 account, now commonly referred to as the Biddle edition, carried no mention of Biddle anywhere. He might never have existed so far as the reader could tell. On the title page, where his name should have appeared in bold letters, we find instead, "Prepared for the press by Paul Allen, Esquire." And in the preface, written by Allen, we again fail to find the name, only an oblique reference to it: "After a considerable and unavoidable delay, the papers connected with the Expedition were deposited with another gentleman [*viz.*, Biddle], who, in order to render the lapse of time as little injurious as possible, proceeded immediately to collect and investigate all the materials within his reach."

The only logical explanation of this incredible omission is that Biddle wanted it that way, insisted on complete anonymity.[38] It is utterly inconceivable that Allen, without a specific directive from Biddle, however guilty of "slovenly inaptitude" he may have been, would have presumed to substitute his own name. Providing credence to the above explanation is the circumstance that Biddle rarely if ever attached his own name to any of his several contributions to *Port Folio*, but wrote, as earlier mentioned, under the pseudonym of Oliver Oldschool.

We must assume that Clark and Biddle had agreed on some kind of financial arrangement at Fincastle, for Clark would surely have insisted on it. However, in records available to us, we have found no mention of payment until September, 1812, more than two years later. At that time Clark offered Biddle "half of every profit" derived from sales of the finished work.[39]

As things turned out, Biddle received nothing for his months of

[38] Nicholas Biddle Wainwright, great-grandson of Nicholas Biddle, with whom I have discussed this point, leans toward the same explanation.
[39] Jackson, *Letters*, 579.

unremitting labor, for the simple reason that he refused to accept as much a penny. At least that was the case if we believe what Biddle told Clark in a letter dated March 23, 1814, and, to us, it allows of only one interpretation. Said Biddle, "I am content that my trouble in the business should be recompensed *only by* the pleasure which attended it, and also by the satisfaction of making your acquaintance, which I shall always value."[40] It was a particularly magnanimous gesture, since Biddle, in addition to contributing his time and talents as editor, had given Allen $500 out of his own pocket and had incurred other expenses, such as those incidental to his trip to Fincastle. But his magnanimity did not end there, as a letter he wrote to Bradford and Inskeep attests: "The chief purpose of my writing at present is to ask your attention to the affairs of my friend General Clarke. . . . After all the toils & hazards which he has undergone, the only remuneration he expected was from the profits of his book, and I should be sorry that he should not derive all the emolument from that source to which he is entitled."[41]

The fact that Biddle seems to have been financially independent takes nothing away from the handsomeness of these gestures by him, and dampens not at all our increased respect and admiration for this man because of them.

Regrettably, in spite of Biddle's wish expressed to the publishers, Clark apparently received no royalties from sales of the book, received only the copyright, some copper plates (of engraved maps),[42] and the right to bring out a second edition.[43] Contributing further grief to this unhappy editorial finale was the circumstance, now a matter of record, that Clark, two years after publication, was still looking for a copy of the book,[44] and, six months later, continuing to look, had been able only to *borrow* one.[45]

Reviews soon began to appear in various contemporary periodicals,

[40] *Ibid.*, 598.

[41] *Ibid.*, 604.

[42] At least four of these copper plates are today housed in the library of the American Philosophical Society. Three are small, each measuring 5 by 8 inches. The other, a beautiful piece, is 13 inches wide and 29½ long. Engraved on it is Clark's large map delineating the West from the Mississippi to the Pacific.

[43] Coues, *History*, I, xciii.

[44] Jackson, *Letters*, 610.

[45] Coues, *History*, I, xciii.

one of the first in Philadelphia's *Analectic Magazine and Naval Chronicle*. Herein the reviewer had this to say:

> The style and manner of the work are such as they always ought to be in compositions of this nature; unostentatious and perspicuous; the language is expressive, without a redundancy of epithet; the observations and reflections occasionally introduced, are sensible and well timed; and the descriptive parts, simple and precise, without appearing to be aided by the arts of exaggeration.[46]

Other contemporary reviewers provided equally bootless assessments. Many years later Reuben Gold Thwaites was more explicit. The work to him was "comparable in many respects with *Astoria* and *Bonneville's Adventures*—of course lacking Irving's charm of style, but possessing what Irving's two western classics do not, the ring of truth."[47]

—4—

When Jefferson learned that Dr. Barton had failed to prepare the projected scientific volume, no one was more unhappy than he. An immediate concern, as expressed in a letter to Alexander von Humboldt, the great German naturalist, was that the "botanical & zoological discoveries of Lewis will probably experience greater delay, and become known to the world thro' other channels before that volume will be ready."[48]

Dr. Barton died in 1815 and, soon afterward, Jefferson addressed himself to José Correa da Serra, fellow member of the American Philosophical Society.[49] To him he said, "The death of Dr. Barton revives my anxiety to recover the MS. journals of Capt. Lewis. . . . Knowing nothing of what is doing, or intended to be done as to the publication of the papers respecting the natural history & geography

[46] *Analectic Magazine and Naval Chronicle*, Vol. V (1815), 233.

[47] *Original Journals*, I, xlv–xlvi.

[48] Jackson, *Letters*, 596. Henry Muhlenberg (1753–1815), talented American botanist of Lancaster, Pennsylvania, had earlier expressed to a friend the same concern: "I am afraid the descriptions will be made in England, and Lewis's work will come too late" (*Ibid.*, 354n.).

[49] José Correa da Serra (1750–1823), a Portuguese botanist who resided in the United States, 1812–20.

of the country, you will oblige me by any information you can obtain on this subject."[50]

As this and subsequent letters make clear, Jefferson had two immediate objectives in mind: one, that the scattered Lewis and Clark journals, maps, and other documents be brought together and turned over to the American Philosophical Society, and two, that the society, with these in hand, would then proceed to publish the scientific results of the Expedition.

José Correa da Serra shortly reported to Jefferson that, from what he could learn, all Lewis and Clark documentary material then in Philadelphia was in the hands of Nicholas Biddle, excepting a few notebooks held by Dr. Barton's widow. But Biddle, Correa da Serra went on to say, refused to part with manuscripts in his possession until authorized to do so by Clark, who had entrusted them to him.

In an effort to resolve this problem as expeditiously as possible, Jefferson promptly wrote to Clark. His letter, dated September 8, 1816, reads in part:

> The travelling journal of Govr. Lewis and yourself having been published some time ago, I had hoped to hear that something was doing with the astronomical observations, the Geographical chart, the Indian vocabularies, and other parts not comprehended in the journal published. With a view to have these given to the public according to the original intention, I got a friend [*viz.*, Correa da Serra] to apply for them to Mr. Biddle, in whose hands I understand them to be. . . . He said he could not deliver them even to the War-office, without an order from you. It is to sollicit this order that I now trouble you, and it may be given in favor either of the war office or of myself. If the latter, I should deliver the Astronomical observations to the Secretary of War . . . and I should deliver the papers of Natural history & the Vocabularies to the Philos. society, at Philadelphia, who would have them properly edited, and I should deposit with them also for safe keeping the travelling pocket journals as originals to be recurred to on all interesting questions arising out of the published journal. I should receive them only in trust for the War Office to which they belong, and take their orders relating to them. I have received from Dr. Barton's ex[ecuto]rs 4. vols. of the travelling pocket journals, but I think

---

[50] Jackson, *Letters*, 607–608.

there were 11. or 12. The rest I suppose Mr. Biddle has. I hope
the part I have had in this important voyage, will excuse the interest
I take in securing to the world all the beneficial results we were
entitled to expect from it, and which would so fully justify the expenses of the expedition incurred by the United States in that expedition.[51]

We have reproduced most of this letter because it reveals salient
information on at least three counts: (1) it makes plain that Jefferson regards the American Philosophical Society as the proper depository for the majority of the Lewis and Clark papers; (2) it
strongly implies that he expects the society to publish the scientific
data not included in the Biddle narrative; and (3) it leaves no doubt
that Jefferson regards all records resulting from the Expedition as
government property.[52] We should mention, too, in light of later
revelations, that Jefferson, in this letter, includes not even a hint that
he knows, or suspects, that Clark then has in his possession documents brought back by the Expedition other than those alluded to
above, such as the numerous maps Clark had made of western ter-
rains and valuable field notes. In due course, we shall have much to
say about these items.

On receipt of Jefferson's communication, Clark, on October 10,
1816, wrote to Biddle instructing him to deliver to Jefferson (not to
the War Department), "all the papers you may have received in my
behalf relating to the Astronomical Observations, the Geographical
Charts, the Indian Vocabularies, and other papers not comprehended
in the journal of Lewis & Clarke Travils which have been latterly
published, and the Specimins which were in the possession of Doctor Barton—also the travelling pocket journal.[53]

[51] *Ibid.*, 619.

[52] In his original letter to Correa da Serra (January 1, 1816), Jefferson had
been even more explicit: "The right to these papers is in the government, as may
be seen by the instructions to Capt. Lewis" (*Ibid.*, 608). Since we are far from done
with this matter of rightful ownership, these statements should be kept in mind.

[53] *Ibid.*, 623. To Jefferson, on the same day, Clark wrote, "It is with pleasure
that I enclose you an Order on my friend Mr. Biddle for the papers in his possession.
. . . From the mortification of not having succeeded in giving to the world all the
results of that expedition, I feel relief & gratitude for the interest which you are
willing to take, in affecting what has not been in my power to accomplish" (*Ibid.*,
624).

For reasons unexplained, an interval of more than one year ensued, with Biddle seemingly insensible to Clark's instruction. As a result, in January, 1818, Clark sent a reminder to Biddle and, with it, a request: "The journal of Serjeant Ordway I must request you to send me by the first convenient opportunity."[54]

It was April 8, almost three months later, when Biddle finally complied with Clark's instructions. On that date, as records attest, he delivered the following items to the American Philosophical Society:

> Fourteen volumes of the Pocket Journal of Messrs. Lewis & Clark.
> A volume of astronomical observations & other matter by Captain Lewis.
> A small copy book containing some notes by Captain Lewis.
> A rough draft of his letter to the President from St. Louis announcing his return.
> Two statistical tables of the Indian tribes west of the Mississippi river made by Governor Clark.[55]

Beyond question Nicholas Biddle was an extremely busy man, and perhaps a forgetful one, too. Neither then nor later did he, as requested, send Sergeant Ordway's journal to Clark. As a result, it completely disappeared for almost a century, with no one knowing that Biddle had thoughtlessly retained it, as he did the diary kept by Lewis during his 1803 descent of the Ohio River. When, in 1913, this diary came to light, at the same time Ordway's journal was rediscovered, it created much excitement among historians; they had had no inkling that such a document existed.

We must applaud, of course, Jefferson's efforts to bring together in one place the "Pocket Journals" and other priceless records of the Expedition, even though, as we know, he was only partially successful. Whether he had good reason for believing that the Philosophical Society would publish the accumulated scientific data is conjectural. If he did, it follows that he was much disappointed. To the best of our knowledge, the society took no positive steps in that direc-

---

[54] Ibid., 634–35.
[55] See April 8, 1818, entry of minutes of Historical and Literary Committee of American Philosophical Society.

tion until 1901. By then Jefferson had been dead seventy-five years.

Having presented the several Lewis and Clark documents to the American Philosophical Society, Biddle's accountability to Jefferson and Clark ended. Terminating soon afterward, too, was the youthful phase of his life which had brought him much deserved acclaim as a lawyer, legislator, and litterateur of exceptional promise.

In 1819 a new and entirely different phase of his career had its inception. In that year President James Monroe named him as one of the directors of the Bank of the United States, Philadelphia. Four years later, as a result of his vigorous and competent attention to financial matters as a director, the bank chose him to be its president, as did, in 1836, its successor, Bank of the United States of Pennsylvania. Biddle continued in that office until his retirement in 1839, five years short of his death.

We can't profess surprise that Nicholas Biddle's biographers have consistently addressed most of their biographical delineation to that portion of his life given over to banking. We do profess surprise, however, that they have paid such slight attention to his significant and distinguished role in preparing the Lewis and Clark journals for publication. For instance, the author of the only full-length biography of Biddle limits his consideration of that role to barely more than a page—in a volume of 413 pages altogether.[56]

Hopefully, Biddle's future biographers will take a longer, more approving look at this interim, historiographical period of his life, and through so doing, reinvest his paraphrase of the Lewis and Clark journals with the aura of importance and permanence that once surrounded it. No student of the Expedition needs to be reminded that, from 1814 to 1905—almost a full century—the Biddle edition was the only authorized, authentic account of the Expedition, that it quickly took its place among the world's classics of exploration and discovery, and that it was reprinted again and again, not only in the United States, but also in such European countries as England and Germany.

Writing in 1893, Elliott Coues said, "The story of this adventure

[56] Govan, *Nicholas Biddle*, 22–23, 34, 36–37.

stands easily first and alone. This is our national epic of exploration, conceived by Thomas Jefferson, wrought out by Lewis and Clark, and given to the world by Nicholas Biddle."[57]

[57] Coues, *History*, I, v–vi.

CHAPTER VI
Elliott Coues

Stranger things have happened, of course; but a period of almost eighty years followed Biddle's 1814 publication of the Lewis and Clark journals before a scholar came forward to extend appreciably the existing knowledge of the Expedition. It was 1892–93 when Elliott Coues (pronounced "cows") edited the reissue of Biddle which is today, because of Coues's abundant commentary, of such value to all historians of Lewis and Clark. Between 1814 and 1893, it is true, publishers had reprinted the apocrypha, Biddle, and Gass, but these reissued editions, without exception, adhered closely to original formats and thus provided nothing new of tangible import about the Expedition.[1]

Elliott Coues (1842–99) was born in Portsmouth, New Hampshire, on September 9, 1842, the son of Samuel Elliott Coues and Charlotte Haven (Ladd) Coues. From an early age he demonstrated an intense interest in natural history. According to one writer, "As soon as he could exhibit a preference for any subject, his taste for ornithology was manifested, and even when only able to toddle about the nursery ... no book nor story interested him unless animals were their subjects."[2]

[1] Between 1814 and 1893, apocryphal editions appeared in 1840, 1841, and possibly other years; editions of Gass in 1847, 1852, 1854, and 1859. There were several reissues of the Biddle edition, notably in 1815, 1817, 1818, and 1842. For a fuller treatment of the above, see Thwaites, *Original Journals*, I, lxiii–xciii.

[2] D. G. Elliot, "In Memoriam: Elliott Coues," *The Auk*, Vol. XVIII, No. 1 (January, 1901), 2.

When Coues was eleven years old his father accepted a position with the Patent Office in Washington, D.C., and moved his family to that city. Becoming a resident in the nation's capital proved to be a circumstance of rare good fortune for young Coues. It afforded him access to the zoological collections at the Smithsonian Institution and made possible his acquaintance with prominent naturalists there. One in particular, S. F. Baird,[3] who later became secretary of the Smithsonian, befriended him and provided "incentive and opportunities which he early and enthusiastically embraced."[4] Coues was not slow in acknowledging his high regard for and indebtedness to Baird. When, in 1861, he described for the first time a bird new to science, he called it *Arctodromas Bairdii*,[5] and just a few years later he named his first son Elliott Baird Coues.

In his student days, at Gonzaga Seminary and Columbian College (now George Washington University), Coues's best friends were naturalists. One of them later declared that Coues loved birds more than any other animals, delighted to talk about them, and to debate the various questions that a discussion of them invariably aroused; and he further declared that Coues's mind "dwelt continuously upon them."[6]

Meantime Coues's ornithological enthusiasm and capabilities had so impressed Baird and other men at the Smithsonian that in the summer of 1860—even before Coues had attained his eighteenth birthday—they sent him on a collecting trip to Labrador. It was an exciting and rewarding experience for him, and the following year he responded by publishing three papers, the first of literally hundreds that in time came from his pen. One of the three, a report on his previous summer's industry, was titled "Notes on the Ornithology of Labrador," while the other two were monographs, one on

---

[3] Spencer Fullerton Baird (1823–87) was born in Reading, Pennsylvania, and, before going to the Smithsonian, was professor of natural history at Dickinson College. It was through his efforts that Congress established the Bureau of Fisheries. He wrote *Mammals of North America* (Philadelphia, 1859) and, in collaboration with T. M. Brewer and Robert Ridgway, *History of North American Birds* (Boston, 1875–84).

[4] Joel Asaph Allen, "Biographical Memoir of Elliott Coues 1842–1899," National Academy of Sciences *Biographical Memoirs*, Vol. VI (June, 1909), 400.

[5] Today it is *Erolia bairdii* (Coues) and, in the vernacular, Baird's sandpiper.

[6] D. G. Elliot, "Recollections of Elliott Coues," *Bird-Lore*, Vol. IV (January–February, 1902), 3–5.

redpolls and one on sandpipers.[7] According to a contemporary ornithologist, Coues's monograph on the sandpipers was "notable for the care and completeness with which the subject was treated, and would have been credited to an author of much greater experience. It fully foreshadowed the high character of his subsequent work in systematic ornithology."[8]

At Columbian College, after graduating with an A.B. degree, Coues studied medicine. Receiving his M.D. in 1863, he was shortly commissioned assistant surgeon, United States Army.

During much of his army service, Coues was stationed at posts in the West, the first being Fort Whipple, a remote military base situated near Prescott, the capital of Arizona Territory.[9] It was during the last stage of his journey to Fort Whipple, where he arrived in late July of 1864, that a young infantry officer, Lieutenant C. A. Curtis, first met Coues and was immediately so impressed with him as an individual, and with his extraordinary activities as a field naturalist, that he later wrote in some detail about him:

> He was at that time still some months short of being twenty-two years old, and had but recently been commissioned as assistant surgeon in the army. He was a man of good features and figure, a little above medium height, with light brown hair and no beard or moustache. . . . Ornithology was the Doctor's special cult, but he was also prepared to make collections in other branches of natural history. . . .
>
> From the beginning of the march on the 16th day of June [at Santa Fe, New Mexico] until its close, on the 29th day of July, Doctor Coues never ceased, except for a brief interval, making excursions along the flanks of the two columns and arriving in camp with many specimens. Clad in a corduroy suit of many pockets and having numerous sacks and pouches attached to his saddle, he regularly rode out of column every morning astride of his buckskin-colored mule, which he had named Jenny Lind on account of her musical bray. . . . He usually brought in all his pockets and pouches filled with the trophies of his search, and when he sat upon the

[7] All three papers were published in the Academy of Natural Sciences of Philadelphia *Proceedings*, Vol. XIII (1861).

[8] Allen, *op. cit.*, 400.

[9] Named for Lieutenant A. W. Whipple, Corps of Topographical Engineers, who early surveyed a railway route from Fort Smith to Los Angeles. He died in 1863, from wounds received at Chancellorsville.

ground and proceeded to skin, stuff and label his specimens, he was never without an interested group of officers and men about him. . . . When we reached the most dangerous part of our march and frequent attempts to stampede our grazing flock and herds were made by the lurking red men, the Doctor was cautioned to remain near the escort, but the flitting of rare plumage or the utterance of a strange note would often tempt him away and give us great anxiety until he returned. In three collisions with the Indians he showed us he was possessed of true soldierly spirit.

At one point the danger became so great that the discharge of firearms by any member of our party was strictly forbidden and all were told that should a shot be heard we were all to rally in its direction. One day we rallied in hot haste to the rear, only to meet the ornithologist holding up a beautiful and rare specimen, saying, "I really could not allow this bird to escape without causing a serious loss to science."

"Well," replied the commanding officer, "I shall deprive science of any further collections for a week by placing you under arrest and taking possession of your gun and ammunition."

The arrest, however, did not last until the next morning, when the colonel, having slept off his vexation, delivered Doctor Coues a lecture on military science, with particular reference to service in an Indian country. . . . Professionally, the Doctor was a good surgeon, and never neglected his duty. In Arizona for a year he continued his collecting throughout a large part of the territory, and, when he was relieved duty and ordered to Washington in November of 1865, he told me he should take with him over two hundred and fifty distinct species of birds and six hitherto unknown to science.[10]

It should be mentioned that in September, 1864, Coues made a trip from Fort Whipple down the Colorado River to Fort Yuma, at the mouth of the Gila River, and on his return to Washington, by way of San Francisco and Panama, he spent time among the birds at the Bay of San Pedro in southern California. The following year he published a paper about his journey from Fort Whipple to the Pacific and his observations on the avifauna of San Pedro.[11]

Returned to Washington, Coues was placed on special duty for a

[10] Captain C. A. Curtis, "Coues at His First Army Post," *Bird-Lore*, Vol. IV (1902), 6–7.
[11] Elliott Coues, "From Arizona to the Pacific," *The Ibis*, Vol. II, n.s., No. 7 (July, 1866), 259–75.

brief period at the Smithsonian. In June, 1866, he was ordered to Columbia, South Carolina, where he served more than two years as post surgeon. From February, 1869, until November, 1870, he served in a similar capacity at Fort Macon, North Carolina,[12] after which he was ordered to Fort McHenry, Baltimore, Maryland.

It was in 1872, while at Fort McHenry, that Coues completed and published *Key to North American Birds*. This was, according to J. A. Allen, ". . . beyond question . . . his greatest service to ornithology."[13] Designed as a popular handbook, it was much more than that, primarily because it introduced to zoologists the "key" method of the botanists. Indicative of its success, it ran through six editions (the last in 1927 twenty-eight years after the author's death) and was the forerunner of similar keys in other zoological fields.

—2—

Coues's next army assignment took him into Lewis and Clark country. In 1872, about the time his *Key* came from the press, he received orders to report to Fort Randall, Dakota Territory. After spending the winter of 1872–73 at this army post, situated where modern Randall Creek empties into the Missouri in Charles Mix County, South Dakota, Coues was attached to the Northern Boundary Commission as naturalist and surgeon. The primary responsibilities of the commission were to survey (in company with a like Canadian commission) the forty-ninth parallel from the Red River of the North to the Rockies, a distance of about eight hundred and fifty miles, and at the same time to study the fauna, flora, and topography of the region on either side of the parallel. Coues had reason to be happy with this assignment, not only because he had been designated as naturalist, as well as surgeon, to the survey, but also because he would have the opportunity of exploring an area of our country parts of which, especially the westernmost, were still relatively unknown. That white men had been active with their guns in the eastern part Coues disclosed when he wrote, "There were no buffalo . . . though

[12] See Elliott Coues and H. C. Yarrow, "Notes on the Natural History of Fort Macon, North Carolina," Academy of Natural Sciences of Philadelphia *Proceedings*, Vol. XXI (1878), 21–28.

[13] Allen, *op. cit.*, 401. The publisher was the Naturalists' Agency of Salem, Massachusetts.

the country was still scored with their trails, and skeletons were plentiful from the Mouse River westward."[14]

Coues spent the summer months of two years (1873–74) with the Boundary Commission. These months provided experience and knowledge that would be invaluable to him when he later undertook to edit a reissue of the 1814 Biddle version of Lewis and Clark. In years ahead he would declare that during his stint with the commission he had followed the Lewis and Clark route a full one thousand miles. It was while following the route, too, that he first developed an abiding interest in Lewis and Clark, and furnished proof by writing an article, "An Account of the Various Publications Relating to the Travels of Lewis and Clarke, with a Commentary on the Zoological Results of the Expedition."[15] This article, published in 1876, is not as well known to students of the Expedition as might be expected, for it was the first paper of consequence *written about* Lewis and Clark, the first to attempt a Lewis and Clark bibliography, and the first to appraise technical results of the journey. Thus Coues was an innovator—far in advance of a host of other writers who have since contributed so voluminously to an increased knowledge of this outstanding American venture.

—3—

With his labors on the Northern Boundary Commission fulfilled, Coues soon afterward (1876) received appointment to a position in a larger program. The army stationed him in Washington, where, for the next four years, he served as naturalist and secretary to the United States Geological and Geographical Survey of the Territories, the "Territories" then including the vast western area that ultimately would be carved into seventeen states of the Union. During those four years, he made two trips to the West, both to Wyoming and Colorado, the first in 1876 and the second in 1878.

In the seventies Coues's literary output, both quantitatively and

[14] Elliott Coues, "Field Notes on Birds Observed in Dakota and Montana . . .," United States Geological and Geographical Survey of the Territories *Bulletin*, Vol. IV (July, 1878), 546–47.

[15] *Ibid.*, Ser. 2, No. 6 (February 8, 1876), 417–44.

qualitatively, was little short of remarkable. He wrote several books and scores of articles. Among the former (in addition to *Key to North American Birds* earlier mentioned) were *A Check List of North American Birds* (1873), *Birds of the Northwest* (1874), *Field Ornithology* (1874), *Fur-bearing Animals* (1877), *Monographs of North American Rodentia* (1877, in collaboration with J. A. Allen), and *Birds of the Colorado Valley* (1878).[16]

Of these books, *Birds of the Colorado Valley* received unusually favorable notices. It was a much-needed treatise of the birds of the then little-known Colorado River watershed. It contained a bibliography of North American ornithological writings which, because of its accuracy and completeness, became at once a model for future bibliographies (Coues himself, in 1879–80, extended the North American bibliography of birds with three additional installments) in this field. And it attested throughout (as had *Birds of the Northwest*) to Coues's prowess as a writer of superlative bird biographies.

Now and then prominent naturalists have been induced to prepare anthologies of "the best ornithological prose." Donald Culross Peattie and John Kieran are two Americans who have done so, and both men included among their selections bird biographies by Elliott Coues. Kieran chose just one, "The Burrowing Owl,"[17] but Peattie, himself a literary stylist of no little ability, chose four: "The Cowbird," "The Plumbeous Bush-tit," "The Cliff Swallow," and (with Kieran) "The Burrowing Owl."[18]

Coues once wrote, "It is possible to make natural history entertaining and attractive as well as instructive, with no loss in scientific provision."[19] His numerous avian word pictures, replete with felici-

---

[16] *Check List* and *Field Ornithology* were published in Salem, Massachusetts, by the Naturalists' Agency; the others, in Washington by the Government Printing Office.

[17] John Kieran, *Treasury of Great Nature Writing* (Garden City, Hanover House, 1957), 219.

[18] Donald Culross Peattie, *A Gathering of Birds, an Anthology of the Best Ornithological Prose* (New York, Dodd, Mead & Co., 1939), 267–90. "The Burrowing Owl" and "The Cowbird" are from *Birds of the Northwest* and "The Plumbeous Bush-tit" and "The Cliff Swallow" from *Birds of the Colorado Valley*.

[19] Coues, *Birds of the Colorado Valley*, vi.

tous phrase and sentence, come as close to proving his theses as any comparable writing we have encountered.

In November, 1880, the War Department ordered Coues to report again to Fort Whipple. He was extremely unhappy with this order, for, due to his labors there in 1864–65, he felt that he could contribute little more ornithologically by his return. He reported for duty late in December and remained at Fort Whipple until he received a leave of absence in early September, 1881, which allowed him to return to Washington. On October 11 he resigned his commission, one he had held for seventeen years, and on November 17 it was accepted.

During the remainder of the eighties, Coues busied himself variously. He lectured in anatomy to medical students of Columbian College, continued to produce articles about his beloved birds, and, for a time, delved into the vagaries of theosophy and spiritualism. In 1883 he played a leading role in the founding of the American Ornithologists' Union, which in almost no time became the most important organization of its kind in the United States. Coues served as its first vice-president and, 1893–95, as its president.

Beginning in 1884, and for seven years succeeding, Coues almost completely divorced himself from the out-of-doors and, in large measure, from the birds and other animals that up till then had dominated his life. He agreed to collaborate with other authors in producing the first edition of *The Century Dictionary*. Most likely financial considerations dictated this move, for by now Coues had a wife and three children to support.[20] His specific obligation to the dictionary entailed writing definitions for more than forty thousand zoological and anatomical terms that went into its several quarto volumes. That he succeeded admirably, at least with the matter pertaining to birds, seems evident from J. A. Allen's expressed opinion that this matter was "practically an encyclopedia of ornithology."[21]

[20] Coues's married life had its ups and downs. In 1864 he was granted a divorce from Sarah A. Richardson. In 1867 he married Jane Augusta McKenney, who bore him five children: Edith Louise (1868), Elliott Baird (1872), Beverly Drinkard (1878), and two others who died in infancy. Following a divorce in 1886 from his second wife, Coues married Mary Emily Bates in 1887. There were no children by this last marriage. See Michael J. Brodhead, "A Dedication to the Memory of Elliott Coues," *Arizona and the West*, Vol. XIII (Spring, 1971), 2.

[21] Allen, *op. cit.*, 421. The first edition was published in 1889.

—4—

It was in June, 1891, that the New York publisher, Francis P. Harper, inquired of Coues if he would be interested in editing a reissue of Biddle's 1814 edition of Lewis and Clark. Enthusiastic about the prospect, Coues replied promptly:

> In regard to your proposition to publish "Lewis and Clarke,"[22] under my editorial supervision.
>
> Some years ago I made a special study of the L. & C. literature,[23] and I could therefore undertake the desired work with confidence. It could also be congenial work.
>
> I will therefore do it with pleasure, if circumstances justify you in making me an offer that I could afford to accept. Literature is my profession; and other things being equal, I must choose the most remunerative. I have for several years been forced to decline all proffered engagements; owing to my absorption in the "Century Dictionary," and shall not be able to undertake anything else until some time next autumn.[24]

For this job Harper could not have made a better choice. During Coues's years as lexicographer with *The Century Dictionary* he had absorbed much editorial experience and, in earlier years while on duty in the West, he had gained a knowledge of western topography and zoology equal if not superior to that of any other man then alive.

As the year 1891 neared its end, Coues, with health impaired by his recent definitional labors, left for California. Here, free from pressing responsibilities, he expected quickly to regain his customary vigor. Before leaving, however, he had written Harper, "This reprint [of Biddle] I think you will agree with me should be *verbatim et literatim et punctuatim* after the original, even to copying typographical errors, and should indicate also the original pagination." A commendable proposal by Dr. Coues, but, as we shall see, his

[22] Coues, though generally familiar with Lewis and Clark history, still had a few things to learn, such as the correct spelling of Clark.

[23] See footnote No. 15 in this chapter for this "special study."

[24] The Elliott Coues-Francis P. Harper correspondence quoted here and afterwards consists of more than one hundred letters and is an integral part of the Western Americana Collection, Yale University Library. The substance of only one or two of these letters has previously been published.

thinking, like the plumage of his highly cherished birds, was often subject to change.

Coues's health returned tardily, and we learn nothing further about the proposed reissue of Biddle until June of the next year, when Harper again wrote to Coues: "How about Lewis and Clarke? We are anxious to have this matter under way, as I am informed that another publisher has under consideration the republishing of this work."

Coues, who by now had returned to his home in Washington, replied that he would like very much to have his name connected "with a reissue of that memorable book," that he presumed Harper contemplated using his [Coues's] name on the title page, and that he had in mind explanatory notes and a new critical, bibliographical preface. He concluded, "If you think we can come to terms make your offer . . . and I will give you a final answer at once."

Harper responded with an offer of $500 to $750 for a bibliography and "such explanatory and historical notes as would make the edition a valuable book for reference." Perhaps fearful that Coues might refuse his offer (one that certainly seems modest today), he minimized the need for extensive research—because of Coues's special knowledge of the West—and praised him as "the best person living for such a work."

Coues accepted Harper's offer, and soon afterward transported himself and his "desk" to a summer home in Cranberry, North Carolina, a small town situated in the mountains near the Tennessee line. He chose this place because it provided the seclusion and quiet his temperament demanded.

Coues was now approaching his fiftieth birthday. From various sources, we learn quite a bit as to his appearance and disposition. According to one, he was a tall man of fine physique, with bushy brown hair and full beard, and "one who usually became the center of attention when he joined any group."[25] Another said that he possessed an attractive personality, was genial and vivacious in conversation and an altogether kindly man, though "impulsive and sometimes indiscreet, having some of the failings that usually accompany genius."[26] A third source said that he delighted his asso-

[25] Kieran, *op. cit.*, 219–20.
[26] Allen, *op. cit.*, 424.

ciates with a ceaseless flow of humor, even nonsense, which was most unusual "for an impeccable scientist."[27]

After Coues began work on the reissue, he was struck almost at once with a compelling thought, that "this History, which has held its own for nearly a century as a standard work of reference, has never . . . until now been subjected to searching and systematic criticism."[28] It was indeed a compelling thought, and one from which he derived immediate and sustained motivation.

Harper quickly learned that his editor was a spirited and often demanding correspondent. Coues's letters to him, all in longhand, averaged two to three weekly, and the majority contained requests and/or directives. For instance, on July 30, 1892, Coues wrote:

> I enclose 5 maps, from Lewis & Clarke, which we shall reproduce, and which you may as well take in hand at once. They can be cheaply reproduced by process work . . . maybe reduced to ¾ present size if desired; have them gone over by a skillful hand, to sharpen and define any blurred letters or lines of the impression from which we take a plate.
>
> Where is the missing map? That is the most important of all. I need it here to go by in tracing the route, and we shall have to get hold of one for final reproduction, please look up one now and send it to me without delay.
>
> I hope a copy of the Gass Journal which I requested is already on its way to me.
>
> Please see if you can find a copy of the original State Paper, 1806, being "Message of the President of the U.S. communicating discoveries, etc., Washington, A. & G. Way, 8vo pp. 171 + 3, 1806; reprinted New York, Hopkins & Seymour, 8vo pp. 128, 1806." We have to incorporate some matter from this, and I want to have it in hand as soon as possible.
>
> I am hard at work, and expect by the time I leave here to have done all that I can do outside of Washington, where I have a good deal of official, ethnographic and topographical matter to look up in the Congressional Library. So it will expedite matters if you can send me what is here requested.

A few days later Coues wrote Harper again, saying, "It will ex-

---

[27] Peattie, op. cit., 270.
[28] Coues, History, I, vi.

pedite matters if you can attend to several things I note in this letter." He asked that a manuscript enclosed be typewritten in duplicate and that a portrait of Sergeant Gass be redrawn by some competent artist. He requested Harper to look for portraits of Lewis and Clark, and to locate and copy a biographical sketch of Clark. He wrote for reference works, and, before the summer ended, Harper had mailed to him such books as the 1814 Biddle, Sergeant Gass's *Journal*, Washington Irving's *Astoria*, Major Stephen H. Long's *Account of an Expedition from Pittsburgh to the Rocky Mountains*, Rev. Samuel Parker's *Journal of an Exploring Tour Beyond the Rocky Mountains*, and a number of the apocryphal editions of Lewis and Clark.

The most important of these works to Coues was, of course, the 1814 Biddle, or *editio princeps*, as he often called it. On receiving it from Harper, he promptly advised him that he proposed to go through it "line by line, make my marks and put in what notes I can here, where I am without any of the authorities." After pursuing this procedure for a time, he relayed to Harper additional thoughts on the matter of editing:

> [The Biddle edition was] very badly edited from the rough field-notes of the explorers, after these notes, in a chaotic state, had had a precarious existence for seven to ten years & went through various hands after Capt. Lewis blew his brains out in 1806 [1809] or thereabouts. The printer, Inskeep, probably did the best he could with the copy furnished him, but it is wretchedly set up, the pointing in particular being terrific, the spelling often very funny, and the "parts of speech" dislocated in a thousand places. . . . While I think you will agree with me that it would *not* be desirable, even if it were possible, to "recast" or "rewrite" the book—for you must be able to assure your public that you are giving them the original genuine "Lewis and Clarke," without abridgment or alteration— yet I can in going over the book put in the necessary touches, to make "the nouns and verbs agree," etc., and thus insure some degree of literary excellence, without presuming to so much as recast a single sentence.

Thus, at this early stage, Coues adopted a stance contrary to the one he had taken beforehand, namely, that the reprint "should be

verbatim et literatim et punctuatim after the original.[29] By choosing
to "put in the necessary touches," he created a crack in his editorial
armor that later, after the crack had widened, would admit justified,
outspoken censure.

As the summer progressed, Coues and Harper exchanged opinions
about what new material should be incorporated into the reissue. In
their letters they gave serious consideration to such likely addenda
as illustrations, maps, memoirs of Clark and Gass, index, bibliography, and, of course, the nature and quantity of footnotes. As to
the footnotes, Coues argued vigorously and successfully for "identification of places [along the Lewis and Clark route] as they were
then with what they are now." This would offer no problems, he
assured Harper, since in 1873–74 he had traveled "nearly a thousand miles in the very tracks of L. & C." In respect to the quantity
of the notes, Harper thought that about two hundred pages of them
—to accompany some thousand pages of text—would be about right.
Coues, more sanguine (for the moment), believed something less
than two hundred would be ample. If Harper had then had so much
as a glimmering of how many pages of annotation Coues would ultimately produce, he might well have given up all thought of the reprint then and there.

That Coues labored hard throughout that summer there can be
no doubt. Shortly before he left his mountain retreat to return to
Washington, he told Harper, "You will be surprised, and I think
much pleased, to find how much more and of what kind I have put
into the edition. It has interested me deeply; I have worked con
amore, and done little else than this for a couple of months. Have
already more than filled up my side of the work—I never stint
work once I take it up." He admitted to being surprised at "how
much was required in the way of topography, ethnology and natural
history."

Coues's interest, keen from the outset, soon took a sharp upswing.
Writing to Harper on September 29, he exulted:

> You will rejoice to hear that I have found out all about [the loca-
> tion at the American Philosophical Society of] the original manu-
> scripts [of Lewis and Clark] through Judge Craig Biddle (son of

[29] Author's italics.

Nicholas Biddle). Also lots of letters of Clarke, &c.—and the original copper plates of the ed. of 1814. I am also in correspondence with Clarke's *son* [Jefferson Kearny Clark].

Incredible as it may seem to us today, except for a few informed members of the American Philosophical Society, no one else then appears to have had even the vaguest notion as to the whereabouts of the original Lewis and Clark journals. As Coues himself subsequently said, when addressing the Philosophical Society, "few could have told" where they were kept.[30]

And only those few members of the society had knowledge, too, of the fact that in 1818 Nicholas Biddle had deposited the manuscripts with the society, and that there they had remained, virtually unknown, unheralded, and untouched, for three-quarters of a century.[31] Today, appraised by scholars as among the most priceless of American historical documents, they are guarded with something of the care ordinarily afforded crown jewels. Their "discovery" by Coues, measured by most any yardstick, was an event of incalculable consequence to the further history of the Lewis and Clark Expedition and, indeed, to the history of the country as a whole.

Coues returned to Washington from North Carolina in early October and at once began haunting the archives of the Library of Congress and of the War and State departments in search of additional unpublished Lewis and Clark material, as he had previously informed Harper he would do. Reporting on October 14, he said, "Have examined all the War Department archives. Some nuggets, a few of which we shall print as historical curiosities." Again, a few days later, "Have discovered a lot more precious historical material, never published."[32] In days ahead he benefited from visits to the Bureau of American Ethnology of the Smithsonian Institution and to the United States Geological Survey.[33]

[30] Elliott Coues, "Description of the Original Journals and Field Notes of Lewis and Clark, on which was based Biddle's History of the Expedition of 1804–1806, and which are now in the possession of the American Philosophical Society of Philadelphia," American Philosophical Society *Proceedings*, Vol. XXXI, No. 140 (1893), 17. Coues read this paper at a meeting of the society held January 20, 1893.

[31] See the letter of transmission bearing the date of April 6, 1818 in the Library of the American Philosophical Society.

[32] Included in this material was "much official correspondence" between Clark and Henry Dearborn. See Coues, *History*, I, lxxiv.

[33] On these visits Coues met scientists who would later be of much help to him,

Shortly thereafter Coues began sending copy to Harper. With it went his latest reflections on editing:

> No *rule* can be laid down in the reprinting of historical works; but each case must be editorially decided on its own merits. . . . I have taken some liberties with the original text, and gone as far as I dared in capitalization, spelling, punctuation, etc., if we are to advertise "a faithful reprint." But we must not go too far in that direction; and in general, we must be scrupulously particular in the cases of all *proper* names, which, when "wrong," must be left so in text, and explained in notes.

With Coues thus further tipping his hand, it becomes apparent that he is increasingly altering the text, making changes that no reputable historian today would even consider making.

The desirability of soon visiting the American Philosophical Society to examine the original Lewis and Clark manuscripts now began to assume increased importance in Coues's mind. Until he had done so, he told Harper, he felt "a little shaky about sending back proofs," for an inspection of these documents might "put quite a different aspect on our arrangements." Harper's reply jolted Coues: "Let the Phila. original manuscripts go for the present. You have been so fortunate in finding so much important additional material that I think we have enough for the purpose."

Throughout this period of joint effort, editor and publisher understandably did not always see eye to eye. In a number of instances, as the correspondence attests, the former courteously deferred to the wishes of the latter. However, when Harper suggested that they disregard the originals for the time being, he discovered that Coues could, and would, take a positive stand. Replied Coues:

> It would be inexcusable not to *consult* the original mss., in case it is accessible, and when such a work as ours is going through the press. To what extent, if any, we should then wish to utilize it, or work it up, is another question. I may not want to do *anything* with it. But the fact of being able to say that I had examined it, in our prospectus, would be an advertising point that I should think you would be quick to recognize the advantage of.

among them John Wesley Powell of the Bureau of Ethnology and G. Brown Goode and F. H. Knowlton, both of the Smithsonian. For instance, Coues leaned heavily on Knowlton in identifying plants discovered by Lewis and Clark.

On the eve of his proposed trip to Philadelphia, Coues discovered a matter demanding prompt attention. He forthwith explained it to Harper:

> I have discovered that the name printed Clarke throughout our book should be Clark. I have copies of the Clark genealogies from the family Bible back to 1724, and have lately examined many signatures of Mr. [William] Clark. There is no sign of an *e* anywhere. I have private letters from the son [Jefferson Kearny Clark] & grandson [Meriwether Lewis Clark], both now living, & they both sign Clark. So we must adopt the correct spelling in our edition.

Oddly enough, Clark *is* spelled correctly on the title page of the *editio princeps*, and in Paul Allen's preface to it. Throughout the text, however, Biddle had rendered it Clarke, and that despite his meetings with Clark and the several letters he had received from him signed William Clark. So, until Coues set the matter right, we find the name appearing in important literature as both Clark and Clarke, even Clarck. Lewis consistently spelled the name correctly; Jefferson incorrectly.

Delayed by illness, Coues did not get to Philadelphia until near mid-December. Once there, and armed with a requisition from Jefferson Kearny Clark, he petitioned the American Philosophical Society for permission to take the Lewis and Clark manuscripts with him to Washington, where he would have them readily available for close study. The minutes of the society for December 16 include this terse entry: "Dr. Elliott Coues presented a request for the loan of the Lewis & Clark Mss. which was granted."

Coues promptly advised Harper that he would be going home the next day with "all those Manuscripts of L. & C.," and urged him to say in his prospectus that they contained "much new matter of the utmost importance" which would be incorporated into his notes, since the Biddle narrative differed appreciably from the originals.[34]

---

[34] In reporting later to the Philosophical Society, Coues said, "I do not find quite all of the Biddle deposit, as itemized in the receipt given him by the Society; for example, no [Indian] vocabularies and no maps." (See Coues's "Description of the Original Journals . . .," *loc. cit.*, 19.) Neither then nor later did Coues learn of the existence of additional Lewis and Clark material which was then in the hands of descendants of William Clark. If Biddle deposited any Lewis and Clark vocabularies or maps with the society, they have disappeared.

Returned to his Washington home (1726 N Street), Coues worked overtime scrupulously examining the valuable manuscripts that had been entrusted to him, and then considering how best to use them. He soon informed the secretary of the Philosophical Society, then Henry Phillips, that he would "return the papers in better order" than he had received them and that, unless there was specific objection, he would remove the old brass clasps from the journals. "Most of them," he declared, "are broken off already, and I have taken away the stumps of them. They injure the covers, and are a nuisance. The loose papers I will furnish with covers."[35] Presumably Coues received no restraining order from Phillips; at least I find, on examining the journals today, no trace of brass clamps on any of them. Coues's removing them was, of course, just another example of his tampering with valuable documentary material.

In his next letter to Harper, Coues described the manuscripts in some detail and explained what he had been doing with them, as well as what he thought should be done with them in the future:

> I have been working the mine opened in Phila., and now have all the Mss. in perfect order for reference and when necessary for citation by vol. and page. There are 18 bound note books, and 12 small parcels of other Mss., making in all 30 codices, and I think something like 2,000 written pages. Of course we shall not be idiotic enough to ever let the Mss. go out of our hands without keeping a copy. I have an expert copyist already at work, making an exact copy, word for word, letter for letter, and point for point. I do not know how the expense will come out; if you will authorize the expenditure of $150, I will make up the balance, whatever it will be, and the copy thus become[s] our joint property. I think most probably, *after* our present edition, you will want to bring out another vol. reproducing the orig. Mss. *verbatim*. It would be such a curiosity as the world has never yet seen and make a great sensation.

After continued study of the originals, Coues displayed even greater enthusiasm. To Harper he confided: "You know the dis-

---

[35] The Coues-Phillips correspondence quoted here and afterwards is held by the American Philosophical Society. After obtaining the journals, Coues must have labored day and night with them, for it was less than a month later, on January 20, that he described them at a meeting of the society.

covery and utilization of the Mss. puts a new complexion on the whole enterprise. I regard it now as one of the greatest and most novel things in literature, sure to make a great sensation, and be the corner stone of a great reputation for you as a publisher. . . ."

Coues's above description and appraisal of the original journals were, of course, the first to be written—Biddle had provided nothing comparable. Coues included, too, his estimate of their literary and historical worth, his conviction that Harper should publish them verbatim, and his tacit admission that he would like to have a hand in introducing them to the world. In view of the fact that other Lewis and Clark manuscript material would later be discovered elsewhere, it should be understood that Coues's evaluation extended only to that in the American Philosophical Society.

What Coues next did with the manuscripts deserves commendation. He shortly told Henry Phillips about it:

> The 18 bound vols., as you know, are in perfect order. The loose Mss. (66 pieces) I have gone over with the utmost care, pressed and put in the best possible shape, interleaved with onion skin writing paper, and made up in twelve parcels in smooth stiff paper covers. I have paginated each book, and each parcel, and arranged the whole in a series of 30 "Codices" (Codex, A, B, etc.). The entire material is now in perfect permanent order, *citable* by codex and page like the vols. of a published work.
>
> In doing this work, I have elaborately indexed the contents of every bound book and Ms. parcel, and prepared for publication a short paper on the L. & C. manuscripts. Of course the A.P.S. should have the refusal of this; so will you please offer it for publication to the Society's *Proceedings*. On notification of acceptance, I will send it to you at once.

Although Dr. Coues, certainly one of the most astute and energetic of editors, had in his hands "one of the greatest and most novel things in literature," he was unawed by it, as his summary actions described above amply testify. It should be particularly noted that he said nothing whatever to Phillips about his copying the journals. Harper seems not to have questioned the propriety of this action. In responding to Coues, he manifested concern only about the expense involved: "If the work is really much different and would not conflict with our 1812 [*sic*] reprint, you can call on me for $150 for copying. I to own half interest in the Mss., then if our L. & C. is a success, we can talk about the publishing of this afterwards."

Coues immediately assured Harper that the amount of new matter in the codices was large, that it differed significantly from Biddle, and that it would conflict in no way with the work in progress. He then added, "Meanwhile, however, let us simply possess ourselves of the copy, and we can talk about printing it later. . . . Better keep very dark about this."

Whatever interpretation we may place on Coues's motives for covertly transcribing the manuscripts, or the seemliness of his action, the fact remains that the documents in question had been acquired from the American Philosophical Society and he had no license to copy. From his counsel to Harper advocating secrecy, it is evident that he himself knew perfectly well that he could not rationally defend his action.

From January (1893) until the reissue came from the press in early fall, Coues continued to labor indefatigably. As the publication date drew ever nearer, he and Harper faced final decisions about maps, illustrations, and other probable inclusions to which we have already alluded. Constantly nibbling away at Coues's time and strength, in addition to the vitally necessary annotations, were frequent visits to federal agencies, consultations with Smithsonian and other scientists, and the inevitable nerve-biting surfeit of letters. In time he complained to Harper of feeling heavily the stress and strain "in performing in less than four months an amount of labor probably greater than Mr. Biddle's in the original writing of the whole book." He went on to say, however, that he experienced a just pride in having brought to the work a full measure of his talent. "Nothing short of that," he declared, "would have enabled me to edit the text at such 'lightning express' speed, sift and digest the 3,056 pages of the manuscript of the codices, and hold in mind every one of the thousands of minutiae requisite for my commentary."

If Coues had had his way, he would have livened the reissue with numerous illustrations, deeming them as "almost essential," because "no previous edition had had any." To Harper he repeatedly expressed his desire for likenesses of Lewis, Clark, and Gass, as well as drawings of plants, animals, and Indians. He very much wanted, too, a photograph of the monument erected at the site of Lewis' death and burial, and would have made the trip to Tennessee to obtain it if Harper had not withheld permission and requisite funds.[36] Locating satisfactory likenesses of the two captains proved to be difficult, in spite of the fact, as we now know, that at least a half-dozen portraits of Lewis were then extant and more than twice that number of Clark.[37] Coues did find sketches of the two in one of the apocryphal editions, but they were quite rightly "wretched blotches" he did not care to touch;[38] and Harper discovered, in an early periodical, St. Mémin's now well-known full-length portrait of Lewis dressed in Indian garb.[39] Coues thought they might use this sketch "simply as a historical curiosity," but not "as *our* portrait of Lewis." He objected to it on the grounds that it was poorly executed and an unsatisfactory likeness of Lewis' face.

When the reissue finally appeared, it displayed just two portraits, engravings of Lewis and Clark prepared especially for the edition from the original paintings by Charles Willson Peale. Coues preferred them because they were "the most 'historic' of all the likeness[es], and best for our purpose, as they show the men as they were just off the trip."[40]

As to maps, Coues was eager to reproduce what he referred to as "the famous Mandan map of 1804–5," even though it was "geographically worthless—simply a precious historical relic." After receiving a proof of it, he told Harper that it carried so many names misspelled or omitted that he would have to "go over all of them with a magnifying glass, and make quite a number of corrections. It must be as nearly as possible a facsimile, to be of any account;

[36] Coues was disappointed at this rebuff. He wanted to obtain not only the photograph, but also information on the manner of Lewis' death. At one point he wrote Harper, "I am going to raise the whole question of murder vs. suicide." And this he did, in "Supplement to Jefferson's Memoir of Meriwether Lewis." See Coues, *History*, I, xliii–lxii.

[37] For current data, see Cutright, "Lewis and Clark: Portraits and Portraitists," *Montana, the Magazine of Western History*, Vol. XIX, No. 2 (Spring, 1969), 41–53.

[38] Apparently Coues found these sketches in the Dayton, Ohio, apocryphal edition of 1840. Another set, equally "wretched," appeared, as we know, in William Fisher's 1812 edition.

[39] The original, a small watercolor, is now the property of the New York Historical Society. Harper had seen a reproduction of it in an 1816 number of *Analectic Magazine and Naval Chronicle*.

[40] These engravings were done by a London-born artist, Samuel Hollyer.

and since that is now impossible, the next thing is to secure a literally accurate copy."

Even more, Coues wanted a modern map, one on which he might trace, in red, the Lewis and Clark route. Through the good offices of men associated with the United States Geological Survey (especially its director, John Wesley Powell), he finally obtained what he wanted. Writing to Harper in late April, he said:

> By the enclosed correspondence . . . you will see we have struck it rich, and you will be glad to accept Mr. Bien's terms of $135.00 for the edition of 1000 copies.[41] This map I selected as being almost the duplicate in size of our 1814 [of Biddle], and of showing detail enough to answer our purpose by marking the L. & C. trail. I will mark the red lines, and Mr. Bien will print these upon the map.

When the Coues-Harper reissue came from the press, it contained three large folding maps: (1) the 1814 original of Biddle, (2) the "Mandan" map, and (3) the modern one obtained from Bien "to show what wasn't known beyond the Mandans in 1805." The reissue reproduced, too, the five small charts present in the original Biddle.

Coues was emphatic when he wrote, "There ought to be a law against indexless books, with heavy penalty."[42] Since none of the earlier editions of Lewis and Clark (including those of Gass and the counterfeits) had an index, it was doubly imperative, as Coues saw it, that his reissue should be provided with one. When finally printed, it was another first in the annals of Lewis and Clark literature—thanks to the insistence of Elliott Coues.

Coues prevailed upon Harper to reproduce autographed letters of both commanders. Writing to Harper on April 9, he enclosed a letter by Clark he had received from Judge Craig Biddle. He had chosen it from about fifty "as being important and interesting in itself, a good specimen of Clark's handwriting, and a characteristic autograph." This was the January 27, 1818, letter from Clark to Nicholas Biddle directing him to deposit with the Philosophical Society the Lewis and Clark material he had in his possession. Lewis'

[41] Julius Bien (1826–1909), for years chief lithographer of the United States government, and especially active in the preparation of maps and illustrations of western surveys.

[42] Coues, *History*, I, cxxv.

letter which Coues singled out to reproduce bore the date of March 2, 1807, and was Lewis' resignation from the First U.S. Regiment Infantry submitted to Henry Dearborn.

Editor and publisher pondered closely every change or supplement, such as pagination, title page wording, dedication, and table of content. As to the last mentioned, Coues thought it should be limited to brief chapter headings, should be shorn of the "nonpareil synopses," since nobody reads the latter "except unhappy authors and editors & proofreaders." When considering the dedication, Coues asked Harper what his reaction would be to inscribing the edition to Henry Villard, a journalist and financier who held a controlling interest in the Northern Pacific Railroad. It would appear that Harper objected, for another, happier, inscription was finally agreed on: "To the People of the Great West."

Coues thought the title page might remain the same as in the original Biddle except for the addition of "edited by Elliott Coues, A.M., M.D., and Ph.D." and the deletion of the word "Captains" preceding Meriwether Lewis and William Clark. He would excise this word, he said, because "these men are in 1893 illustrious historical characters whose names eclipse all possible titles—it is only poor devils of editors and such that need to be tagged." Having evidenced a bit of transparent conceit by suggesting that "A.M., M.D., and Ph.D." be appended to his name, Coues may have been irked when someone, perhaps Harper himself, saw fit to blue-pencil their inclusion.

First and last Harper manifested concern about Coues's prolific output of footnotes. Originally, as we know, he thought some two hundred pages would be about right. Later, on receipt of Coues's initial copy, he expressed himself in no uncertain terms. At the rate he was starting out, "the notes would outrun the original text." Even after the discovery at the Philosophical Society of the original Lewis and Clark manuscripts, and the obvious resultant necessity for additional notes, Harper nevertheless continued to press Coues to curb his annotative ardor. Coues maintained his calm; following one such caveat, he replied, "You can sleep the sleep of the just about my notes. I know pretty well what I am about, and I expect to fetch you out the 300 pp. or so near it you will have nothing to say. I fully recognize the reasonable limitations of the case." Nevertheless, Coues's notes did come close to outrunning the original text.

It was perfectly natural that Coues should wish to include a bibliographical introduction; as we know, he was an old hand at such. His attention to the apocryphal and other early editions of Lewis and Clark—as expressed in his letters to Harper from North Carolina—stemmed from his eagerness to add to his earlier list. In midsummer, for instance, he remarked to Harper on a rare and "worthless" counterfeit edition just received, "the full title of which has never been given in any bibliography correctly."

As publication date neared, a wind blew in from the West kicking up waves on the Coues-Harper sea of tranquillity. One of the heirs of William Clark created the storm on learning that Harper had failed to reserve for members of the Clark family first copies of the limited, numbered edition of the reprint. On hearing of this, Coues wrote to Harper:

> Item, about W. H. Clark [William Hancock Clark, grandson of William Clark], who has evidently got a fishbone crosswise in his throat. Of course we don't want to hurt his feelings, and could not afford to offend him. He must be pacified—if not for his own sake, then for the memory of his illustrious grandpa. It would never do to get the numerous and influential Clark family down on the book! They have no doubt got enough of old William's stuffing in them to raise hell, if they took a notion. I fancy Jeff. C. [Jefferson Kearny Clark] in St. Louis when he discovered I had 18 codices to his one, got a little grumpy. Now you do this: write to W.H.C. the politest and most deferential letter you can concoct. Illuminate his grandfather, & let the reflected glory alight on his own head. Say how infinitely you value his genealogical charts, which you could hardly have got along without, and that you know your editor prizes them not less highly. Say how very sorry you are you did not ascertain his wishes sooner regarding Nos. 1 and 2 of the large paper copies; but that No. 1 had been sold long before; but that the moment Dr. Coues heard of his wishes regarding early copies, he, Dr. Coues, "generously relinquished" Nos. 2 and 3 for himself and Jeff. C. which therefore you have the pleasure of placing at his disposal, etc., etc. In fact, unless No. 1 itself has "really and truly" gone beyond your control, it might be worth while to recover it. I had

supposed you preempted it for yourself! For myself, I don't care a rush what no. I receive.

In the absence of any word to the contrary, we presume that Harper removed the fishbone lodged crosswise in W.H.C.'s throat. Coues's letter brings to mind John Kieran's remark prefacing his inclusion of Coues's "The Burrowing Owl" in his aforementioned anthology of great nature writing. Wrote Kieran, "The author of this piece about this odd bird was something of an odd bird himself!"[43]

The Coues edited and annotated reissue of Biddle, *History of the Expedition Under the Command of Lewis and Clark*, came from the press early in the fall of 1893.[44] Coues at once lauded Harper (and inferentially himself):

> [You have] launched the *only* "Lewis and Clark," warranted "all wool and a yard wide," fast color, to wash and wear for the next hundred years, as Biddle's fabric did for his century. . . . You have on hand a noble, enduring work, in stately and sumptuous form, on which you can safely build up your reputation as a publisher. I am as thoroughly pleased with the whole affair as you yourself can be. So every thing is lovely.

Revealing his pleasure on another score, Coues soon informed Harper that the job of copying the original journals had been completed, and that this copy, the only one in existence, was "a very valuable piece of property!" He further told Harper, "I shall in a few days, as soon as I catch up with my correspondence, take the originals back to the Philos. Soc. and deliver them over. I want to time myself to catch a public meeting of the Society, and make a few remarks on the occasion."

Minutes of the society for January 5, 1894, record the safe return of the manuscripts by Coues in person. They further state that these documents "were correct in number and condition; that Dr. Coues had arranged them in a most-excellent and careful manner, so as to

---

[43] Kieran, *op. cit.*, 219–20.

[44] On September 9, 1893, Coues wrote Harper, ". . . if quite convenient, I wish you would make the ostensible date of publication Sept. 9. That is my 51st birthday, and the sentiment of the date would please me."

facilitate all further reference; in fact that they were in a much better condition than when loaned by the Society."

But in one significant respect, as historians of the Expedition now know, these manuscripts were not in "a much better condition." During the time Coues had had them in his possession, a period of more than a year, he had freely interlined pages with words of his choice calculated to improve the text. For instance, in Codex A alone (that is, Clark's journal from May 13 through August 14, 1804), I find more than a hundred such interlineations.[45]

Knowledge of the liberties Coues had taken with the original journals remained undetected until Reuben Gold Thwaites, some ten years later, assumed editorship of these priceless documents. Since then, by harshly criticising Coues's editorial indiscretions, historians have beclouded his significant, positive contributions to the Biddle reissue. They have described his interlineations as shocking, indefensible, and irresponsible. One critic wrote that Coues, instead of treating the manuscripts with the scrupulous care and inviolability ordinarily accorded valuable documents by reputable scholars, had treated them like "mere copy for the printer, which might be revised with impunity."[46]

Such censure was, of course, justified. However, if it is possible to put out of mind Coues's tampering with the originals long enough to allow opportunity for an unhurried, objective appraisal of his editorship of Biddle, we should experience no particular difficulty in discovering his numerous benefactions to that work, and to the sum of Lewis and Clark history. For one thing, Coues must be credited with rediscovering the original journals (if he had not, it is anybody's guess as to how much longer they would have remained in relative obscurity at the Philosophical Society). For another, while he had the journals on loan from the society, he arranged them, as we know, in an orderly fashion, thus facilitating their use by future students. For still another, he heightened the value of Biddle's work by adding such supplementary material as bibliography, index, and the memoirs of Clark and Gass.

Finally, and most importantly, Coues increased immeasurably the

---

[45] These interlineations are in black ink. Others, in red ink, have been attributed to Biddle.

[46] Thwaites, *Original Journals*, I, xlix–l.

worth of the Biddle version by contributing extravagant commentary and, in so doing, focused attention for the first time on the vast amount of unpublished and virtually unknown scientific data in the original journals and, thereby, on the salient roles played by Lewis and Clark as outstanding pioneering naturalists. Heretofore most people had regarded them only as explorers, woodsmen, and exemplary military leaders.

Coues amassed his abundant commentary in less than a year—a triumph in itself. Enhancing tremendously its worth, and attracting immediate attention, was the inclusion (for the first time anywhere) of carefully selected verbatim quotations from the original journals. Also, looked at from most any angle, Coues's documentation evidenced the workings of a highly organized, inquisitive mind bent on wringing from the fabric of recorded history every drop of knowledge pertinent to his subject. His notes constituting the commentary, though running into the hundreds, fall logically into three main categories: geography, natural history, and ethnology.

Coues's abundant geographical notes preclude adequate concise summarization. For the most part, he limited them to facts about rivers and creeks, the tributaries large and small of the Missouri and Columbia alluded to by Lewis and Clark. To obtain his data, he studied maps and other source material available to him. For instance, following a reference by Clark to Little Manitou Creek,[47] Coues, in footnote, provided the information that this creek was "the R. au Diable of D'Anville, 1752; the Petit Manitou of Perrin du Lac, 1805 (whence *Little* Manitou of our text); Maniteau creek of Nicollet, 1843; Manitoo of Brackenridge, 1814. . . ."[48] Hence Coues, before writing this note, had consulted the charts of Jean Baptiste d'Anville, Perrin du Lac, and Joseph N. Nicollet, and Henry Marie Brackenridge's *Journal of a Voyage up the Missouri in 1811*.[49] Patently, as a reading of his commentary reveals, this is

[47] *Ibid.*, I, 40.

[48] Coues, *History*, I, 15n. Coues consulted many other technical works, among them the books of such naturalists as Frederick Pursh, Sir John Richardson, Alexander Wilson, George Ord, Richard Harlan, C. L. Bonaparte, S. F. Baird, and Prince Maximilian of Wied-Neuwied.

[49] Pittsburgh, 1814. The French royal cartographer D'Anville published his *Atlas Général* between 1737 and 1780, with maps based on travelers' reports. François Marie Perrin du Lac ascended the Missouri River to the White River in

no isolated example of his thoroughness in ferreting out facts for his geographic annotations. We know, for instance, that he studied other maps, among them those of Aaron Arrowsmith, General G. K. Warren, Captain W. F. Raynolds, Governor I. I. Stevens, Major W. J. Twining, the Geological Survey, and the Missouri River Commission.[50]

Since we know that Coues went to such lengths to acquire geographic data, we are not at all surprised with his confidently worded statement that "... if there is anything I do know, it is exactly where Lewis and Clark were on every day, almost every hour, from start to finish of their famous expedition."[51]

Coues had learned, too, that latter-day cartographers had changed many of the names Lewis and Clark had given to topographic features. That he was unhappy about this, as many students of the Expedition since have been, is evident from his statement: "Hundreds of names ... should be restored, not only in equity, but on the plainest principles of the law of priority, which geographers pretend to obey."[52]

While preparing his commentary, Coues turned denominator himself. Noting that the Expedition's campsite of 1806 on the Clearwater River, near present-day Kamiah, Idaho, had no name, he called it Camp Chopunnish (Chopunnish being the Indian equivalent of Nez Percés).[53] This name is now firmly fixed in Lewis and Clark literature.

In concluding our assessment of Coues's geographical commentary, we would be culpably remiss if we did not stress the fact that Coues, to the best of our knowledge, was the first person to bring forefront Clark's native talent as a maker of maps. In a particularly striking footnote, Coues said that Clark was "one of the greatest

1802; the English edition of his *Voyages dans les Deux Louisianes* appeared in 1807. Nicollet, a French scientist, emigrated to the United States in 1832; his report on his explorations of the Upper Missouri was published in 1843.

[50] Arrowsmith, hydrographer to the British royal court, put out many editions of his map, "Interior Parts of North America," beginning in 1795.

[51] Elliott Coues, "Notes on Mr. Thomas Meehan's Paper on the Plants of Lewis and Clark's Expedition Across the Continent, 1804–1806," Academy of Natural Sciences of Philadelphia *Proceedings*, Pt. 2 (April–September, 1898), 291.

[52] Coues, *History*, I, 324n.

[53] *Ibid.*, III, 1010n.

geographical geniuses this country ever produced."[54] Since 1893 a number of professional cartographers have evaluated Clark's maps and not one of them, so far as I am aware, has taken exception to Coues's statement.

As a naturalist of proven ability, Coues was in a position to recognize natural history abilities in others. In his footnotes to the Biddle reissue, by crediting Lewis and Clark with the discovery of numerous species of plants and animals then unknown to science, Coues left no room for doubt as to how he viewed the natural history instincts of the two leaders of the Expedition. By way of illustration, he credited them with the discovery of cutthroat and steelhead trout among fishes; the prairie rattler and horned toad among reptiles; the black-billed magpie, western tanager, mountain quail, Nuttall's poor-will, whistling swan, Clark's nutcracker, and Lewis' woodpecker among birds; and the coyote, prairie dog, pronghorn antelope, mule deer, and mountain goat among mammals.

One typical footnote reads, "This is the ring-necked scaup duck [*Aythya collaris*]. . . . L. & C. are again discoverers of a new species; for this duck was unknown to science in 1806."[55] And another states, "This is the original and easily recognizable description [by Lewis] of this bird [the western grebe, *Aechmophorus occidentalis*], which was not formally characterized till many years afterward."[56]

In like manner Coues, in footnote, apprised his readers of many herbs, shrubs, and trees discovered by Lewis and Clark, among them the bigleaf maple, Engelmann's spruce, ponderosa pine, Oregon grape, buffalo-berry, various species of sagebrush, mariposa lily, mountain lady's slipper, bear grass, Lewis' wild flax, and, of course, ragged robin (*Clarkia pulchella*) and bitterroot (*Lewisia rediviva*).[57]

Unfortunately, Coues then had no knowledge (nor did anyone else) that more than two hundred dried, preserved plant specimens were at that moment stowed away in a forgotten recess at the American Philosophical Society.[58]

---

[54] *Ibid.*, II, 421n.

[55] *Ibid.*, III, 889n.

[56] *Ibid.*, III, 882n.

[57] For a much fuller listing of plants discovered by Lewis and Clark, see Cutright, *Lewis and Clark: Pioneering Naturalists*, 399–423.

[58] These plants were found, by Thomas Meehan, at the society just three years later (1896). Meehan was a botanist at the Academy of Natural Sciences of Phila-

Coues was much impressed, and rightly so, with the enormous body of ethnographic data Lewis and Clark had accumulated, and he was full of praise for their untiring efforts to portray the Sioux, Arikaras, Mandans, Shoshonis, Flatheads, Nez Percés, Chinooks, and other Indians as they found them. He declared, for instance, that Lewis' description of the Shoshonis "will be forever the best,"[59] and he was clearly struck by Lewis and Clark's observation that the Eneeshur Indians, who resided immediately above Celilo Falls, understood only a few words of the Echelutes, who resided just below. The observation, he wrote, "well illustrates the great attention paid by Lewis and Clark to ethnology, and the discernment they showed in discriminating similar appearing Indians who were nevertheless of distinct linguistic stocks, at a time when modern scientific classifications had no existence."[60]

In composing his ethnographic commentary for the Biddle reissue, Coues had to pull out most stops, not because Lewis and Clark were ill-informed about Indians,[61] but because so much had been written about them since 1806. For instance, Coues had available to him manuals providing systems of classification which did not exist at the time of Lewis and Clark's transit of the West, including the very latest, *Indian Linguistic Families of America North of Mexico*, by John Wesley Powell,[62] as well as earlier works by Henry Schoolcraft, Albert Gallatin, George Catlin, and Maximilian. Lewis and Clark were quick to note language differences, but lacked taxonomic terms yet uncoined with which to designate the differences. If they had had those available to Coues, they would have indicated that the Eneeshurs belonged to the Sahaptian linguistic family and the

delphia. With others, these plants constitute today the Lewis and Clark Herbarium, which is housed at the academy. In the summer of 1966 this writer, with the help of Dr. A. E. Schuyler, the academy's current curator of botany, attempted to locate and bring together in one place (they had been scattered) the specimens of this valuable collection. With job completed, the herbarium totals at least 216 herbarium sheets.

[59] Coues, *History*, II, 479n. See also Thwaites, *Original Journals*, III, 161–62.

[60] Coues, *History*, II, 672n.

[61] Because of experiences in border warfare, particularly under General Anthony Wayne in Ohio, both Lewis and Clark surpassed most of their countrymen in knowledge of Indians. Lewis had had the benefit, too, of his intimate two-year association with Jefferson, a dedicated student of the American Indian.

[62] Washington, D.C., Bureau of American Ethnology, 1891.

Echelutes to the Chinookan linguistic family. Coues's lengthiest foot-notes were about Indians, one alone (about the Sioux) covering four pages and consisting of more than two thousand words.[63]

In a particularly cogent footnote, Coues explained why Biddle had passed over the technical matter contained in the original journals:

> When about to bring out the work, after the death of Governor Lewis, General Clark made a contract with Benj. S. Barton, of Philadelphia, by the terms of which the latter was to produce a formal work on the natural history of the Expedition. In conse-quence of which, Mr. Biddle, of course, passed over such points in the codices. Dr. Barton soon died, having done nothing . . . . This is the simple explanation of the meagerness of the History in scien-tific matters with which the codices are replete—to the keenest regret of all naturalists, and the great loss of credit which was justly due these foremost explorers of a country whose almost every ani-mal and plant was then unknown to science. My notes may in some measure throw back upon them a reflection of what is their just due—but it can never be more than reflected glory, for in the mean-time others have carried off the honors that belong by right to Lewis and Clark.[64]

Regrettably, limitations of space disallow further consideration of Coues's annotations. In comprehensive compass, as I view them, they provide yet another convincing example of the whole being greater than the sum of its parts.

Coues completed his labors on the reissue in something like four-teen months. On August 1, 1893, he acknowledged receipt of a check from Harper in the amount of $750, this being payment "in full for all editorial and other work done." On occasion, to Harper, Coues may well have been like a bee on a hound's nose. Yet Harper subsequently said of him, "He had a capacity for work that was al-most beyond belief, and was always prompt and business-like. He was a firm and trustworthy friend, and an ideal author for a pub-lisher to have business relations with."[65] As further evidence of his high regard for Coues's abilities, in years immediately ahead, Har-

[63] Coues, *History*, I, 97–101.
[64] *Ibid.*, II, 400 n.
[65] Frances F. Victor, "Dr. Elliott Coues," *Oregon Historical Quarterly*, Vol. I, No. 2 (1900), 191–92.

per called upon him to edit reissues of five other books about the West: *The Expeditions of Zebulon M. Pike*, *The Manuscript Journals of Alexander Henry and David Thompson*, *The Journal of Major Jacob Fowler*, *The Personal Narratives of Charles Larpenteur*, and *The Diary and Itinerary of Francisco Garcés*.[66] These five reissues alone would have been sufficient to give Coues a position of high standing in the literary world, but when we add his reissue of Biddle, his definitional contributions to *The Century Dictionary*, and his publication of several hundred books, articles, and reviews on birds and other animals, it becomes evident that he was not only one of the most prolific writers of his century, but also, at least ornithologically, a literary giant.

And we must not disregard Coues's prodigious output of letters. Someday, surely, an ornithologist will awake to the fact that Coues's letters about birds, if assembled and competently edited, would provide an extremely interesting and significant chapter to the history of American ornithology.

After Coues's death, his widow revealed something of his habits as a correspondent: "He never neglected a letter, although from a stranger, asking for assistance. He gave it if he could, most generously, and if unable, gave a courteous answer, and a reason. I myself have counted sixty letters he had written in about six hours—not merely a reply of a few lines."[67]

Elliott Coues was a remarkable composite: ornithologist, mammalogist, surgeon, lecturer, lexicographer, correspondent, editor, teacher, critic. Bemused by the uncommon character and versatility of the man, this writer finds it strange that his biography has yet to be written.

Coues died all too soon, on Christmas Day, 1899, in his fifty-seventh year. In eulogies, contemporaries paid him high tribute, emphasizing in particular his many distinguished contributions to the advancement of ornithology. Regrettably, they said little, or nothing at all, about his success in building the solid base on which many later scientific studies of the Lewis and Clark Expedition now rest.

[66] *Pike*, 1895; *Henry-Thompson*, 1897; *Fowler*, 1898; *Larpenteur*, 1898; and Garcés, 1900.
[67] Victor, "Dr. Elliott Coues," 192.

CHAPTER VII
Reuben Gold Thwaites

Early in 1901 the American Philosophical Society, with simultaneous centennials of the Louisiana Purchase and the Lewis and Clark Expedition fast approaching, approved plans to publish the original manuscript journals of Captains Meriwether Lewis and William Clark. The society soon interested the New York publishing house of Dodd, Mead and Company in this undertaking, and the latter presently engaged Reuben Gold Thwaites to serve as editor.

Born in Dorchester (now a part of Boston), Massachusetts, May 15, 1853, Reuben Gold Thwaites obtained his education at the Universities of Wisconsin and Yale. In 1876 he was named editor of the *Wisconsin State Journal*, leading Republican newspaper of Madison, the state capital. A special interest in history often took him to the State Historical Society of Wisconsin, then presided over by Lyman C. Draper, distinguished collector of Western Americana. When Draper retired from his post in 1886, he named Thwaites as his successor. Soon after assuming the duties of his new position, Thwaites began editorial work on a new edition of *Jesuit Relations and Allied Documents*, a comprehensive series which ran to seventy-three volumes. This monumental task, completed in 1901, established his reputation as one of the foremost historical editors of his day.[1] Consequently, when Dodd, Mead and Company officials be-

---

[1] Prior to 1901 and immediately thereafter, Thwaites added to his literary reputation with other publications. He edited Alexander Withers' *Chronicles of Border*

gan casting about for a man qualified to undertake the role of preparing the Lewis and Clark journals for publication, their eyes soon
focused on Thwaites.

This ambitious, historically important project may be said to have
had its origin on May 22, 1901, when the American Philosophical
Society, through its secretary, Isaac Minis Hays, wrote Dodd, Mead
and Company in part as follows: "This Society possesses the original
journals of Lewis & Clark. . . . I write to inquire if you would care
to consider the advisability of publishing them in extenso."[2] We
have been unable to find any immediate reply of the publisher to
this communication; however, five months later (October 14), Robert E. Dodd, who in ensuing months was to take a more active role
as correspondent for his firm than any other person, informed Hays
that he would visit Philadelphia in a day or two to examine the
Lewis and Clark manuscripts. Following that visit, Dodd, Mead
and Company gave this answer:

> We will print the Lewis & Clarke [sic] Journals under the fol-
> lowing arrangement, provided that we can arrange the matter of
> copyright with Francis Harper. Some arrangement we think can
> be made with him. We will print the Journals in appropriate shape
> and pay the Society a royalty of ten per cent on the retail price of
> the books for their use in this edition. The copyright of the Journals
> it is understood remains with the Society, but the Society is not to
> allow another reprint of the Journals until four years after the issue
> of our edition.[3]

At about this same time, when the publication of the journals by
Dodd, Mead seemed to be successfully launched, the calm of Isaac
Minis Hays was disturbed. He learned that the Boston publishing
house of Houghton, Mifflin Company had also taken steps to publish the Lewis and Clark journals and had even gone so far as to
interest Reuben Gold Thwaites in editing them. Hays received news

Warfare (Cincinnati, 1895) and wrote two biographies, *Daniel Boone* (New York,
1902) and *Father Marquette* (New York, 1902).

[2] All correspondence between Isaac Minis Hays (for the American Philosophical
Society) and Dodd, Mead & Co. is from the Library of the American Philosophical
Society.

[3] No other reprint was made until more than fifty years had elapsed. In 1959,
the Antiquarian Press, Ltd., New York City, published a reissue.

of this development from Thwaites himself, who wrote the society requesting access to the Lewis and Clark papers in order that he might begin editing them for Houghton, Mifflin. On hearing from Hays of the society's executed compact with Dodd, Mead, Thwaites sent his regrets and, with it, his personal reflection that "historical scholars will be very glad to have the MSS. at last available, and it matters not what agency undertakes the publication, so long as it is really well done—and to this the Society will no doubt see. I have notified Messrs. Houghton of this conclusion of our negotiations."[4]

Originally, the American Philosophical Society had in mind one of its own members to edit the journals. Attesting to this fact is a letter from Hays to Dodd, Mead dated October 15, which reads:

> In reference to the Lewis & Clark Journals it has occurred to me that either Mr. Owen Wister or Prof. Angelo Heilprin might be suitable editors. The former has seen considerable of life in the far West, and you are familiar with his stories of wild life on the prairies. . . . Prof. Heilprin is something of an explorer himself, and has considerable scientific attainments. He was formerly President of our Geographic Society and held a professorship in our Academy of Natural Sciences.[5]

A few days later Robert Dodd agreed with Hays that the journals "would be well edited by Heilprin." His failure to approve Wister similarly—in his letter he ignored him completely—may have been due to any one of several reasons, though, if Hays's recommendation had been made a year later, after Wister had received wide acclaim with his publication of *The Virginian*, Dodd's attitude might have been entirely different. Wister's name did not come up again in any of the correspondence between Hays and Robert Dodd; but the fact that, for one brief moment at least, Wister was considered as editor for the journals cannot fail to be of interest to the rapidly expanding legion of Lewis and Clark devotees.

Another month went by, with no editor agreed upon. That the

---

[4] Letters from Thwaites to the American Philosophical Society, Dodd, Mead & Co., and other parties are from the Library of the State Historical Society of Wisconsin, Madison.

[5] Heilprin had earlier been much in the news when he led the Peary relief expedition to the Arctic.

matter was uppermost in the minds of both the society and publisher was revealed December 7, when the latter addressed Hays:

> We shall be very glad to select an editor from the members of the Society if this can be done advantageously, but we must be at liberty to select our editor with reference to his availability, all things considered, rather than to the fact that he is a member of the Society, and we presume to this proposition there will be no dissent on your part or members of the Society.
>
> We had already before the receipt of our letter, corresponded with a gentleman who is peculiarly well qualified to act as an editor for the new edition, but he is not, we believe, a member of the Society. He has not yet signified his acceptance of the position and in his reply made one or two conditions which may perhaps make it impossible for us to use his service.

The gentleman referred to may possibly have been Thwaites. In any event, Dodd, Mead soon afterward contracted with him to undertake the role as editor, even though, unlike Wister, he had had no personal experience with the Far West and, unlike Heilprin, no scientific attainments. The first documentary proof I have found confirming his selection is a letter Thwaites himself wrote to Dodd, Mead the following September requesting them to assure the American Philosophical Society that the library building of the State Historical Society of Wisconsin contained fireproof vaults in which the Lewis and Clark manuscripts could be lodged with safety.

—2—

Thwaites began his editorship at the age of forty-nine. Even before he started work, Dodd, Mead had ascertained that Francis Harper held no copyrighted interest in the original journals, and, with that matter settled, they considered possible methods of copying them. If a copy were made, it could be sent to Thwaites instead of the originals, which they feared might be lost in transit. However, on receipt of unexpected news, they quickly dropped all thought of copying. In a note of February 18, 1902, Robert Dodd informed Hays:

> We have discovered that when Dr. [Elliott] Coues had in his possession the Lewis & Clark manuscripts, he made a verbatim tran-

script of them. . . . This manuscript . . . is now under the control of Mr. [Francis] Harper of this city and Mrs. Cowes [*i.e.*, Mrs. Elliott Coues]. They have approached us with reference to using this manuscript and we are considering the question of doing so. If it turns out to be as represented, and if we can agree on price, we shall use it.

Perhaps this was the first the American Philosophical Society had heard about Coues's arbitrary, unauthorized copying of the original manuscripts (it will be recalled that he had charged Harper at the time to keep very dark about it). If so, it would be interesting to know how the society responded to this intelligence. Of course, having received it belatedly, and with Coues dead, they were hardly in a position to do anything. Dodd, Mead, however, could do something; they promptly purchased the transcript and shipped it to Thwaites.

After a brief examination of the copy, Thwaites revealed to Dodd, Mead his initial impressions of it:

> I have just been making a preliminary survey of [Coues's transcript of] the Lewis & Clark MSS. It is evident that great care has been taken in making the transcript; it bears the mark of intention to be literal in all matters. But I can see that I shall certainly need to have the originals at hand, as we go along, especially as to interlineations by other hands, and as to proper names. My Secretary, Miss Nunns, who did some copying from the transcript this summer, and is herself quite expert in "crooked" chirography, tells me that there are here and there places where the copy does not make sense, giving rise to the suspicion that the transcriber misapprehended some words, especially in proper names—which is not to be wondered at, for I understand that the originals are very crabbed.[6]

Since Thwaites recognized the expediency of having the originals in hand for ready reference and for comparison with the transcript, he applied to the society for them at once. Hays replied that he had been authorized to send them, but only two volumes at a time, and

[6] In a postscript to this letter Thwaites added, "A case has arisen since I dictated the above. My assistant has raised the interesting query whether or not it was Lewis himself that made certain corrections and erasures in Clark's Journal, but we cannot now decide, for we have no Lewis Ms. as yet of even date with the Clark Ms." Later, with samples of Lewis' handwriting before him, Thwaites determined that Coues had been the culprit.

that they were to be returned through the Money Order Department of the American Express Company.

When the first shipment arrived in Madison, it was evident to Thwaites that Hays was sending the volumes in chronological order, since it consisted of Codices A, Aa, B, and Bb. Only a brief examination was necessary to convince Thwaites that this procedure was unsatisfactory. As a consequence, he forthwith wrote Hays asking that he be accorded "the same courtesy shown to Mr. Coues in 1892—that of being sent the entire collection of Lewis and Clark codices at one time." At the same time, this procedure seeming of such exigency to him, he wrote similarly to Dodd, Mead, urging them to give his request full support.

Thwaites's reasons, to him, were simple enough: (1) The transcript was "a wretched piece of work," the transcriber apparently having been unaccustomed to work of this kind and, therefore, with no idea "of the pin-point exactness necessary in reproducing manuscripts for publication." (2) With the codices arriving chronologically, it often happened that material needed for collating with Codex A might be far down, in Codex C, for example. (3) It was frequently necessary for him to examine a later entry, perhaps one about the return trip, and he was frustrated by the absence of ensuing codices. (4) Under such a procedure, it was impossible for him to complete any one section of the work until the last codex was available to him, a situation he found difficult to contemplate.

The society, thus pressed by both Thwaites and Dodd, Mead, acted affirmatively and promptly. Within less than a month after receiving Thwaites's request, Hays informed the publisher that Thwaites would have the complete set of codices in his hands within a few days. To Thwaites, in a similar notification, he advised that they would be transmitted in installments, with each being "valued in shipment both coming and going at $100."

It is evident by now that the society's evaluation of the Lewis and Clark manuscripts, and their attitude about safeguarding them, had altered appreciably since 1892, when Coues, with no imposed restrictions, took the entire lot with him to Washington. Then there was no insistence that they be insured against loss or damage, or that they, when not in use, be stored in fireproof vaults. Also, it would appear, the society had given little or no thought to their worth either monetarily or historically. By 1902, just ten years later, the society, as we now see, parted with the manuscripts reluctantly, and then only after stipulating that they be transmitted by express in installments and that each codex be insured for $100.

Today, some seventy years later, these same Lewis and Clark documents are regarded by the society as "select," to use a term employed by the British Museum to define any holding that is particularly precious. Since 1902, when they were shipped to Thwaites, they have not been lent to anyone, and no doubt never will be again, except under extraordinary circumstances.

With all of the codices at last in his hands, Thwaites began to give them the attention they required. Almost at once he was struck by Coues's numerous interlineations and expressed his initial reaction to Hays: "Private—Dr. Coues' emendations appear in pencil across the Codices, hundreds of times. What a pity that he thus defaced these splendid old manuscripts! I should never have thought this of him, but for the evidence he has left. To my thinking, such conduct is sacrilege!" After further examination of the manuscripts, being struck by the care someone had given to their arrangement, pagination, and the like, Thwaites inquired of Hays if Coues had been responsible. In the same letter, he requested a brief history of the codices for those years since the society had acquired them.[7]

Thwaites held an advantage over Coues in one important scientific respect: he knew (as Coues did not until after 1893) that a collection of pressed plants brought back by Lewis and Clark was extant, that it had been discovered in 1896 at the American Philosophical Society, and that soon afterward it had been placed on loan to the Academy of Natural Sciences, which had the facilities for taking care of it.[8] As a consequence, Thwaites wrote to Stewardson Brown, then assistant curator of botany at the academy, requesting him to prepare a brief description of the collection (now generally referred to as the Lewis and Clark Herbarium).

[7] Hays referred him to Coues's preface in the 1893 Biddle reissue, and to Coues's article about the Lewis and Clark manuscripts he had published in the society's *Proceedings* of 1893.

[8] This discovery was made by Thomas Meehan, academy botanist, who wrote a paper about his find, "The Plants of the Lewis and Clark Expedition Across the Continent, 1804–1806." Academy of Natural Sciences of Philadelphia *Proceedings*, Pt. 1 (January–March, 1898).

In due course, Brown outlined for Thwaites the history, as he knew it, of the collection and said that it consisted of 173 "recognizable species."[9] Thwaites subsequently printed Brown's description verbatim and without comment.[10] This is the kind of material on which Coues, with his technical background, would surely have elaborated if he had served as editor of the original journals instead of Thwaites. Indeed, in all likelihood, he would have insisted on an appendix listing all species of the herbarium and giving time and place of their discovery.

Before long a sharp difference of opinion arose between Thwaites and the society. The latter, as Hays wrote Thwaites on January 12, 1903, wanted one sentence of the title page to read, "Published from the original journals in the library of the American Philosophical Society and under the supervision of the Committee on Historical Documents." Thwaites objected strenuously to the word "supervision," as implying that the committee had regulated his editing. He suggested instead the words, "by arrangement with its Committee," or an equivalent phrase. This affair of words ran on for some time, with Thwaites an ultimate loser, even though Dodd, Mead, siding with him, told Hays that "Mr. Thwaites feels exceedingly sensitive on this point." When the journals finally came from the press, the title page bore the originally suggested wording except that "Published under the supervision of" had been changed to "Printed by direction of." Perhaps this slight alteration was more acceptable to Thwaites.

At about this same time, Hays informed Thwaites that he had been "delving" here and there in the society's library and had made some discoveries. These, it soon came out, were major discoveries, namely, Lewis and Clark manuscripts that had not come to the attention of Coues in 1892–93 and, until now, were unknown to historians. Among them were several letters, including the one by Biddle to the society dated April 6, 1818, listing the Lewis and Clark documents he was then, in compliance with Clark's directive,

---

[9] The author's count of "recognizable species" (reported in *Lewis and Clark: Pioneering Naturalists*) approximates that by Brown, though, due to duplication, Lewis' plant collection at the academy contains at least two hundred and sixteen herbarium sheets.

[10] For Brown's description, see Thwaites, *Original Journals*, VI, 151–53.

depositing with the society.[11] Of greater importance, Hays had located two large statistical tables (viz., "Estimate of the Eastern Indians" and "Estimate of the Western Indians") and another valuable document, "Diary and Thermometrical Observations."[12]

On receipt of this intelligence, Thwaites urged Hays to forward these manuscripts to him so that he might supervise their copying. "I do not like to trust any unknown person to copy these things for me," he explained. "My experience with transcribers has been very unfortunate . . . the thing has to be done with pin-point exactness; then again, it requires long experience, which very few copyists have, together with a knowledge of typographic values, and an ability, born of long practice, to decipher old manuscripts." Even so, when one of the "Statistical Tables" reached him, he admitted, ". . . it is a 'tough one,' and is going to require some typographical ingenuity to reproduce it."

In mid-April, 1903, Thwaites advised Hays that in May he expected to come east to confer with Dodd, Mead and would, of course, drop in at the society to see him and to

> take another look through your vault . . . to see that we have made a clean sweep of everything. . . . The scientific and miscellaneous material which I have extracted from the Journals proper is of very great importance, and a fresh contribution to science. One becomes more and more, in the course of editing, impressed with the magnificent courage of the explorers and the splendid results of the expedition. Mr. Brown and Mr. [Witmer] Stone [academy ornithologist] have both of them sent me excellent notes upon the botany and zoology of the expedition and I am gathering [additional scientific] material from men upon the Pacific coast and elsewhere.[13]

After Coues, Thwaites was the first person to recognize the vast

---

[11] In his listing of items Biddle included "The Manuscript Journal of Sergeant Ordway." In light of subsequent events, it would appear that he did not deposit the diary with the society then or at any other time.

[12] Thwaites printed the "Estimates" in Volume VI of the *Original Journals* and the letters in Volume VII.

[13] The "men upon the Pacific coast and elsewhere" were botanists C. V. Piper, Washington State University, and William Trelease, director of the Missouri Botanical Garden, St. Louis. The notes of ornithologist Witmer Stone appear in Thwaites, *Original Journals*, VI, 121.

amount of technical data Lewis and Clark had recorded, and it is much to his credit that he understood its value. Farther along in this chapter, we will consider the attention he gave to it.

With an eye to illustrative material, Thwaites shortly wrote to Hays for information about the likeness he remembered seeing at the society of an Indian chief who had been known to Lewis and Clark. The likeness turned out to be that of the Mandan chief, Big White, one of the better known of several sketches of Indian leaders done by the French-born artist, St. Mémin. Big White and other Indian chiefs had formed a delegation that came east in 1806 with Lewis and Clark to pay their respects to Jefferson. Henry Marie Brackenridge, who visited the Mandan villages in 1811, described Big White as "a fat man, not much distinguished as a warrior, and extremely talkative."[14] Lewis and Clark had more to say about him than about any other native chieftain they encountered on their entire trip. St. Mémin's portrait of Big White today adorns a wall at the Philosophical Society. For reasons unknown, Thwaites did not see fit to reproduce it.

Looking further for illustrations, Thwaites learned that the copper plates used by Biddle in reproducing the five small maps which appeared in his 1814 edition and subsequent reissues were now the property of Judge Craig Biddle. On request, Judge Biddle sent these plates to Thwaites, who, however, did not make use of them. Instead, he employed Clark's original maps, and thus is explained the evident differences between the five charts of Coues and Thwaites.

Students of Lewis and Clark know that the *Original Journals* contain the diaries of Sergeant Charles Floyd and Private Joseph Whitehouse. Thwaites experienced no trouble in gaining permission to publish the former, since it was the property of the Historical Society of Wisconsin. The converse proved true with Whitehouse's journal, which was privately owned. Thwaites's first reference to it is contained in a letter to Hays of April 13, 1903: "You will be pleased to know no doubt that we have at last secured the original Whitehouse Journal and I am expecting it within a few days. This with the Floyd Journal is going to make our series a splendid one."

[14] *Ibid.*, I, 212n.

It was Thwaites who had conducted the successful search for this journal, as is proved by his own words: "The Whitehouse diary was secured by me for Dodd, Mead & Co. expressly for this publication, at a considerable expenditure of time and money." While engaged with his search, he learned quite a bit about what had happened to it in the interval between 1806, when Whitehouse received his discharge from the Expedition, and 1903, when Thwaites obtained it. Thwaites summed it up in a letter to Olin D. Wheeler, a friend who was then completing for publication *The Trail of Lewis and Clark, 1804–1806*:[15]

> As I understand it, Whitehouse upon his death gave the manuscript to Canon de Vivaldi, an Italian priest; I think it was about 1860, although my information upon this point is still a little foggy. The Canon owned a newspaper in Arkansas and a Mrs. Gertrude Haley of San Francisco loaned him money. He gave her this journal as a recompense. It was kept for some twelve or fifteen years in the Archives department of the New York Historical Society, and has since drifted from pillar to post until a few years ago it was returned to Mrs. Haley's possession. She has endeavored to sell it to the Library of Congress, but they thought the price too high, and finally my publishers have secured it. It is somewhat on the order of the Floyd journal although more interesting and written by a better educated man. In a good many small particulars it admirably supplements the journals of the chiefs. On account of the large price which Dodd, Mead & Co. paid for the journal, they desire to keep it from use by anyone else until they have had the publication of it. . . . the journal covers only the trip out, from March 14, 1804 to Nov. 6, 1805.

When Thwaites wrote the introduction for the *Original Journals*, he added to the above information and clarified certain points. The canon himself, he said, had deposited Whitehouse's diary with the New York Historical Society, about 1860, at the time ecclesiastical duties had called him to Patagonia. There it remained until the canon returned to the United States in 1893 and found himself stopping at the same Los Angeles hotel occupied by Mr. and Mrs. Haley. It was on this occasion that Mr. Haley advanced money to the canon and was, in turn, given an order on the New York His-

---

[15] New York, G. P. Putnam's Sons, 1904.

torical Society for the journal. Haley obtained it the following year and, on his death, it went to Mrs. Haley, who kept it until she sold it to Dodd, Mead and Company. Thwaites added that he first learned of its whereabouts upon Mrs. Haley's effort to sell it to the Library of Congress.[16]

What happened to Whitehouse's diary after Dodd, Mead published it? They sold it to Edward Everett Ayer, a Chicago collector of rare books. From him it passed to Newberry Library, Chicago, where it has since remained. However, the story of Whitehouse's journal does not end there. In 1966, a paraphrase of the original was discovered in a Philadelphia bookstore. For a detailed account, see Appendix A.

Thwaites's argument with Hays about the title page wording was trifling when compared to another which developed soon after his spring visit to Philadelphia. It centered on library policy about permissions to use historical material, specifically, in this case, Lewis and Clark manuscripts. Thwaites advocated a generally free, unrestricted policy in dealing with reputable scholars; Hays took a stand against such liberality. The controversy. which ran on for more than a month, represented honest differences of opinion. The first inkling we have of it is in a letter from Thwaites to Hays dated May 23, 1902:

> Until your remark the other day, I was quite unaware that the Philosophical Society took the attitude toward the Lewis and Clark Journals that not even a photograph of a page of the manuscript could be permitted to appear in an historical publication without express permission. I had supposed that the MSS. being the official report of a government expedition, and simply deposited by the President of the United States with the Society, the latter would be only too glad to have them known to the public, not only for public information but for the credit of the Society as their keeper. Taking this view, I had proposed to use in a magazine article several of the photographs taken of sample pages, incidental to communications with Dodd, Mead & Co. relative to illustrations, etc. I will confess that I had only taken into consideration, in this matter, the interests

[16] Thwaites, *Original Journals*, I, lv–lvi. Whitehouse's *Journal* was, of course, incomplete. It ended November 6, 1805, and contained several hiatuses, notably January 21 to April 30, 1805, inclusive.

of the house. Assuming that a magazine description of the journals would help the sale, I had agreed to write such an article.

There was more to Thwaites's letter. As he continued, he made it plain that he had planned to use illustrations not only in the article referred to, but also in a book he had in preparation, *Brief History of Rocky Mountain Exploration*.[17] He informed Hays, too, that he had promised Olin D. Wheeler "the privilege of photographing a few of the pages of Lewis and Clark, as well as of our Floyd Journal." He regarded this as proper, particularly so since Wheeler had provided him with essential data about the route Lewis and Clark had followed across the Bitterroot Mountains. Also, he was considering the request of Dr. Guy Carlton Lee, who was then writing a history of the United States, that he be allowed a print or two. Thwaites saw nothing wrong in acceding to Dr. Lee's request because, at the State Historical Society of Wisconsin, they had given him permission to photograph anything in their collections—"a privilege we always grant with entire freedom to all scholars."

On receipt of the above, Hays lost no time protesting to Dodd, Mead about Thwaites's arbitrary use of the Lewis and Clark material. After considering their own position, as well as that of Thwaites and the society, Robert Dodd replied, "I think that Mr. Thwaites should not give anyone permission to facsimile any portion of the Journals without first consulting us, and we certainly would not feel justified in giving such permission without in turn consulting you."

Robert Dodd addressed himself similarly to Thwaites, but at greater length. He told him that his house disagreed with Thwaites's stated policy "of allowing free access to the Journals on the part of anyone who may wish to see them," and they felt no one should be permitted to photograph portions without first consulting them, and this feeling extended particularly to the request from Dr. Lee. Dodd then softened his posture by saying, "In regard to Mr. Wheeler's book and your own History . . . we certainly cannot object as they propose to give us a return for the use of the Journals. . . . We understand, of course, that in all this matter you have acted with our interests in mind and with a desire to further our interests."

[17] It was published in 1904.

Thwaites yielded to the demands of Dodd, Mead and the society, but not to the point of agreeing with them. He continued to maintain that recognized scholars should have free access to the Lewis and Clark documents and to any other official reports of government expeditions, for, as such, they belonged to the people. In a subsequent letter to Hays he declared, "Our points of view in regard to these matters are so radically different that perhaps I have been rather strong at times in stating my own." And in another:

> In all my experience of editing, this is the only disagreeable incident that has ever arisen. I will confess that I felt rather nettled over it—but let that pass. It is simply a matter of differences in point of view —we in the West think somewhat differently about the nature of archives, and the responsibility of such archives to the scholarly public than do some of the eastern institutions; so if I am to be blamed at all, you must blame my western training.

Throughout this controversy, both Dodd, Mead and the society utterly ignored Thwaites's oft-repeated insistence that the Lewis and Clark papers belonged to the government. The matter of rightful ownership would be raised again, but not until half a century later.[18]

—3—

Though Thwaites had succeeded in locating Whitehouse's journal, he had no luck at all in his search for Sergeant John Ordway's. He knew, of course, that Biddle had used it when making his paraphrase of 1814, but since that date it had vanished as completely as had Private Robert Frazer's journal. At one time, thinking he had a lead to its whereabouts, he wrote Hays, "I have located this [journal of Ordway's], I fancy, and am not without hopes of being able to publish it in our work."

The lead proved spurious, but it was Thwaites's energetic search for this journal that led eventually to the most important discovery of Lewis and Clark material since Coues's rediscovery, a decade earlier, of the original journals. Thwaites reported this event on August 8, 1903, in a letter to Hays. His tone was surprisingly casual: "We have just discovered in New York some half dozen note

[18] This followed the discovery of Clark's "Field Notes" in 1953.

books, chiefly by Clark, similar to those which are in possession of the Society, together with a considerable mass of other material bearing upon the expedition. I expect to leave here next Monday personally to look into the matter. This will make a very important addition to our collection."

At a somewhat later date Thwaites wrote that his protracted search for Ordway's journal among descendants of William Clark had led to an "unexpected situation." He explained the situation thusly:

> The third son and fourth child of General Clark and his first wife, Julia Hancock, was George Rogers Hancock, born at St. Louis in 1816. This son was his father's executor, and as such came into possession of the explorer's papers and numerous other family records, many of which he appears to have arranged and labelled with some care. Upon his death, in 1858, they descended to his eldest child, now Mrs. Julia Clark Voorhis of New York City, whose proprietary rights are at present shared with her daughter, Miss Eleanor Glasgow Voorhis.[19]

Thwaites's anticipated visit to New York for the purpose of examining the papers had to be postponed, Mrs. Voorhis and her daughter having chosen this moment to leave the city on vacation. Also, as Dodd, Mead informed Hays,

> We could not persuade them to let the material be gone over until they had first had time to go through it with reference to certain private letters which they thought might be included. The matter promises to be most valuable and important and we feel that some arrangement should certainly be made to include it in our publication. The decision made by Mrs. Clark [that is, Mrs. Julia Clark Voorhis] delays matters until Autumn and brings everything to a standstill. This we regret very much, as otherwise we should be able to go to press, Mr. Thwaites having completed his editing of the journals in his hands.

It was late October, some ten weeks after the discovery of the Voorhis collection, before Thwaites finally had the opportunity of examining it. Immediately thereafter, he provided Hays with a detailed description, one that assumes increased significance when we

---

[19] *Scribner's Magazine*, Vol. XXXV (June, 1904), 689.

reflect that historians had no prior knowledge of this material. Thwaites's tone in this letter was anything but casual:

There are five note books by Wm. Clark—four of them the red morocco variety such as you have in Philadelphia, and one an actual field book bound in elk, and carried upon the expedition by Clark himself. Of course you are aware that the books in your possession were all of them copied by the explorers from the field books which they carried in their pockets. Among the Voorhis manuscripts is one field book actually written by Clark in the field and carried by him. It is the only one of the kind that I know of in existence. To reproduce it in all of its crudity would be of exceeding interest. It contains something like fifteen or sixteen small maps showing their route from day to day across the mountains, and would be of immense value in settling the vexed question of the exact route. In addition to these five note books I personally discovered in the mass of material the order[ly] book frequently referred to by Lewis and Clark in their journals. There are also in the collection about fifty maps made by Wm. Clark varying in size from six inches square to 1 x 9 feet in extent. There is also a considerable mass of material relative to the expedition which it would be exceedingly interesting to reproduce in our series, but Mrs. Voorhis and the other members of the family in New York have golden dreams concerning their cash value. . . . Unfortunately we are so situated that we cannot very well go to press without their material. While it is in no sense necessary to our publication, for the note books which you have in your possession and which I have already edited for the press contain the entire story of the expedition day by day from beginning to end, Clark's note books are in large measure mere copies of Lewis's note books, for Lewis was the literary man of the expedition. Nevertheless some rival publisher could take hold of this material—and Mrs. Voorhis it seems has three such publishers on the string—and by skillful editing with extracts from the Biddle narrative so make it appear that our series was of no use without theirs to fill in the gaps. You can see that the publishers are up against a very difficult proposition. Judge [James T.] Mitchell [chairman of the society's Committee of Historical Documents, and related to Mrs. Voorhis] has done his best to induce the ladies to allow the publication of the manuscripts which are in their possession but which are really and honestly the property of the United States government; but his advice appears to have no effect upon them. I really do not know what the outcome will be. I have carefully examined the material and have given my opinion of it to Dodd, Mead & Co.; but the actual financial negotiations I of course have had to leave to them.

Of course you will understand that this communication is entirely confidential. But I thought you ought to know the exact situation.

It was indeed a "difficult proposition," more so than either editor or publisher envisioned at the moment. Negotiations dragged along for more than three months, and it was February 17, 1904, when Robert Dodd informed Hays, "We have at last entered into an arrangement with Mrs. Voorhis for the use of her material in the Lewis and Clark Journals." Prior to that date, Thwaites corresponded regularly with Mrs. Voorhis and made at least two additional trips to New York to confer with her, while Dodd, Mead held an indeterminate number of interviews with her and were intermittently in touch with the Philosophical Society as they tried to arrive at a monetary solution agreeable to all parties. And with each passing week the publication of the journals, of course, was delayed by just that much.

At times the demands of Mrs. Voorhis and her daughter seemed beyond reach. On one occasion, Thwaites wrote Wheeler, "I am thinking that we will have to go ahead regardless of them and on the lines which we have already sketched out." Dodd, Mead persisted in their negotiations only because they regarded the material as "very highly desirable if this is to be a definitive edition of the Journals," and because they feared, as Thwaites had indicated, that some rival publisher would grab it if they did not.

As the days and weeks had gone by, with no agreement reached, Thwaites had spoken out forthrightly, even immoderately, about the refusal of the Clark heirs to come to terms. To one friend he had written, "They want a large sum of money for the use of their stuff, when it really belongs to the United States government. They are simply conducting a holdup game." To others, because of the continuing frustration, he used much stronger language.

Once Thwaites had the Voorhis material at hand, he lost no time incorporating parts of it into the first volume of the set, doing so in little more than a month. And he was sanguine enough to predict, as he told Dodd, Mead, that he would have this volume out by late spring or early summer. In this labor he had been handicapped by a severe eye trouble that had developed during the winter, with his doctor insisting that he avoid "every stitch of work under artificial light." The condition had so far improved by spring that he was fit for six to seven hours each day, but he was still forbidden to work at night.

This was not the last of Thwaites's problems; he had a final tangle with Hays. In his introduction to the set, he had stated that the original journals had slumbered "unnoticed and forgotten" for nearly seventy-five years in the vaults of the Philosophical Society. Hays, on reading this, took vigorous exception to it. Members of the society, he informed Thwaites, were and always had been quite aware of the presence of these journals in the library of the society. Attempting to patch up the matter, Thwaites replied:

> I have your kind note of the 24th [of May]. By my phrase "unnoticed and forgotten" I of course did not mean that the Society itself had forgotten the existence of its own treasures. Obviously that would be absurd. The idea which I intended to convey was that it had remained "unnoticed and forgotten" by historical students. If I find on reading the proof that this needs explanation, I will of course do so—but it had seemed to me impossible that anybody would conceive the idea that I should suppose the Society had forgotten its own possessions. . . . I am very sorry that you have taken offence when certainly no offence was intended.

Publication of the first volume was delayed until October, by which time it had become apparent that the total number of volumes would be eight, instead of four or five as originally planned.[20] By then, or soon afterward, Thwaites had completed his editorial labors. By terms of his original contract with Dodd, Mead, he was to have received $1,500. However, because of considerable additional work, mainly that resulting from the acquisition of the Voorhis material, the publisher increased the sum to $2,500. In explanation of this figure, Dodd, Mead told Thwaites:

---

[20] In addition to the quantity, eight-volume edition, Dodd, Mead published two limited editions of fifteen volumes quarto, one of two hundred copies, on Van Gelder handmade paper, and the other a de luxe edition of fifty numbered copies on imperial Japan paper, with many of the illustrations colored by hand.

While you have put in more editorial time than you foresaw, we have been put to greater expense and risk than was contemplated in the beginning. . . . The initial sale has been disappointing, and we shall have to use our best efforts to come out whole upon the venture. We will say now that when we sell enough to cover expenses we will pay you a further sum of $500. . . . We congratulate you heartily on your editorial work. We are in a position to realize, to some extent, its difficulties. As far as the mechanical side goes, we have never had to do with an editor who so thoroughly understood the typography and make-up of a book and that, too, a very difficult one.

Thwaites's contributions to the publication history of Lewis and Clark were many and varied. He transcribed the original journals of Lewis, Clark, Floyd, and Whitehouse, as well as many collateral documents—a sizable task in itself, in spite of whatever help the Coues transcript may have been. He organized this wealth of material into what must be regarded as an entirely acceptable whole. He gave it the benefit of collation and annotation (as much as Dodd, Mead would allow). To him must go the credit for discovering Whitehouse's journal and the Voorhis collection of papers and maps, the latter a discovery of the utmost importance. Also, during the course of his editing, Thwaites brought to light a number of facts not fully understood before; for instance, that Clark—not Lewis— designed all of the illustrations in their journals, those of birds, fish, plants, Indian head-flattening, and many others, and that Clark often copied Lewis' diary, almost word for word, particularly from early January to July of 1806.

In any comparison of Thwaites's editorial capabilities with Coues's —and such a comparison seems called for at this point—it should be kept in mind that the former was essentially a historian by training and that the job he had been hired to do centered largely on compilation. Conversely, the latter was a scientist whose basic duty in editing the 1893 reissue of Biddle was to annotate. We should be sensible of the fact, too, that the *Original Journals* differed appreciably from Biddle's paraphrase in that they contained a vast amount of geographical, ethnological, and biological data.

This writer might be satisfied in saying that both Thwaites and Coues succeeded admirably in their respective editorial roles, and let it go at that, except that Thwaites wrote Dodd, Mead that his annotations from beginning to end "bring out a great wealth of topographical and other scientific information." The statement simply does not hold up, at least when we compare Thwaites's wealth with that provided by Coues. Numerically, the latter's footnotes on technical matters exceed the former's by two to one and, of course, cover far more ground. We can be more specific, by considering, for instance, the notes of both men for the period of April 9 to 27, 1805, as the corps moved from Fort Mandan to the mouth of the Yellowstone. During that period, Coues employed a total of seventeen notes about plants and animals and bracketed twenty-four scientific names. Thwaites, to the contrary, appended just six biological notes and bracketed no binomials whatever.

That Thwaites did not make fuller use of Coues's notes may be ascribed to his over-all unfamiliarity with the sciences and to limitations of space—if he had been allowed full rein, the eight-volume production could well have grown into one of nine or ten. His use of certain of Coues's plant and animal notes, to the exclusion of others, would baffle if we did not know of his lack of training in biology. For example, on April 11, 1805, Lewis wrote, "Saw some large white cranes pass up the river—these are the largest birds of that genus common to the country through which the Missouri and Mississippi pass. They are perfectly white except the large feathers of the first two joints of the wing which are black."[21] Coues correctly identified these as whooping cranes (*Grus americana*); Thwaites ignored them completely, as he did other animals Lewis and Clark had encountered between Fort Mandan and the Yellowstone, such as the snow goose, Canada goose, gray wolf, coyote, and spermophiles, and such plants as Jerusalem artichoke, box elder, and juniper. And thus it went from start to finish of the entire trip.

How would Coues have handled documentation of the original journals if he had been privileged to edit them? Of two things I think we may be certain: his notes would have been greater numerically, and they would have been lengthier. Also, because he had traveled extensively in the West and therefore possessed a personal familiarity with its geography, biology, and ethnology, it seems

[21] Thwaites, *Original Journals*, I, 295.

logical to presume that he would have brought a greater enthusiasm, as well as knowledge, to his task.

How did Thwaites himself view the end product of his editorial labors? He exuded general enthusiasm, as we learn from a letter to Dodd, Mead dated January 6, 1906, wherein he stressed specific features that he thought their agents should emphasize when offering the series to the public: (1) they should make much of the fact that "the Biddle edition contains exceedingly little upon the scientific side of the expedition; whereas our version contains literally every scrap of explanation which the explorers brought back, together with a great mass of additional material and comments thereon by some of the leading scientific experts in this country;" (2) "The Appendix should especially be called attention to, containing as it does a great mass of subsidiary matter that throws light upon the expedition and upon the times;" (3) "Then let them dwell upon the Index, which is exceedingly full and detailed from every point of view;" (4) "Especial stress should be laid upon the Atlas volume. In the Biddle edition are a few small modern maps made up from data furnished by Clark. But in our volume we have not only the maps that the explorers themselves carried upon the expedition, but practically every scrap of topographical data which they themselves collected. . . . These maps have not been copies, but are reproduced with the most faithful photographic process exactly as Clark proposed them. They are not only maps, but they are covered with data of all sorts and descriptions. Their actual camping places day by day are given—this is of very great importance to local antiquarians and historians. . . . The Atlas is alone worth the cost of the entire series."

Reviewers, after all eight volumes had been made available to them, had only praise for both editor and publisher. One notice, more or less typical of others, went, "As regards the work of Dr. Thwaites in arranging the vast and chaotic mass of material, and in providing it with proper introduction and notes, it is all that could be expected from a scholar so able and painstaking."[22]

A final question arises: what dispensation was made of the Voorhis collection after Dodd, Mead had finished with it? According to a provision of the will of Mrs. Voorhis, the journals, letters, and other

[22] *The Nation*, Vol. LXXIX (September 15, 1904), 216–18.

documents went to the Missouri Historical Society, St. Louis, and that is where they may be found today.[23] Surprisingly, Mrs. Voorhis

[23] Minutes of the Missouri Historical Society for April 1, 1923, read

Gift—Clark collection to be known as the ELEANOR GLASGOW VOORHIS MEMORIAL COLLECTION:

Original Journal kept by Lewis and Clark on their Expedition to the Pacific Ocean 1804–06, bound in buffalo [elk] hide.

Four red bound books compiled by Lewis and Clark relating to their Expedition, in which they have drawn Indians, fish, birds, leaves and maps of rivers &c., which they encountered.

Letter of Credit from Thomas Jefferson dated July 4, 1803, in which he informs Lewis and Clark that they are authorized to draw on the Secretaries of the Army and Navy for whatever funds they may need to pay individuals or nations to facilitate their progress, that he solemnly pledges the faith of the U.S. that these drafts will be paid punctually.

Wm. Clark's "Orderly Book" including names of the men who were on his expedition.

[Letters] To Clark:—

ALS, T. Jefferson, Sept. 10, 1809, ack. receipt of Mastodon bones.

" " " Dec. 10, 1807, regarding placing of above bones.

" " " Sept. 8, 1816, wishing permission to obtain the Lewis and Clark Journal for the purpose of using the astronomical observations, geographical charts, maps, &c. for publication.

ALS, Gen. Lafayette to Wm. Clark, Paris, March 1830, letter of commendation on the good conduct of six Osage Indians, 4 men and 2 women, while on a visit to Paris.

Letter to Clark with a copy of the resolutions passed requesting the President to appoint Clark Governor of the Territory, Apr. 1809.

ALS, Wm. H. Harrison, Vincennes, Nov. 13, 1803, regarding a map which he forwards and says that news received that the Senate had advised the ratification of the French treaty 24 to 7.

ALS, Wm. Carr Lane, Mayor of St. Louis, May 16, 1823, to Clark, with resolutions passed by Mayor and Board of Aldermen to rename the streets of St. Louis and asks Clark's support.

Oaths of office taken by Wm. Clark as Chief Magistrate of Missouri Territory 1813–1816–1817–1820.

ALS, Andrew Jackson, Hermitage, Jan. 7, 1829, to Clark, introducing Mr. John G. Anderson who with his family goes to St. Louis to settle.

ALS, [Prince Paul of Württemberg], dated Fort Clark, Mandans, Apr. 25, 1830, to Clark thanking him for letters he gave to present to the government agents who have treated him well.

Collection of miscellaneous invitations to Clark, including one from Auguste Chouteau, undated.

ALS, James Monroe, Dept. of War, Mch. 11, 1815, regarding a Commissioner to treat with the Indians with whom we were at war, in which he gives the highest praise to Alexander McNair.

ALS, Jas. Monroe to Wm. Clark regarding statement of Boilvin, 1816.

willed the extremely valuable collection of Clark's maps to her attorney. On his death they passed to his wife and she, without loss of time, offered them for sale. Bids came in from several sources, including the Library of Congress, but the highest was from the Old Print Shop, New York City. That firm, before long, sold the maps to Edward Eberstadt & Sons, dealers in Western Americana, who in turn sold them to the collector, William Robertson Coe. In 1951 Coe presented the entire collection to Yale University, and there, it would appear, these historically priceless charts have found a permanent home.[24]

—4—

During the remaining years of his life, Thwaites continued to edit earlier published classics of trans-Mississippi exploration, notably the series of thirty-two volumes which appeared in 1904–06 under the title *Early Western Travels*.[25] Students of Lewis and Clark have long since learned the collateral value of a number of these volumes, such as Major Stephen H. Long's *Account of an Expedition from Pittsburgh to the Rocky Mountains*, Maximilian's *Travels in the Interior of North America, 1832–1834*, John Bradbury's *Travels in the Interior of America, in the years 1809, 1810 and 1811*, and Gabriel Franchère's *Narrative of a Voyage to the Northwest Coast of America*.

Thwaites died October 22, 1913. In an obituary notice one writer said, "The wider reading public of the country knew him as the

---

ALS, Same to same Apr. 21, 1820, introducing his younger brother, Joseph Monroe, who goes to settle in the new state of Missouri.

ALS, Same to same, Oak Hill, Va., Sept. 28, 1828, encloses a copy of his "Memoires."

Locket of hair of Wm. Clark. His Watch Chain. Wax Seal of Family.

Watch Chain given Wm. Clark by his son Meriwether L. Clark.

Gold Locket owned by Wm. Clark with picture of Geo. R. Clark.

Original Journal of the Lewis & Clark Expedition, kept by Capt. Clark, also Orderly Book (fragmentary) of same.

[24] The Missouri Historical Society had reason to understand that these maps were to have been willed to them. For more about the disposition of the Voorhis Collection, see Calvin Tomkins, "The Lewis and Clark Case," *The New Yorker*, October 29, 1966, 105–48.

[25] Cleveland, The Arthur H. Clark Co.

author of admirable histories and biographies related to the Middle West, and particularly as the editor of the famous 'Jesuit Relations,' in 73 volumes; of the 'Journals of Lewis and Clark,' and 'Early Western Travels'."[26] Historian Frederick Jackson Turner, in a memorial address, declared that Thwaites, while preparing the *Original Journals*

> met and conquered difficulties in a way that proved him an editor of the very first rank. He ferreted out from their concealment missing documents necessary to complete the journals; deciphered the difficult writing and spelling of these historic frontiersmen . . . mastered the problem of correlating and printing the several journals of the expedition; drew upon all of his resources of typographic and editorial skill to give an absolutely faithful reproduction of the originals.

In conclusion, Turner described Thwaites as "Short in stature, but with a compelling personality, his cheery, winning spirit shining out behind his twinkling eyes, always ready with a joke or a story that impressed a point upon his hearers; alert, decisive, receptive, helpful, a man of honor and of character."[27]

---

[26] *American Review of Reviews*, Vol. XLVIII (December, 1913), 670.

[27] Frederick Jackson Turner, *Reuben Gold Thwaites: a Memorial Address* (Madison, State Historical Society of Wisconsin, 1914).

CHAPTER VIII
Milo Milton Quaife

The years immediately preceding and following 1900 yielded an extraordinary succession of discoveries and rediscoveries of Lewis and Clark documents. The sequence began in 1892 with Coues's rediscovery of the original journals and, the next year, with Thwaites's disclosure, among papers of Dr. Lyman C. Draper at the State Historical Society of Wisconsin, of Sergeant Charles Floyd's journal.[1] It was continued in 1903 with Thwaites's discovery of Private Joseph Whitehouse's journal and the Voorhis windfall of letters, maps, and journals; and it terminated—on a high note—in 1913 with the discovery of Meriwether Lewis' "Ohio Journal" and the rediscovery of Sergeant John Ordway's journal. That so many manuscripts of such tremendous consequence should have been brought to light and made available to historians in such a brief span of years is surely one of the most incredible and fortunate happenings in the entire aftermath of the Lewis and Clark Expedition —and, obviously, one full of import for the future.

Since, in earlier chapters, we described the finds of 1892, 1893, and 1904, we may now turn to those of 1913, and limit our remarks for the moment to the rediscovery of Ordway's journal. In St. Louis right after the Expedition ended, it will be recalled, Lewis and

[1] Sergeant Charles Floyd's "Journal," edited by Dr. James D. Butler, was originally printed in 1894 in the American Antiquarian Society *Proceedings*.

Clark had bought the sergeant's diary, paying him $300 for it.[2] In 1810, Clark had lent it to Biddle, who found it of much value while he was editing the official account of the Expedition. Still later, in 1818, Clark had requested Biddle to return Ordway's journal to him. Thereafter it vanished, like a burned-out meteorite. Thwaites had presumed that Biddle had returned it to Clark; but when Thwaites failed to find it among the Voorhis documents, as he thought he might, he despaired of its ever being found.

Biddle was always a busy man, and perhaps a forgetful one, too. In any event, he did not return Ordway's journal to Clark, and following his death it passed to his nearest of kin. These facts, however, did not come to light until 1913, when grandsons of Nicholas Biddle, Charles and Edward Biddle, unearthed the journal while going through "the thousands of papers accumulated by their grandfather and still in the possession of the Biddle family."[3] Its disappearance had lasted, as simple arithmetic reveals, exactly ninety-five years.

News that Ordway's journal had reappeared created much excitement among American historians, one of whom was Milo Milton Quaife (1880–1959), at that time superintendent and editor for the State Historical Society of Wisconsin, in Madison. Influenced perhaps by the earlier successes of Coues and Thwaites in editing the journals of Lewis and Clark, Quaife immediately entertained notions of laboring in this same literary vineyard. As evidence, he wrote to Charles Biddle inquiring if he had plans to publish Ordway's journal and, if so, would he consider putting it in the hands of the State Historical Society of Wisconsin for that purpose. He made it clear, of course, that he himself would assume responsibility for editing the journal. In due time, Biddle replied affirmatively to both of Quaife's questions.

—2—

Until Quaife intruded his journalistic pen, the men who had

[2] Lewis and Clark paid equal amounts. From Lewis' "Account Book" we learn that he paid his portion April 18, 1807 (Jackson, *Letters*, 462).

[3] Milo M. Quaife (ed.), *The Journals of Captain Meriwether Lewis and Sergeant John Ordway* (Madison, State Historical Society of Wisconsin, 1916), 26. Hereinafter cited as *Ordway*.

figured most prominently in editing and publishing the Lewis and Clark journals—M'Keehan, Biddle, Coues, and Thwaites—had their roots deep in eastern soil, at least initially. Quaife was born west of the Mississippi, on a farm near Nashua, Iowa, a small town perhaps best known because the hymn, "The Little Brown Church in the Wildwood," originated there.

Quaife received his adult education from Grinnell College (Ph.B., 1903), the University of Missouri (A.M., 1905), and the University of Chicago (Ph.D., 1908). From 1908 through 1913 he taught history at Lewis Institute, Chicago. It was in 1914 that the State Historical Society of Wisconsin induced him to come to Madison to serve as its superintendent and editor. In those capacities he continued until 1922.

In Quaife's own words, "In the spring of 1914 the present editor was permitted, through the courtesy of Charles Biddle, to make a copy of the journal with a view to securing its ultimate publication."[4] Quaife was then just thirty-three years old. As for his editorial qualifications, he had done well academically in college and university, had five years of successful teaching behind him (having been advanced from an initial instructorship to a full professorship), and he had written and published one book, *Chicago and the Old Northwest, 1673–1835*.[5]

If I interpret correctly statements made by Quaife,[6] it was Charles Biddle who discovered the mass of papers originally belonging to his celebrated grandfather, but Edward Biddle who, while later scanning individual items (preparatory to shipping the whole to the Library of Congress as then planned), actually spotted the "manuscript contained within loose covers which proved, upon examination, to be the long-lost journal of Sergt. John Ordway."[7]

Once Quaife had the manuscript in his hands, he examined it closely and was much distressed with what he found. As he subsequently wrote:

.... the manuscript in hand constituted but a portion of the original

[4] *Ibid.*, 26.

[5] Chicago, University of Chicago Press, 1913.

[6] Quaife, *Ordway*, 26; also Milo M. Quaife, "Some New-found Records of the Lewis and Clark Expedition," *Mississippi Valley Historical Review*, Vol. II, No. 1 (June, 1915), 108–109.

[7] Quaife, *Ordway*, 26.

journal. Contained within loose covers, the record had been kept with the greatest possible degree of regularity from the time the expedition departed from River Dubois, May 14, 1804, until the headwaters of the Columbia were reached, September 30, 1805 [at which date the party, after crossing the Bitterroots, had halted at Canoe Camp on the Clearwater River, Idaho, to build dugouts]. A variety of considerations seemed to render it unlikely that Ordway had suddenly laid down his pen and abandoned his journal at this point. A request was forwarded to Mr. [Charles] Biddle, therefore, that a further search be made among the family papers for the continuation of the journal.[8]

The results of the further search exceeded Quaife's most sanguine expectations. Another look by the Biddle brothers brought to light

> four volumes of varying size and significance, all being narrative journals, kept in the usual form of such records. Of the four records the three largest proved on examination to pertain to the Lewis and Clark expedition. Two of these were the continuation, to its conclusion, of Sergeant Ordway's journal. The third volume contained the journal . . . of the river trip in the summer and autumn of 1809 [1803, rather], first of Lewis and later of Clark, from Pittsburgh to the camp on River Dubois.[9]

Thus, in what must be regarded as one of the great moments in the literary history of Lewis and Clark, the two grandsons of Nicholas Biddle had unearthed not only the latter half of Ordway's journal but, also, Lewis' "Ohio Journal," a document previously unheard-of by students of the Expedition, or by any one else.

With Ordway's complete diary now at hand, Quaife began work on it at once, first transcribing and then collating and annotating. The deeper he dug into it, the more impressed he became. He cited reasons: it contained an entry for each of the 863 days the Expedition had been in progress and was, therefore, the only *complete* record among the several kept by members of the party;[10] it was

[8] *Ibid.*

[9] *Ibid.* The fourth volume was a journal kept by Clark in 1808 while on a trip up the Missouri which resulted in a treaty with the Osage Indians and the construction of Fort Osage.

[10] Clark's journal, almost complete, lacked entries for just ten days. These had been omitted while he was away from Fort Mandan on a hunting trip. On his return to the fort, he did, however, summarize events of those ten days.

the only journal describing the July, 1806, descent—by Ordway and nine others—of the Missouri from Three Forks to Great Falls; it was the only journal except Gass's to recount events at Great Falls on the return journey; and, of journals kept by subordinates, it was far and away the fullest and most informative.[11]

To underscore his point that Ordway's journal contained more information than that by any of the other subordinates, Quaife called attention to a number of statements found only in that record. For instance, on July 14, 1804, Ordway had written, "Capt Clarks notes & Remarks of 2 days blew overboard this morning in the Storm, and he was much put to it to Recolect the courses &.C."[12] No other journalist reported this incident, not even Clark himself. Jefferson had feared contingencies such as this, hence his insistence on multiple accounts.

Ordway alone gave details of a visit he and three companions made August 13–14, 1804, to an Omaha village that had been burned and abandoned in the wake of a smallpox epidemic.[13] Ordway, too, in describing a council with the Yankton Sioux on August 30–31, 1804, included near verbatim reports, entirely missing from other diaries, of speeches delivered by the Yankton chiefs.[14]

In citing these instances of Ordway's conscientious reporting, Quaife overlooked one that has an especial appeal to this writer. It described an event of October 11, 1804, at which time the explorers had halted just above the Grand River, South Dakota, to confer with the Arikara Indians. There followed the usual exchange of talks and gifts, after which, as Ordway reported, ". . . one of the chiefs lost all the goods he Recd from us in the River, Going home, the Skin cannoe [*i.e.,* bullboat] got over Set [and] turned everry thing out of it he Grieved himself considerable about his loss &.C."[15]

---

[11] According to Quaife, Ordway's journal contained approximately one hundred twenty-five thousand words; Gass's, eighty-three thousand; Whitehouse's, sixty-seven thousand; and Floyd's, twelve thousand five hundred. See Quaife's "Some new-found Records," *loc. cit.,* 110. Thwaites estimated the words written by Lewis and Clark at some million and a half (*Original Journals,* I, xlv).

[12] Quaife, *Ordway,* 97.

[13] *Ibid.,* 109–10.

[14] *Ibid.,* 119–23. Whitehouse used only about two hundred and twenty-five words descriptive of the Yankton Sioux, Gass some four hundred, Clark about a thousand, but Ordway near two thousand.

[15] *Ibid.,* 151.

Biddle, it will be recalled, had found Ordway's journal more helpful to him than Gass's. Quaife regarded it as more important than
those of Gass, Floyd, and Whitehouse combined, and, in some respects, superior even to Clark's.[16]

—3—

Particularly frustrating to today's historian of the Expedition is
the scantiness of information available to him about the lives of the
men who accompanied Lewis and Clark. For instance, only four of
them, George Drouillard,[17] John Colter,[18] George Shannon,[19] and
Patrick Gass,[20] have attracted biographers. But these biographers,
unable to find more than a modicum of information about the pre-
and post-Expeditionary years of their subjects, have perforce devoted most of their space to yet another retelling of the Lewis and
Clark transit. Sergeant Ordway, certainly one of the four or five
most valuable members of the party, has yet to find a biographer,
and probably will never find one, such is the poverty of data about
his early and late years.[21]

John Ordway (c.1775–c.1817) was born in New Hampshire, one
of ten children. According to one source, "He came of a good family
and some of his brothers and sisters emigrated to Ohio and Kentucky."[22] Another source says that in 1804 his parents and one son,
Stephen, lived near Hebron, New Hampshire.[23]

Lewis and Clark found Ordway at Kaskaskia, where he was attached to Captain Russell Bissell's First Infantry Company. Proof

[16] Quaife, "Some New-found Records," *loc. cit.*, 112.
[17] M. O. Skarsten, *George Drouillard, Hunter and Interpreter for Lewis and
Clark and Fur Trader.*
[18] Three biographies of Colter have been published: Burton Harris, *John
Colter, His Years in the Rockies*; Stallo Vinton, *John Colter, Discoverer of Yellowstone*; and Ethel Hueston, *The Man of the Storm, a Romance of John Colter Who
Discovered Yellowstone.*
[19] Grace Voris Curl, *Young Shannon, Scout with Lewis and Clark.*
[20] Jacob, *The Life and Times of Patrick Gass.*
[21] For biographical information about Ordway, see (1) William Clark's "Cash
Book" for 1825–28 in Jackson's *Letters*, 638–39; (2) Coues's *History*, I, 254; (3)
Wheeler's *The Trail of Lewis and Clark, 1804–1806*, I, 91–92; (4) Jackson's
Letters, 370 *et passim*; and (5) Charles G. Clarke's *The Men of the Lewis and
Clark Expedition*, 40–41.
[22] Wheeler, *op. cit.*, I, 92.
[23] Clarke, *op. cit.*, 40.

that Ordway was then a sergeant is found in a letter still extant that he wrote in Kaskaskia in September, 1803, to his brother Stephen in Hebron.[24] Two months earlier Henry Dearborn had written Bissell, "You will be pleased to furnish one Sergeant & Eight good Men . . . to go with Capt. Lewis."[25]

The first reference to Ordway I have been able to find in any of the journals is in Clark's "Field Notes." Therein, on December 30, 1803, Clark wrote, "Drewyer & Serjt O[r]dway set out for Kohokia."[26]

In point of command during the crossing of the continent, Ordway was next to Lewis and Clark. According to one writer, "Of all the men who enlisted or volunteered for the expedition he was the best educated."[27] Obviously, the two commanders regarded him as the most valuable and trustworthy of their noncommissioned officers, for, on those rare occasions when both found it necessary to be away from the main party at the same time, they yielded the command to him. One such instance, perhaps the first, occurred in mid-March, 1803, when Clark left Camp Dubois for St. Louis to join Lewis at the ceremonies attending the formal transfer of Louisiana Territory to the United States.[28]

Further testifying to their confidence in Ordway, Lewis and Clark had entrusted him with at least two important missions, both occurring on the return from the Pacific. One, already mentioned, was his command of the party which ran the boats from Three Forks to Great Falls. The other took place earlier (May 27–June 2, 1806), while the party marked time for a month at Camp Chopunnish on the Clearwater River waiting for the snows to melt in the Bitterroots, and was occasioned by a shortage of food when salmon failed to appear as expected. Learning, however, that these fish had started running in the Snake River, Lewis and Clark dispatched Ordway, with Privates Frazer and Wiser, to "precure some salmon on that river."[29]

[24] Jackson, *Letters*, 120–21.
[25] *Ibid.*, 103.
[26] Osgood, *Field Notes*, 9.
[27] Wheeler, *op. cit.*, I, 92.
[28] This was the transfer of the upper part of Louisiana. Transfer of the lower part had occurred earlier, December 20, 1803, in New Orleans.
[29] Thwaites, *Original Journals*, V, 71.

Lewis and Clark, from information supplied by the Nez Percés, understood the distance from the Clearwater to the Snake to be "but half a day's ride."[30] As Ordway quickly determined, the distance was much farther (some seventy-five to eighty miles), necessitating a three-day ride through hazardous terrain. I have consulted Ralph S. Space, formerly superintendent of Clearwater National Forest, as to the character of the country Ordway traversed. According to him, it is "terribly rough and steep. I don't see how he made it. It is much worse than Ordway's diary would lead one to believe."[31] But Ordway did succeed in crossing this badlands country, and he brought back with him several salmon, though, due to the time required to return them (three days), they spoiled in transit—hardly the fault of the sergeant and his two companions. They accomplished their mission and, in so doing, were the first white men to traverse portions of Lewis, Idaho, and Nez Perce counties of Idaho. Thus, the recorded history of this rugged, fractured region of Idaho begins, quite manifestly, with Ordway's account.

We know but little of Ordway's life after the Expedition had returned to St. Louis. Later that same year (1806), he was one of the men who accompanied Lewis and a delegation of Indians to Washington. From there he allegedly went to New England to visit his parents. By 1809 he was back in Missouri, where he married, settled down on a farm,[32] and soon became sufficiently prosperous to make extensive land purchases, including "two plantations under good cultivation [with] peach and apple orchards, good buildings & &."[33] If, as reported, Ordway did die about 1817, he enjoyed his prosperity—and apples and peaches—but briefly.[34]

---

[30] *Ibid.*, 68.

[31] Letter of Space to author dated December 20, 1970. Space subscribes to Ordway's route as laid down by John J. Peebles: "From Camp Chopunnish, it was west up Lawyer's Creek, south along Deer Creek to the Salmon River, west up China Creek, and down Coral Creek to the fishery at Wild Goose Rapids [on Snake River]." See Peebles, "The Return Journey of Lewis and Clark," *Idaho Yesterdays*, Vol. X, No. 2 (Summer, 1966), 21.

[32] Quaife, *Ordway*, 27–28.

[33] *Ibid.*, 28.

[34] Following Ordway's name in Clark's "Cash Book" for 1825–28, we find the one word, "Dead." Jackson, in *Letters*, 370n., is more explicit as to year: "c.1817."

—4—

The Journals of Captain Meriwether Lewis and Sergeant John Ordway appeared in published form in 1916, exactly 106 years after Nicholas Biddle had informed Clark that Ordway's journal was "much better than Gass's."[35]

Like many other editors in a similar capacity, Quaife displayed strengths and weaknesses. As to the former, he had been trained in the rigors of postgraduate study, doctoral dissertation, and classroom presentation, so that he was able to approach his initial editorial effort with the confidence and expertise these disciplines had developed. His *Chicago and the Old Northwest*, published in 1913, proved that he could put words together felicitously and that, as he said in his preface to that work, he could "produce a readable narrative without in any way trenching upon the principles of sound scholarship."[36]

On the debit side, Quaife lacked the practiced editorial hand of a Coues or Thwaites. Also, like Thwaites, he was unable to bring to his task a knowledge of natural history or a personal familiarity with the trail Lewis and Clark had followed, both grievous liabilities to anyone editing accounts of the Expedition.

Knowledge of Quaife's labors experienced during his editing of Ordway's journal is limited, primarily because we have been unable to locate even a single letter that he might have written in that period, and his correspondence may well have been heavy. The little we do know derives mainly from his annotations. For instance, we learn from these that he leaned heavily on such important reference sources as Coues's reissue of Biddle (especially Coues's notes therein), the *Original Journals*, the thirty-two-volume, Thwaites-edited *Early Western Travels*, and the maps of J. N. Nicollet, Perrin du Lac, the United States Geological Survey, and the Missouri River Commission.

Quaife's footnotes approach numerically those of Coues, but lack the latter's flood of words. He bolstered the 323 pages of Ordway's text with close to eight hundred notes, the great majority of them being geographical. Of the first one hundred, seventy-eight relate

[35] *Ibid.*, 551.
[36] *Chicago and the Old Northwest*, v.

to geography, eight to history, five to ethnology, two to natural history, and the remaining seven to other topics. He derived much, but not all, of his geographical data from Coues. For example, following Ordway's statement of July 7, 1804, that "my Capt." named a stream "Ordway Creek," Quaife commented, "Unfortunately for the fame of Ordway Creek, Lewis' journal for the day, if he kept one, is lost, and Clark makes no mention of the stream or its name. The party passed the site of St. Joseph, Mo., this day."[37]

Quaife employed botanical and zoological notes so sparingly as to make this writer wonder why he bothered at all. Perhaps he was wise, as one example indicates. Throughout his commentary he used just four binomials, one being that for the pack rat, which should have been rendered *Neotoma cinerea*. But it wasn't, for the reason that Thwaites, in copying from Coues, had misspelled both words so that they read *Neotama cinera*.[38] Then Quaife, borrowing from Thwaites, altered the words still further to *Montana cinera!*[39]

Though handicapped in areas mentioned, Quaife, on balance, edited Ordway's journal commendably. His introduction and commentary have proved valuable to Lewis and Clark scholars, and his collation deserves unstinted praise. Indeed, he compared Ordway's account with those of Lewis, Clark, Gass, Floyd, and Whitehouse so meticulously that only a minimum of differences and contradictions escaped him.

—5—

Quaife failed to exhibit the excitement we might expect at the discovery of Lewis' "Ohio Journal," and the opportunity afforded him to edit it. In comparing it with Ordway's, he said only that it was "a more unique contribution to the records of the expedition."[40] The statement is remarkably casual, considering the fact that Quaife, after reading the journal, knew all too well that, except for a handful of letters Lewis and Clark had written to each other and to Jef-

[37] Quaife, *Ordway*, 93n. Months later, in western Montana, Lewis and Clark did name a stream Ordway's Creek (Thwaites, *Original Journals*, II, 244, 244n.). Regrettably, it appears on modern maps as Little Prickly Pear Creek.

[38] Thwaites, *Original Journals*, II, 205.

[39] Quaife, *Ordway*, 242n.

[40] *Ibid.*, 27.

ferson, it contained the only information available about Lewis' trip from Pittsburgh to Camp Dubois.

Soon after he had received the "Ohio Journal," Quaife wrote a magazine article in which he gave a brief description of it. He said, in part:

> The document before us is a leather bound volume containing 258 pages 4⅝ by 7¾ inches in size; 37 pages are blank, 93 pages are devoted to notes and observations, and 128 pages to the journal of the river trip. The latter begins at Pittsburgh, August 30 [1803], and concludes at River Dubois with the entry for December 12. Unfortunately, however, entries are lacking for over half of the total period of the voyage. The principal omission is that of Sept. 19 to Nov. 12, a period of fifty-four days. The reason for this hiatus is not apparent; possibly the journal was kept in another book and still awaits discovery by some future, fortunate researcher. . . . Lewis's portion of the narrative covers thirty-six days, and Clark's contribution eleven days. The change in authorship from Lewis to Clark is due to the fact that on November 28, at the mouth of the Kaskaskia River, Lewis turned boat and journal alike over to Clark, and proceeded thence overland to St. Louis. . . . The journal contains, as it has come down to us, about 15,000 words, chiefly the handiwork of Lewis.[41]

Easily overlooked in the above is the clause, a most important one, which reads, "93 pages are devoted to notes and observations." With that allusion to these pages, Quaife seems to have dismissed them from his mind, for he did not again refer to them. He thus missed the enviable opportunity of determining that these "notes and observations" had been written by Nicholas Biddle when Biddle, in 1810, visited Clark in Fincastle, Virginia. As I reported earlier, it was Donald Jackson who made that determination (after he had rediscovered them at the American Philosophical Society), but not until fifty years after Quaife had alluded to them.[42]

The value of Lewis' "Ohio Journal" is evident from the beginning. In his initial entry, Lewis supplied information heretofore un-

---

[41] Quaife, "Some New-found Records," *loc. cit.*, 113–14.

[42] Not all of the Nicholas Biddle notes were written in the leather-bound volume described by Quaife. Biddle jotted down others in a separate, smaller notebook (Jackson, *Letters*, 497 f.).

Meriwether Lewis, water color by Charles de St. Mémin, painted probably in 1807.

William Clark, water color by Charles de St. Mémin, painted probably in 1810.

Thomas Jefferson, painting by Rembrandt Peale, 1800.

Mathew Carey, who published three editions of Sergeant Gass's journal illustrated with fanciful engravings that have since often appeared in Lewis and Clark literature.

From Thomas Payne Govan, *Nicholas Biddle, Nationalist and Public Banker*

Nicholas Biddle, miniature by Henry Inman painted probably about the time Biddle was editing the Lewis and Clark journals.

From *Bird-Lore*, January-February, 1902

Elliott Coues, photographed at the age of twenty-one in his lieutenant's uniform when he was serving as an assistant surgeon in the U.S. Army.

From *Missouri Historical Society Collections*
Reuben G. Thwaites.

Courtesy State Historical Society of Wisconsin
Milo M. Quaife.

Ernest S. Osgood, pointing toward Lewis and Clark Pass, near his summer home on Alice Creek, Montana.

Donald Jackson.

Julia Clark Voorhis, granddaughter of William Clark, who had in her possession many of his maps, letters, and other effects.

Eleanor Glasgow Voorhis, daughter of Julia Clark Voorhis and co-owner with her of the Clark papers brought to public attention by Reuben G. Thwaites.

"The Gate of the Mountains," pencil sketch by A. E. Mathews of the spectacular gorge in western Montana discovered by Lewis and Clark on July 18, 1805.

Missouri Meadow Lark

Male

Western Meadowlark, drawn from nature by John James Audubon and presented in his *The Birds of America*. Lewis, however, had discovered the species at Great Falls in 1805.

Black-billed Magpies, water color by Titian R. Peale, the first sketch of this bird to be made in its natural habitat. The species was discovered by Lewis and Clark.

Buffalo, drawn by Titian R. Peale about 1819 on the High Plains.

From Harold McCracken, *George Catlin and the Old Frontier*

"Sioux Indians Hunting Buffalo," drawing by George Catlin, 1832.

"Pompey's Pillar," painting by J. K. Ralston. This National Historic Landmark near Billings, Montana, was discovered by Clark on July 25, 1806, and named for Sacagawea's infant son, who had been nicknamed Pompey by members of the Expedition.

Pl. 495.

Nuttall's Whip-poor-will

From J. J. Audubon, *The Birds of America*

Nuttall's Poor-will, drawn in 1843 by Audubon, who was the first to describe the species. Lewis had discovered it in South Dakota on October 17, 1804.

From Olin D. Wheeler, *The Trail of Lewis and Clark*

"Captain Lewis, with Drewyer and Shields, meeting the Shoshoni Indians, August 13, 1805," painting by Charles M. Russell. This was the first illustration to be printed in color in Lewis and Clark literature (1904).

"The Great Explorers—Lewis and Clark," drawing by Frederic Remington published in *Collier's Magazine*, May 12, 1906. The artist depicted the explorers at the mouth of the Columbia dressed in Revolutionary War uniforms and equipped with birchbark canoes!

From Isaac I. Stevens' *Reports of Explorations and Surveys from the Mississippi River to the Pacific Ocean*

The Dalles, with Mt. Hood in the background, drawing by John M. Stanley.

"An American having struck a Bear but not killed him, escapes into a Tree," engraving from Mathew Carey's 1810 edition of Sergeant Gass's journal.

The same subject in the 1812 edition. Both man and bear have changed decidedly.

From R. G. Thwaites, *Original Journals of the Lewis and Clark Expedition*
Sage Grouse, sketch by William Clark. This bird was discovered by
Lewis on June 5, 1805, on the Marias River in Montana.

Lewis' Wild Flax. This specimen, from the Lewis and Clark Herbarium in the Academy of Natural Sciences of Philadelphia, was collected by Lewis on July 9, 1806, near Great Falls, Montana.

known: the date of his departure from Pittsburgh, the number of men accompanying him, and the first mention anywhere of his now celebrated air gun. In subsequent entries, we first learn of Lewis' unusual interest in and knowledge of wildlife, his quite remarkable observational ability, and his adherence to Jefferson's insistence on the recording of events and observations. We discover, too, that Lewis, while stopped at Wheeling, came close to signing on a physician;[43] that he had with him a dog, a Newfoundland, for which he had paid twenty dollars; and that, at Fort Massac, he signed on George Drouillard, who later played such an important role as interpreter and hunter.

In editing the "Ohio Journal," Quaife employed a number of the same maps and other reference sources he had found useful when working on Ordway's journal. But, additionally, he consulted such books as Thwaites's *On the Storied Ohio* (1903) and Zadoc Cramer's *Navigator* (1811). The majority of his footnotes—fewer per page than in Ordway—clarified Lewis' occasional vague or obscure references to streams, villages, forts, and individuals. For example, following Lewis' statement of September 7 that he had "passed Charlestown [Virginia]," Quaife explained, "This is modern Wellsburg, West Va. . . . in 1807 it had . . . a courthouse, jail, stocks and pillory."[44] And two months later, after Lewis had written of visiting "Oald Fort Jefferson," Quaife's annotation read, "Fort Jefferson was built by George Rogers Clark in 1780 as a stronghold in his struggle with the British for supremacy in the West. It was abandoned the following year."[45]

Considering the brevity of the "Ohio Journal," it is remarkable that Lewis managed to enliven it with such a variety of natural history observations. If Quaife had been a man of Couesian bent, he would have footnoted all of them. Instead, he offered no commentary whatever.

Lewis began his natural history observations just below Pittsburgh, near the mouth of the Beaver River. The date was September 2, and already, ". . . the leaves of the *buckeye*, Gum, and Sausa-

---

[43] Dr. William Ewing Patterson, son of Robert Patterson. On his 1803 visit to Philadelphia, Lewis consulted the latter about use of navigational instruments.

[44] Quaife, *Ordway*, 37n.

[45] *Ibid.*, 50n.

fras begin to fade, or become red."[46] If Coues had been editing the journal, he would surely have supplied the scientific names of the trees mentioned here, namely, *Aesculus glabra* for buckeye, *Sassafras sassafras* for "Sausafras," and *Nyssa sylvatica* for gum (undoubtedly black gum); and he might well have made the point that this was the very first recorded natural history observation by Lewis, the first of literally hundreds to appear in ensuing reports.

A few days later (September 11), above Marietta, Ohio, Lewis' entry included the description of an event which may have been unique in his experience:

> . . . observed a number of squirrels swiming the Ohio and universally passing from the W. to the East shore they appear to be making to the south; perhaps it may be mast or food which they are in search of but I should reather suppose that it is climate which is their object as I find no difference in the quantity of mast on both sides of this river it being abundant on both except the beach nut which appears extremely scarce this season, the walnuts and Hickery nuts the usual food of the Squirrell appears in great abundance on either side of the river—I made my dog take as many each day as I had occation for, they wer[e] fat and I thought them when fryed a pleasant food—many of these squirrels were black, they swim very light on the water and make pretty good speed—my dog was of the newfoundland breed very active strong and docile, he would take the squirel in the water kill them and swiming bring them in his mouth to the boat.[47]

Lewis here described an occurrence the like of which few persons, now or in the foreseeable future, will see duplicated, namely, a mass migration of gray squirrels (*Sciurus carolinensis*). Since about 1860 these mass movements have been rare and minor in extent. In Lewis' day gray squirrels were present in vast numbers, and their migrations were commonly witnessed by the early settlers; but that was before riflemen, in increasing numbers, rapidly reduced the gray squirrel population.

Earlier we remarked that the "Ohio Journal" provides examples of Lewis' observational ability. In the above-quoted entry the reader, if attentive, will have noted his statements about the squirrels

[46] *Ibid.*, 34.
[47] *Ibid.*, 42–43.

"universally passing from the W. to the east shore," that they swam "very light on the water," and that many of them were black (instead of gray).[48] He mentioned, too, that, while on both sides of the Ohio beechnuts were in short supply, walnuts and hickory nuts abounded. John Burroughs once remarked that everyone sees the big things, but that the true observer is known by his skill in seeing the little things.[49] Lewis, as his observations here on squirrels and the nuts of forest trees attest, well fulfilled this ideal. The likelihood is remote that any of his several companions on the descent of the Ohio shared his talent in seeing such "little things."

Two days after witnessing the squirrel migration, Lewis and his party arrived at Marietta. While here he wrote, ". . . observed many pigeons passing over us pursuing a south East course."[50] These birds were, of course, the now extinct passenger pigeons (*Ectopistes migratorius*). However disinterested Quaife personally may have been in birds, as an editor he might have demonstrated some interest in this particular species, which in the time of Lewis and Clark and for many years afterward periodically filled eastern and middle western skies with flocks of such magnitude and density as to obliterate the sun. Quaife may not have known that the last passenger pigeon on earth had died on September 1, 1914, at 9:30 A.M., in the Cincinnati Zoo, for at that time he was just beginning to edit the "Ohio Journal." But, with scant effort, he could have found passages in the works of such early ornithologists as Wilson and Audubon to provide a footnote documenting the former unparalleled abundance of the passenger pigeon.

At the mouth of the Ohio, on November 16, Lewis exhibited unusual interest in a catfish caught by one of the party. On weighing it, he found that it tipped the scales at 128 pounds and, with tape line, determined its length to be four feet three and one-half inches long. Having obtained these figures, he wrote, "I have been in-

[48] It is not unusual to find melanistic (black) individuals in parts of the gray squirrel's range. Since writing the above about migrating squirrels, I have learned of a minor migration that occurred in 1968 in parts of the East. See Tom Mayer, "The Case of Migrating Squirrels," *Wonderful West Virginia*, Vol. XXXVII, No. 5 (July, 1973), 6.

[49] John Burroughs, *Camping and Tramping with Roosevelt* (Boston, Houghton Mifflin Co., 1906), 102–103.

[50] Quaife, *Ordway*, 43.

formed that these fish have been taken in various parts of the Ohio & Mississippi weighing 175 to 200 lbs. which from the evidence of the subject above mentioned I have no doubt is authentic."[51] The catfish measured by Lewis was the great blue cat (*Ictalurus furcatus*), which, according to one authority, "abounds throughout the large rivers of the Southern States and reaches a weight of 150 pounds or more."[52] In months ahead, we may interpolate, Lewis would measure and weigh countless other animals.

On this same day, at the confluence of the Ohio with the Mississippi, Lewis wrote additionally, ". . . saw a heath hen or grous which flew of[f] and having no gun with me did not persue it."[53] A few days later he reported seeing more "Heth hen or grows" and that "one of my men went on shore and killed one of them, of which we made some soup for my friend Capt. Clark who has been indisposed since the 16th inst."[54] In those days this bird (*Tympanuchus cupido*) ranged from southern Saskatchewan and Manitoba to Texas and Louisiana, and east of the Alleghenies from Massachusetts to Maryland and Virginia. In the East it was called the heath hen—hence Lewis' use of that name—and farther west the almost identical bird became known as the greater prairie chicken. In time ornithologists created the subspecies *Tympanuchus cupido cupido* and *T. c. pinnatus*, even though the former was only a slight variant of the latter.

Lewis' comment on this species interests us. It proves his familiarity with the heath hen, and suggests that he had hunted it in his boyhood days in Virginia—otherwise, here at the mouth of the Ohio, he could not have identified the quite similar subspecies. Of course, as all ornithologists know, the heath hen is today extinct, having joined that spectral company which now includes the great auk, Carolina parakeet, and the passenger pigeon. According to the American Ornithologists' Union *Check-List of North American Birds*, the heath hen, after 1835, was "confined to the island of Martha's Vineyard, where last seen March 11, 1932."[55]

[51] *Ibid.*, 49.
[52] David Starr Jordan, *A Guide to the Study of Fishes*, 2 vols. (New York, Henry Holt & Co., 1905), II, 180.
[53] Quaife, *Ordway*, 49.
[54] *Ibid.*, 54.
[55] The American Ornithologists' Union, *Check-List of North American Birds* (5th ed., 1957), 136.

Before leaving the mouth of the Ohio, Lewis made two botanical observations, one about mistletoe (*Phoradendron flavescens*) and the other about a species of scouring rush, or horsetail (probably *Equisetum robustum*). Of the former he wrote, ". . . observed a large quantity of Misseltoe on the trees bordering on the river. . . . I first observed this plant about the mouth of the Muskingum river [Marietta, Ohio]."[56] Contrary to popular belief, mistletoe is not limited in its range to states of the Deep South. Indeed, it may be found as far north as New Jersey and, as Lewis indicated, Ohio, Illinois, and Missouri.

Of the latter plant Lewis said, ". . . the banks [of the river] appear every where to abound with the *sand* or *scrubing Rush*. it grows much thicker, and arrises to a much greater hight in the bottoms of this river than I observed it elsewhere. I measured a stalk of it which was 8 feet 2 inches in length & 3⅛ inches in circumference."[57] This was one of several rushlike perennial plants which constitute the horsetail family (*Equisetaceae*) and, most likely because of its size, the species known in the vernacular as the stout scouring rush. Lewis quickly recognized it as a "scrubing Rush" because of its similarity to eastern species, the stems of which, containing quantities of silica, were then much used—perhaps by members of his own family—for scouring and polishing wood and metal.

It is regrettable that not one of the above-cited examples of Lewis' minute attention to plants and animals merited a footnote by Quaife. He thereby let pass the opportunity to emphasize the fact that Lewis, in his "Ohio Journal," proved himself to be knowledgeable both botanically and zoologically and, therefore, worthy of Jefferson's trust in him as a competent naturalist.[58]

[56] Quaife, *Ordway*, 53.

[57] *Ibid.*, 55–56.

[58] Both Ordway's journal and Lewis' "Ohio Journal" have found a home in the library of the American Philosophical Society. Accession records of the society state that Charles Biddle, on November 21, 1913, deposited with the society the manuscript of Ordway's journal carrying entries from May 14, 1804, to September 13, 1805. This, of course, was the abbreviated portion first received by Quaife. The same accession record closes with the sentence: "The same to be kept on deposit by the American Philosophical Society, and subject to recall at any time by Mr. Biddle." After the discovery of the remainder of Ordway's journal, it, too, according to further records (September 2, 1915), was deposited, by Charles and Edward Biddle, at the society. A still later record informs, "Ordway's Journal was pre-

—6—

Quaife filled his remaining years with a variety of activities. He left the State Historical Society of Wisconsin in 1922 and, soon afterward, was elected secretary and editor of the Burton Historical Collection, Detroit Public Library, positions he held until 1947. Concurrently, he applied himself to such other jobs as managing editor of the *Mississippi Valley Historical Review* (1924–30); graduate lecturer, Wayne University (1931–42); advisory editor, *Dictionary of American History* (1937–39); president, Anthony Wayne Historical Association (1941–47); and editor, American Lake Series of the Lakeside Press (1941–47). Also, Quaife found time to write such books as *The Development of Chicago* (1916) and *Wisconsin: Its History and Its People* (1924), and to edit still others, among them a reissue of Josiah Gregg's *Commerce of the Prairies* (1926).[59]

Shortly before Quaife died, a Detroit newspaper paid tribute to him:

> It was a lucky day for Detroit when Dr. Milo Milton Quaife first came to town about 30 years ago. He ranks, in all probability, as Detroit's No. 1 author; he's a nationally known historian, and he undoubtedly knows more about this city's past than any other person.
>
> Tonight is the occasion for acknowledgment of the achievements of this energetic, erudite—and sometimes crusty gentleman of 73, who has earned himself such distinction as a writer, editor, scholar and educator.
>
> It would be hard to find a living American who has been as prolific and prodigious a writer as Quaife. He has been the author or editor of a list of histories and biographies that, by his estimate, contains more than 100 titles.[60]

---

sented to the A.P.S. by Charles Biddle in 1949." See *Guide to the Archives and Manuscript Collections of the American Philosophical Society*, compiled by Whitfield J. Bell, Jr., and Murphy D. Smith (Philadelphia, 1966).

[59] Published Chicago, 1916; Chicago, 1924; and Chicago, 1926, respectively.

[60] "Honoring an Historian, Dr. Quaife: A City's Lucky Break," by Frank B. Woodford, *Detroit Free Press*, April 5, 1954. On that date Quaife delivered the annual "Lewis Cass Lecture" to the Detroit Historical Society.

CHAPTER IX

Ernest Staples Osgood

On a day early in January, 1953, the curator of manuscripts of the Minnesota Historical Society, Lucile M. Kane, received a telephone call from a woman who gave her name as Mrs. Vaclav Vytlacil. Mrs. Vytlacil said that she was in the process of closing down the house of her mother, Mrs. Sophia Hammond Foster, who had recently died. The house, she went on to say, was situated at 117 Farrington Avenue, St. Paul, and had originally belonged to her maternal grandfather, General John Henry Hammond, who had died in 1890. The general's military career had included active participation in battles of the Civil War while on the staff of General Sherman. Following the war, General Hammond had been employed for a brief period by the Indian Bureau as an inspector of agencies in the West.

Mrs. Vytlacil further said that, in going through her mother's effects, she had come upon an old roll-top desk in the attic which recalled an offhand remark by her mother that this desk contained papers of General Hammond that might be of some historical value. Having verified the fact that the desk did indeed contain such papers, she was calling the Historical Society to inquire if they might be interested in having a look at them. This seemingly unexciting telephone conversation proved to be the preamble to a remarkable discovery.

Two days later Miss Kane went to the Farrington Avenue home

and followed Mrs. Vytlacil to the attic. Once there, she later reported, her work "consisted of unpacking the large desk of General Hammond and . . . the desk top [which was] on the floor." The desk itself contained many letters, letter-press books, ledgers, memoranda, and notebooks "packed compactly but unevenly in drawers and pigeonholes." The desk top also contained papers, but they were packed loosely, with the result that she noted immediately a "compact bundle" among them.[1] After completing her inspection, Miss Kane expressed interest in the "bundle" and other papers and asked if she might take them with her for further, closer study. When Mrs. Vytlacil assented, she put the collection in a box and left for the society. The date was January 7, 1953.

Once in her office, Miss Kane unpacked the box and, over a period of days, carefully examined its content piece by piece. When she picked up the "compact bundle," her interest quickened perceptibly, for, as she noted, it had been wrapped tightly in an 1805 copy of the long since defunct Washington newspaper, the *National Intelligencer*. As recently described to this writer, the bundle was flat, about twenty inches long, six wide, and four thick.[2] Removing its wrapping, Miss Kane found several loose sheets of paper covered with handwriting, some of it almost beyond deciphering. To each of these she instantly gave studious attention, which was intensified when she found one sheet bearing an address which read, "General Jonathan Clark, near Louisville, Kentucky," another with the words "Gen. William Clark near Cahokia," and still others with references to Captain Lewis and with listings of names of men whom she recognized as those of the Lewis and Clark party.

When Miss Kane's discovery became generally known, it created profound excitement and widespread publicity. She had brought to life a heretofore unknown diary by William Clark, now customarily known as the "Field Notes," which contained practically every shred of information existing today about the stay of Lewis and Clark at the mouth of the Wood River, Illinois, during the winter of 1803–04. And the excitement and publicity mounted with the unfolding of events which immediately preceded and attended the celebrated

---

[1] *Record in the U.S. Court of Appeals for the Eighth Circuit, No. 15,744, Civil,* 58.
    [2] Ernest S. Osgood to author in interview, May 26, 1970.

court case held to determine rightful ownership of the "Field Notes."

Believing that she had found valuable Lewis and Clark papers, Miss Kane turned at once to the one man of her acquaintance whom she regarded as best qualified to affirm or refute her belief. That man was her former mentor in history at the University of Minnesota, Dr. Ernest S. Osgood. Later Dr. Osgood wrote, "I remember her excitement when she called me . . . she knew that this was Lewis and Clark stuff. . . . All I did was to verify what she knew she had."[3]

Miss Kane has since written that her role in this matter was only "a routine professional one,"[4] but the fact remains that she had made a discovery that forever links her name with Lewis and Clark history. Subsequently, Dr. Osgood gave added significance to the discovery by likening the "Field Notes" to "an ingot of gold in a bale of hay."[5]

Almost immediately following Miss Kane's telephone call, Osgood arrived at the Historical Society, never dreaming that he was taking the first step in an undertaking that would engage much of his attention for the next eleven years, until 1964, when *The Field Notes of Captain William Clark, 1803–1805* came from the press.

—2—

Ernest Staples Osgood (1888–   ), like Coues and Thwaites, is a New Englander by birth. He began life in a then small industrial town, Lynn, Massachusetts, on the Atlantic coast about ten miles northeast of Boston. After attending Lynn Classical High School, young Osgood entered Dartmouth College and, four years later (1912), graduated with an A.B. degree in history.

Parenthetically, I first met Dr. Osgood in 1960 in Wooster, Ohio, where he lived then (and still does). Five years later I had the pleasure of visiting with him once more, at his summer retreat on Alice Creek in western Montana close by Lewis and Clark Pass, and quite recently I met with him again near Winterthur Museum, Delaware, where he was pursuing a historical theme. The first two

[3] Letter from Osgood to author, September 16, 1970.
[4] Letter from Lucile Kane to author, September 22, 1970.
[5] Letter from Osgood to author, September 16, 1970.

147

meetings had been brief, but the third consumed more time, since Osgood had agreed in advance to let me fire questions at him about his long and notable career, and especially about his contributions to the editing and publication of Clark's "Field Notes." While he told me that he was eighty-two, still every word and act belied his age.

One of the first questions I put to Dr. Osgood was whether, by chance, association with any member of his family had encouraged him to study history. To this he replied unhesitatingly in the affirmative. The eminent historian, Herbert Levi Osgood, author of several volumes on the American colonies in the seventeenth and eighteenth centuries, was his uncle and, throughout his life, a continuing inspiration.

After graduating from Dartmouth, Osgood taught for two years in an Ohio private school. Many years later, writing of his experiences in this school, he said, "At the end of the first year there, I got married, and by the end of the second, I got fired. There is always a New Englander about who feels himself fully qualified to start reforming any educational institution he happens to run into."[6]

Not at all disheartened by his dismissal, Osgood and his wife went to Chicago, where he entered the university. He had already made up his mind that he would work in medieval history. However, unexpected ill health put an end to this plan and, some months later, having regained his health, he went to Helena, Montana, a far distance from New England's rock-bound coast. Here he stayed ten years (1914–24), teaching history in the high school of that city. This period of residence in the West, in the eastern foothills of the Rockies close by the Continental Divide, gave new and beneficial direction to his life, just as Coues's years in sage brush and bison country had shaped favorably, and measurably, his future career. For one thing, Osgood gave less and less thought to medieval history and more and more to annals of the western frontier. This newly acquired interest unavoidably included Lewis and Clark, though he gave only passing attention to that field of study until he picked up the packet of Clark's "Field Notes" some thirty years later in the Minnesota Historical Society.

In 1924, yielding to the insistence of friends who knew the quality

[6] Ernest S. Osgood, "I Discover Western History," *Western Historical Quarterly*, Vol. III, No. 3 (July, 1972), 245.

of his mind, and to his own personal desire, Osgood left Helena for the campus of the University of Wisconsin. There, three years later, he received his doctorate in history, his advisor having been Frederick Logan Paxson. He had arrived at Wisconsin, he afterward said, "with a love of the past, and all that Montana had given me."[7] It is not surprising, therefore, that he chose as his subject for his doctoral dissertation the history of the western cattle industry. This thesis was published in 1929 under the title, *The Day of the Cattleman*. Historically sound and well documented, it is today regarded as a classic in its field, and first editions are much sought after by collectors of Western Americana.

After Osgood completed his graduate studies at Wisconsin, he accepted an instructorship in history at the University of Minnesota. During a tenure of thirty years at Minnesota, he was advanced from the rank of instructor to that of full professor. Since his retirement from that institution, he has been associated with The College of Wooster, Ohio, as a lecturer in history. But each summer he returns to the West, a lodestone exerting its annual, irresistible pull. Among his final words to me on my last meeting with him were those stating that he and Mrs. Osgood would soon leave again for the beauty and solitude of Alice Creek. I could but envy him, for just five years earlier, in company with my late brother, I had ascended Alice Creek, a tranquil, white-water, beaver-populated stream, and then climbed to the summit of Lewis and Clark Pass, from which vantage point I had seen for myself this region of satisfying stillness where lovely stands of evergreen forest alternate with beautiful open meadowlands. It was an additional pleasure, too, to reflect that on July 7, 1806, Meriwether Lewis, on his way from Traveller's Rest to Great Falls, had passed that way through what must have been even greater unspoiled beauty along that same way in his day.

—3—

With the foregoing as background, we may now revert to that day in January, 1953, when Osgood first set eyes on the parcel wrapped in the ancient, much-faded copy of the *National Intelligencer*. Osgood afterward described his initial impressions of it in these words:

[7] *Ibid.*, 248.

So tightly was the packet folded that it did not seem possible that it had been opened for years. When I examined its content, there was no question that here was a rough journal by William Clark, the handwriting was unmistakable. Further examination revealed that this journal fell naturally into two parts. The first is Clark's day-to-day account from December 13, 1803 to May 14, 1804, recording the events at Camp Dubois, the winter quarters established by the party opposite the mouth of the Missouri River. . . . The second part, beginning on May 14, 1804, is partly in the form of rough field notes in which Clark recorded the sixteen-hundred-mile trip upriver to the Mandan villages, which the party reached in November. From then on, there are only scattered entries in the journal for the winter of 1804–1805. The journal ends on April 3, 1805, four days before the party resumed the voyage up the Missouri on the way to the Pacific.[8]

During this first examination of the packet, Osgood also ascertained that the number of loose sheets comprising it totaled sixty-seven, and that they were of almost as many different sizes and shapes. The smallest was 3½ by 6⅛ inches, slightly larger than a postal card, and the largest, 13 by 40¾ inches. As Osgood later observed, "At Camp Dubois on December 13, Clark appears to have picked up the first sheet of paper that came to hand, a map that he had made of the junction of the Ohio with the Mississippi, and to have written down on the reverse side his first entry of the Dubois Journal."[9]

To distinguish between the two parts mentioned above, Osgood called the first the "Dubois Journal," and the second the "River Journal." Also, that no confusion might develop between these two and the original manuscript journals that had been edited by Thwaites, he designated the latter the "Notebook Journal."

By now, this early in his examination, Osgood recognized the following primary facts as being incontestable: (1) the material was genuine Lewis and Clark history; (2) the "Dubois Journal" filled a gap in that history about which practically nothing had previously been known; (3) it was, consequently, history of the utmost importance and, as such, should be transcribed and otherwise prepared for publication.

[8] Osgood, *Field Notes*, xiv–xv.
[9] *Ibid.*, xv.

One needs no instant replay to understand something of the excitement stirring in Osgood's mind, particularly when no obstacles arose to prevent his assuming the roles of transcriber and editor. At that moment it was his understanding that Mrs. Vytlacil had presented the "Field Notes" to the society with no strings attached, even though the arrangement had been verbal—and that was the understanding of the society.

During the next few months, with enthusiastic help from Lucile Kane and Robert M. Brown, state archivist, both former students, Osgood succeeded in completing the formidable tasks of arranging the sheets in chronological order and transcribing them. He then began collating and editing.

Only Osgood and his assistants can fully appreciate the difficulties inherent in the transcription of the notes. They discovered at once that Clark used more than one pen.[10] When he employed a blunt-pointed one, he tended to form large, easy-to-read words, but when he picked up a sharp-pointed one he fashioned words of smaller lettering. Some of the latter were exceedingly tiny, particularly when he found himself running out of space, as at the bottom of a page, or when he interlineated, as he did frequently. Obviously, Osgood's transcriptional problems increased as the size of the letters diminished. In general, the "Dubois Journal" was more of a test of his deciphering capabilities than the "River Journal."

Clark muddied the waters of transcription in other ways. He often superimposed his entries on other writings, such as on the name and address of a stampless cover.[11] On the verso of Document 33, for example, he partially obliterated the words, "Captain William Clark, Cahokia or somewhere on the Missouri." In like manner, he obscured to a degree several rough sketches of river courses, such as that of the Big Bend of the Missouri on Document 56. He was care-

[10] Osgood thinks these were quill pens, and he is probably right, since Lewis, while in Philadelphia in 1803, purchased "100 Quils." See Thwaites, *Original Journals*, VII, 240. However, on the same trip, he bought "4 Metal Pens" (*Ibid.*, 232).

[11] Stampless because the United States did not issue postage stamps until 1847. Before that date the sender of a letter would customarily write his message on one side of a sheet of paper, then fold it to form an "envelope," on the outside of which he would write the address. Customarily, too, it was sealed with wax. Paper being a scarce commodity, Clark wrote entries on the address side of a number of letters.

less in his handling of ink, with the result that certain sheets are badly blotched. On Document 1 the smear is so extensive that we can explain it only by presuming that he had inadvertently toppled his inkwell and then, possibly, had tried to remedy the situation by wiping off the overflow with his shirt sleeve. On this and other documents, because of Clark's carelessness, there are a large number of inky fingerprints. One of the most remarkable statements Osgood made to me was that he could, if called on, furnish the FBI with a complete set of Clark's fingerprints.[12] At times Clark may have written his notes on torn pieces of paper, though it seems more likely that the tears had been made at some later date, since certain words are missing. Clark, too, drew outlines of squares, rectangles, hexagons, and circles, also miniatures of plants, animals, and persons, though these did not interfere with transcription. Here and there, too, were graffitilike markings which defy identification or meaning. Clark may have been one of this country's earlier doodlers.

In short, Osgood's task of transcription tested his powers to the limit. Previous experiences of Coues, Thwaites, and Quaife in deciphering other Lewis and Clark documents paled by comparison.

More weeks went by, in which time Osgood continued collating and editing. Then a series of unexpected events brought this phase of his endeavor to an abrupt halt.

—4—

On March 19, some ten weeks after the discovery of the Hammond papers, the St. Paul *Dispatch* carried a front-page, illustrated story announcing that the Minnesota Historical Society had acquired "a priceless collection of papers . . . recovered from a St. Paul attic," and that among them were "long-missing papers covering the first 1,600 miles of the famed Lewis and Clark expedition." The story further asserted that this find represented "the greatest discovery of its kind in decades."

This release immediately spawned a major dispute, with the Hammond heirs vehemently denying that Clark's "Field Notes" had been given outright to the Historical Society, and the society vigorously maintaining that they had been. Thus, it soon became evi-

---

[12] Letter from Osgood to author, September 13, 1970.

dent that, with rightful ownership in question, the matter would probably find resolution only in the courts. Another fact now emerged. Prior to her death, Mrs. Sophia Hammond, widow of General Hammond, had designated the First Trust Company of St. Paul as executor of her estate and, by the time the story of Clark's "Field Notes" broke in the *Dispatch*, an attorney for the trust company, David W. Raudenbush, had already made a formal list of household and other effects preparatory to final disposition of the property. The list did not include, however, Clark's "Field Notes." Learning now, through press releases, that these had a value estimated as high as twenty thousand dollars, Raudenbush promptly wrote the Historical Society "to regard itself merely as custodian of the "Notes" until the question of their ownership was resolved."[13]

As a first step in clearing title, Raudenbush in late September initiated an action in the State District Court of Ramsey County, Minnesota, by listing such claimants as: (1) the living sisters of General Hammond;[14] (2) John Doe and Mary Doe, representing any surviving descendents of William Clark whose true names were unknown to the plaintiff; (3) the Minnesota Historical Society; and (4) the United States of America. The inclusion of the last-named claimant surprised some people, but Raudenbush had knowledge that Jefferson had instructed Lewis to make notes on a wide variety of topics and, on the return of the Expedition, to submit them to the government. He did not expect the United States to intervene, however; in fact he thought that the suit would be solely between the Hammond heirs and the society, and that the matter could be settled simply and expeditiously.

It did not turn out that way, and no one was more surprised than Raudenbush when the government of the United States stepped in to claim permanent title to the documents written by Clark. When this happened, a change of venue proved necessary, and the case was moved from the Ramsey County Court House to the Federal Court in Minneapolis, Hennepin County.

The entrance of the federal government into the case was a significant development on at least three counts. One, it had never pre-

[13] Tomkins, "The Lewis and Clark Case," *The New Yorker*, October 29, 1966, 108.

[14] Margaret Van, S. H. Starr, and Harriet K. Hammond.

viously put in a claim for any of the multitudinous documents emanating from the Lewis and Clark Expedition or, for that matter, for papers from any other government-sponsored expedition. Two, the case was patently clear-cut, that of government versus private ownership. And three, if the government won, then the minor issue between the Historical Society and the Hammond heirs was dead. Initial reactions were near unanimous. What possible chance of winning a court victory did a private party have when pitted against the power and prestige of the United States?

If it had not been for a strong-willed grandson of General Hammond, Louis Starr, partner in a New York financial firm, no one, in all probability, would have contested the government claim. But Louis Starr possessed "a profound sense of family pride and an equally profound belief in the property rights of individual citizens."[15] As evidence, at an earlier date, when the issue had been one solely between his family and the Historical Society, he had gone to St. Paul to hire a lawyer. Then, on being apprised of the federal move, he rushed to St. Paul again. On this visit he met only pessimism. Every law firm he consulted advised that, in a confrontation with the United States, he would be just another Christian in the arena of the lions. Returned to New York, subdued but undaunted, Starr declared, "I just felt that neither the government nor the Historical Society had a right to come in and take away my grandfather's papers."[16]

After considerable deliberation and soul-searching, Starr approached a friend, Donald F. Hyde, partner in a New York law firm. To him he explained the background of the case and asked that he represent the Hammonds in the up-coming trial. At first Hyde refused, but with Starr continuing to press, he later agreed. Actually he had been sympathetic toward Starr's position from the first, for he possessed an intense interest in books and book collecting and held positions on the boards of such institutions as the Morgan Library and New York Public Library. With that as background, he intuitively felt that the government's claim to Clark's "Field Notes" posed a threat to many privately owned historical documents.

Hyde's first move as an attorney for the Hammond heirs was to send an associate to Washington to determine the attitude of the government, specifically, how serious their lawyers were about prosecuting their claim. The associate talked with various men in the Justice Department, including J. Lee Rankin, then assistant attorney general, and he returned to New York with no doubt in his mind; the government was far more determined than Hyde had hoped or suspected.

This intelligence only increased Hyde's earlier premonition of danger to public papers presently in the hands of historical societies, libraries, and private citizens if the government should succeed in winning the pending trial. As a consequence, he and his partner prepared a thoughtfully worded statement outlining the threat as they interpreted it. It read in part:

> We are of the opinion that the pending case is not an isolated one but is an initial move in a plan to assemble in the National Archives all original data and documents which the National Archives Establishment may deem of value and interest and which were compiled or prepared by federal officials of all ranks while in the employ of the United States of America. . . . The implications and ramifications of this lawsuit are so widespread that we feel that a committee should be organized forthwith to resist the claim of the United States.[17]

Hyde sent copies of this statement to leading university libraries, historical societies, and bibliophiles. Those who replied agreed in principle, but only a limited number indicated a willingness to join Starr and Hyde in their declared fight against the federal action. It was the same old story: a near universal conviction that chances of winning held out little or no promise of success.

Prospects soon brightened somewhat, however, primarily as a result of support proffered by the powerful Manuscript Society, an international organization of manuscript collectors, who formed, at Hyde's instigation, a Manuscript Emergency Committee. As a direct consequence, directors of such prominent libraries as those of Harvard, Yale, Princeton, New York Public, New York Historical Association, Morgan, and American Philosophical Society extended moral support. The last-mentioned, as a repository of most of the

[17] *Ibid.*, 120, 122.

original Lewis and Clark journals, entertained considerable anxiety, as did Yale, with its large collection of Western Americana including the majority of the maps drawn by Clark.

Yale, indeed, promptly went beyond moral support. It charged its curator of manuscripts, Robert Metzdorf, to aid the Emergency Committee in getting its program off the ground and fully launched. Thereafter, the committee functioned so well in circulating the "news" that, as Metzdorf said later, "I think the government was just flabbergasted to find that there was so much opposition—they'd really expected to win the case by default."[18]

The allegation leveled by Hyde at the National Archives, that they planned to remove federally prepared documents from libraries, greatly distressed the staff of that institution. As one of them explained:

> We acted in what we believe to be the best interests of scholarship and according to the soundest principles of the archival profession. Our sole interest is in the proper preservation and general availability of Federal records specifically and of public records generally. We do not believe that the National Archives is the only institution competent to administer properly material of national historical interest. . . . The Clark documents lay unidentified in General Hammond's desk in an attic in St. Paul for no one knows how many years, exposed to almost every hazard known to archivists. No one interested in the proper care and preservation of historical material could feel happy about such a situation.[19]

In short, the national archivists thought Hyde was like a child beating the stick it had tripped on.

With hackles raised, the government accelerated its preparations. For example, Dr. Robert H. Bahmer, chief archivist of the United States, devoted full time during the next six months to research alone, "a frightful job," he admitted later, "of going through endless files, never being sure that what we were looking for would ever turn up."[20] Hyde and his associates sweated similarly, as they

---

[18] *Ibid.*, 123.

[19] Robert K. Bahmer, "The Case of the Clark Papers," *American Archivist*, Vol. XIX, No. 1 (January, 1956), 21.

[20] Tomkins, *op. cit.*, 126. Dr. Bahmer, incidentally, had been one of Osgood's students at Minnesota, and the first to obtain a Ph.D. under his direction. Other

meticulously studied copies of the "Field Notes" and became deeply mired in American history. On his own, at Yale, Metzdorf initially experienced similar discomfitures, but eventually, from a mass of clues, formulated a positive theory—about which more later.

—5—

At long last, on December 13, 1955 (almost three years after Clark's "Field Notes" had been discovered), the case came to trial, with Judge Gunnar H. Nordbye presiding. Since the period of gestation had been so prolonged, most persons expressed surprise when the trial ended after just four days of testimony. To many spectators, especially those of academic background, it resembled nothing so much as an unusually lively graduate seminar in history.

Dr. Osgood served as a major witness for the Minnesota Historical Society.[21] Because of his familiarity with the "Field Notes," his testimony, as reported by newsmen, sounded almost as though he had himself been a member of the Lewis and Clark party. He described how Clark, because of a scarcity of paper, saved every scrap and used each one in jotting down his day-to-day chronicle. It was his opinion that Clark had written much of the "River Journal" while on the deck of the keelboat as the Expedition moved upstream, and that he had employed a quill pen (as we know Sergeant Ordway had done). At one point in his testimony, evidencing his close, prolonged scrutiny of the "Field Notes," he asserted, "I think I can identify when he stopped to sharpen his quill pen."[22]

Osgood testified, too, that he had compared the handwriting of the "Field Notes" with Clark's handwriting as found in the original journals housed in the American Philosophical Society, and with other facsimiles in Madison, Wisconsin. As a result, he said, "there was no doubt in my mind, after my first examination, not only was the internal evidence so very strong it was Clark's, but also the writing was clearly Clark's."[23]

former students of Osgood participating in the trial were Lucile Kane, already mentioned, and Clifford James, one of the government attorneys.

[21] About one-seventh of the 356-page published record of the trial is devoted to Osgood's testimony.

[22] *Record, U.S. Court of Appeals,* 77.

[23] *Ibid.,* 78.

From the beginning, the government based its claim to the "Field Notes" on Jefferson's instructions to Lewis. Their witnesses repeatedly came back to the president's insistence that the Corps of Discovery keep several diaries and that these, with mission accomplished, should be placed in the hands of federal officials. Under cross-examination, one government witness admitted that much of the scientific data, as published by Thwaites, had been duplicated; but Clark's "Field Notes" made during the winter of 1803–04 were the only ones extant for that period and, therefore, represented a "missing link" in the otherwise continuous journal that had its inception in Pittsburgh in late August, 1803, and its termination in St. Louis three years later.[24]

One of Hyde's associates, Dermot Stanley, served as trial lawyer for the plaintiff. At once he drew from Osgood his opinion that Jefferson's instructions did not extend to the stay of the party at Camp Dubois, but only to the trans-Mississippi journey which began the following spring. Stanley placed great emphasis, too, on the point that Clark's "Field Notes" were strictly his own personal property—unofficial observations to which the government could lay no valid claim. In support of this contention, he had read into the record that portion of Lewis' letter to Jefferson of April 7, 1805, from Fort Mandan, which said, "You will also receive herewith inclosed a part of Capt. Clark's *private journal*, the other part you will find in a separate tin box. this journal (is *in it's original state*, and of course incorrect, but it) will serve to give the daily detales of our progress, and transactions."[25]

This letter provided ammunition for both sides. The inclusion of the words "private journal" and "in it's original state" supported the argument made by Stanley for the Hammonds; but the government retaliated by insisting that Lewis' reference to "daily detales" was precisely the kind of information Jefferson had instructed Lewis and Clark to obtain. Stanley then countered with the assertion that Lewis, when specifying "daily detales," did not have in mind Clark's "Field Notes" at all, but his clean copy covering the period from May 14, 1804, through April 3, 1805, namely the "Notebook Jour-

[24] Not quite continuous, because of the fifty-four-day hiatus in Lewis' "Ohio Journal."

[25] Thwaites, *Original Journals*, VII, 318. Author's italics.

nal." Stanley attempted to establish as fact, too, that the journals of Gass, Ordway, and Whitehouse were private property, since they had either retained or sold them.

Dr. Bahmer, as a witness for the government, then took the stand and related in detail the history to date of the publication of the Lewis and Clark literature. According to one listener, his recital "became one of the fascinating sidelights of the trial."[26] One phase he stressed in particular was Jefferson's letter to José Corrèa da Serra of April 26, 1816, ending with this sentence: "As to any claims of individuals to these papers, it is to be observed that, as being the property of the public, we are certain neither Lewis nor Clarke would undertake to convey away the right to them, and that they could not convey them, had they been capable of intending it."[27]

This seemed an unusually strong point for the government, but it lost weight when Stanley reminded the court that both Biddle and Clark retained documents, made no attempt to yield them to federal officials, even though specifically requested by Jefferson to do so. Biddle, for example, held on to Ordway's journal (for reasons quite unknown), and Clark seemed to have had no thought at all of parting with a number of the original journals he had written and practically his entire collection of maps.

Why did Clark retain the journals and maps? That was a question Stanley put to Charles Van Ravensway, then director of the Missouri Historical Society. Ravensway replied:

> I feel that Clark kept in his possession all of the original documents relating to the expedition which were duplicated in the material already in the possession of Jefferson and the Philosophical Society, and that he interpreted the President's order to mean that he was not now to send any duplicate material because all the material which we know of that Clark did retain is, for the most part, duplicate material.[28]

To impartial spectators, here was a key issue, namely, the interpretation to be placed on Jefferson's "property of the government." Did he mean to include rough notes, such as Clark's, that were later

---

[26] Tomkins, *op. cit.*, 147. Having related this in even more detail in earlier chapters, I do not repeat it here.

[27] Jackson, *Letters*, 612–13.

[28] *Record, U.S. Court of Appeals*, 279.

copied into the marbled-paper-covered volumes constituting the "Notebook Journal"? The government contended, of course, that he did. Or did he think only in terms of information assembled in final form—of data as opposed to physical documents—as the Hammond lawyers maintained?

As the trial approached an end, the defense presented several witnesses from the rare-book field. Without exception, they testified that numerous federal documents had been solicitously cared for and existed today solely because of private collectors, and they cited examples. Dr. Bahmer, under cross-examination, was forced to admit that all of the presidents, beginning with Washington, had kept their papers, both public and private, and had deliberately taken them with them as they left office. Also, many lesser officials in government had done the same.

With this precedent fixed, Stanley then called to the stand Robert Metzdorf, the Yale manuscript expert. Metzdorf testified that Clark regarded his "Field Notes" as a private diary, but stated that to prove his point it would be necessary to refer directly to these "Field Notes," which were being held in camera, that is, in the judge's chambers rather than in open court. Judge Nordbye then adjourned proceedings to allow Metzdorf, Bahmer, and counsels for both plaintiff and defendant to examine the "Field Notes" held thus far incommunicado.

Holding the "Field Notes," Metzdorf disclosed how one of the documents had been folded to make a packet for others, and that it had been addressed, not to Jefferson or the secretary of war, but to General Jonathan Clark, Louisville, Kentucky. He then expressed his fixed belief that when Lewis wrote Jefferson at Fort Mandan in April, 1805, informing him that he was forwarding Clark's "private journal," he was not referring to Clark's "Field Notes," but to the three marbled-paper-covered volumes comprising the official record. The latter, he was persuaded, had been sent to the president, while the former, folded to make a packet, had been consigned to Clark's brother Jonathan.

Both sides in the court proceedings have since tended to agree that Metzdorf's testimony proved to be a turning point, that it markedly influenced the final decision. For instance, as Bahmer later asserted, "You could almost tell the exact moment when Judge Nordbye began to nod his head in agreement. We were just going through the motions from then on."[29] Stanley also noted the judge's response, promptly decided to call no more witnesses, and rested his case.

In the all-important briefs that followed, Bahmer stressed two points in particular: (1) that General Hammond had obtained Clark's "Field Notes" illegally from the government, and (2) the documents in question, even if obtained legally, had been written, pursuant to Jefferson's instructions, during the course of a military, government-sponsored expedition and, therefore, without question belonged to the government. Stanley's brief likewise emphasized two major issues: (1) Clark's "Field Notes"—after the party abandoned Camp Dubois—had been duplicated and extended, and (2) the government at that time was interested primarily, if not solely, in obtaining information and, with that in hand, regarded all else as superfluous.

—6—

No one can justifiably accuse Judge Nordbye of ruling hastily. He did not hand down his decision until October 8, 1956, more than nine months after the trial ended. While plaintiff and defendant cooled their heels, the judge read history. His ruling proves it, for it contained not only a full-bodied recapitulation of events bearing on the Lewis and Clark Expedition, but also a summary of roles played by leading figures beginning with Jefferson, Lewis, Clark, Barton, Gass, and Biddle and terminating with Coues, Thwaites, and Osgood. He omitted no one of consequence.

In reading his decision, Judge Nordbye left no one long in doubt as to what it would be, early statements plainly indicating the direction of his thinking:

> There is no indication that the notations kept by Lewis and Clark when they were in the United States [*i.e.*, at Camp Dubois] were recorded in response to Jefferson's directions to Lewis. . . . There is no evidence that Clark ever attempted to rewrite these [Camp Dubois] notes in more legible or finished form as he did with reference to the notes kept when the Expedition was under way. . . . It is inconceivable that Clark ever intended that these notes should be

[29] Tomkins, *op. cit.*, 144.

anything more than the basis for a more finished and legible account of the diary which he was keeping. That these notes of the
trip from Camp Dubois to the Mandans were copied later or rather
used by Clark as a basis for his permanent pocket diaries or journals
is convincingly established by the evidence. . . . No one questions
Professor Osgood's conclusion that in Clark's three pocket journals
is to be found substantially all the information to be gleaned from
the portion of the notes in question made when the Expedition was
under way up the Missouri. . . . What possible aid or assistance
could these notes in controversy, which required months of study by
Professor Osgood to transcribe, have been to the Government in
1806? . . . The situation must be considered as it existed after
Clark's return, and not as of today when such original notes and
data may be of great historical interest to scholars or have real
value as collectors' items. The Government was not concerned with
such aspects in 1806. Certainly, every inference to be deduced from
the evidence herein supports the contention that Captain Clark considered these notes as his personal property. . . . It should be noted
that at this time, 1806 to 1818, the Government had no official
depository for such documents. There was no National Archives
. . . and as an observation with reference to the Government's interest in the large amount of material in the Lewis and Clark collection deposited with the American Philosophical Society, it may be
noted that these documents slumbered in the vaults of the Society for
some seventy-five years without the Government or anyone else
having sufficient interest therein to publish any part of this vast
amount of material for the benefit of the public for whom Jefferson
was so much concerned. . . . Moreover, there is no showing here
that the Government ever has made any claim to the documents
which were in possession of the Clark heirs in 1903 and later published in Thwaites' original journals of the Expedition. . . .[30]

Continuing, Judge Nordbye finally arrived at his verdict: "The
Court finds that the Government has not sustained the burden of
proof in establishing its claim to the res in controversy. Therefore,
its claim of a permanent title thereto cannot be, and is not, sustained."[31]

Through its attorneys, the United States later submitted Nord-

[30] *First Trust Co.* v. *Minnesota Historical Society*, 146 F. Supp. (D. Minn.
1956), 658–68.
[31] *Ibid.*, 669.

bye's ruling to the Federal Court of Appeals, which held "that there was substantial evidence to support finding that rough notes of Captain Clark made during the Lewis and Clark Expedition were private papers rather than public documents executed in discharge of official duties."[32] Following this second reverse, the government dropped the case—did not seek a ruling by the Supreme Court. (See Appendix A for a current exposition of legal aspects of the case: *Minnesota Historical Society* v. *United States of America in re Lewis and Clark Expedition Papers.*)

What disposition was made of Clark's "Field Notes" after Judge Nordbye's ruling? With the Minnesota Historical Society and the Hammonds settling their differences out of court, Louis Starr received the "Field Notes" and, soon afterward (for the Hammonds), sold them to Frederick W. Beinicke, a Yale alumnus and wealthy bibliophile interested in great books of the American West. In 1960 Beinicke presented Clark's "Field Notes" to Yale University, where today they constitute an integral part of its library's outstanding collection of Western Americana.

Archibald Hanna, curator of this collection, subsequently wrote, "[When Mr. Beinicke] was able to acquire these field notes of William Clark, his first thought was that they should be published and thus made available to historians everywhere. Dr. Osgood, who had already devoted several years to their editing, was prevailed upon to complete their preparation for the press."[33]

—7—

Since Osgood had already transcribed and collated Clark's "Field Notes," his further responsibilities in preparing them for the press entailed primarily annotation and the writing of an introduction. He approached this work with heightened enthusiasm, not only because the "Field Notes" filled a significant hiatus in Lewis and Clark history, but also because, as a result of the recently concluded trial, they were in the public eye, were momentarily a subject of discussion in all historical circles—and Dr. Osgood was, first and last, a historian.

The "Dubois Journal," as we have made clear, was of far more

[32] 251 Federal Reporter, 2nd series (1958), 687.
[33] Osgood, *Field Notes*, vii.

value historically than the "River Journal." It covered the period from December 12, 1803, through May 14, 1804, except for two or three short breaks and one rather lengthy one (February 10 to March 20), when Clark joined Lewis in St. Louis to witness ceremonies attending the transfer of Louisiana from France to the United States. Therefore, in evaluating Osgood's annotation and introductory remarks, I will limit my comment to the "Dubois Journal."

The majority of Osgood's footnotes (numbering almost a hundred) relate to the precise location of Camp Dubois, and to the more important events occurring there, such as meteorological observations, problems with the enlisted men, identification of visitors, meetings with Indians, map making, estimating distances and travel time from Wood River to the Pacific, and the accumulating and storage of food and equipment.

As to the site of Camp Dubois, Osgood provided evidence that Lewis and Clark had predetermined it and that, in all likelihood, it was on the south side of Wood River within sight of the Mississippi and on what was then called American Bottom. In 1803 Wood River emptied into the Mississippi apparently just below and opposite the mouth of the Missouri. Today, because of changes in river courses since 1803, the original site of Camp Dubois, according to Osgood, is "buried beneath the mud on the Missouri side."[34]

From the first day of January through May 14, 1804, Clark proved himself to be a resolute meteorologist. He jotted down wind directions, rise and fall of water in the Wood and Mississippi, and temperatures at sunrise and 4:00 P.M.[35] For ascertaining temperatures he employed a "Thermometer on the N. Side of a large tree in the woods."[36] Periodically, too, Clark used sextant, quadrant, and chronometer in an attempt to establish latitude and longitude of the mouth of Wood River, thereby providing evidence that Lewis had schooled him, during the descent of the Ohio, in the mechanics of these navigational instruments. Clark's first attempts (December 17–18) put Camp Dubois in latitude 38° 22′ 7″ N. Evincing his

---

[34] *Ibid.*, 3n. See also Roy E. Appleman, "Lewis and Clark: the Route 160 Years After," *Pacific Northwest Quarterly*, Vol. LIX, No. 1 (January, 1966), 8.

[35] Thwaites, *Original Journals*, VI, 166–74.

[36] *Ibid.*, 165.

interest in these figures, Osgood footnoted: "Calculations based on the U.S.G.S. Map, Alton Quadrangle, give the present location of the mouth of the Wood (Dubois) River as latitude, 38° 31′ 42″ N."[37]

Clark referred often, in his "Field Notes" of the winter, to disobedience, fighting, and insobriety among the rank and file. For instance, on April 13 he wrote that one of the men "lo[aded] his gun to Shute S.O. [Sergeant Ordway?]—& Disobyed Orders."[38] Commenting on this and other instances of insubordination, Osgood said, "The task of disciplining the party was Clark's, and these brief notations suggest some of the difficulties encountered in dealing with these tough Kentucky and Tennessee frontiersmen."[39]

Camp Dubois attracted white visitors whom Clark did little more than mention by name. Osgood, after scanning numerous reference sources, identified many of them. For example, a "Mr. Saml Greffeth" turned out to be Samuel Griffith, who owned a farm "located on the Spanish side of the Mississippi ... some ten miles from Clark's camp."[40]

Lewis and Clark may well have been surprised at the number of Americans who had already, at this early date, settled down on the rich farmlands surrounding Camp Dubois. But, as Osgood explained, ". . . after the Revolution came a flood of Americans, to give it the name American Bottom. The first newcomers settled around Kaskaskia; after the Indian danger lessened, following Wayne's victory, others ventured further northward. By 1803–04, farms were numerous above and below the Dubois."[41]

Some of the white visitors to the encampment were prominent men from St. Louis and Cahokia, such as John Hay, Charles Gratiot, Manuel Lisa, Captain Amos Stoddard, and the Chouteau brothers, René Auguste and Jean Pierre. In footnotes, Osgood provided capsulized biographical sketches of these men.

Following an allusion by Clark to "Fort Massacre," Osgood clarified it by saying that this was a name often applied to Fort Mas-

[37] Osgood, *Field Notes*, 4n.
[38] *Ibid.*, 31.
[39] *Ibid.*, 31 n.
[40] *Ibid.*, 3, 4n.
[41] *Ibid.*, 4n.

sac.[42] He said, too, "Here George Drewyer (Drouillard) was engaged as interpreter for the expedition."[43] Drouillard, as we know, became invaluable to Lewis and Clark not only as an interpreter but also as a hunter. He arrived at Camp Dubois on December 22 and during the next two days demonstrated his ability with rifle by killing six deer and five wild turkeys.

Representatives of at least five Indian tribes—Delaware, Maumee, Osage, Sauk, and Kickapoo—called on Clark during the winter, and they must have regarded their visits as highly successful, since they returned to their villages with gifts of whiskey, flour, and other commodities. Clark repayed some of these calls. At one of the villages, on March 26, he undoubtedly was taken aback when he found there the notorious white renegade, Simon Girty, though Clark's only recorded remark was, "Gertey has the Rheumertism verry bad."[44] Osgood was at a loss to explain Clark's matter-of-fact comment on seeing Girty, whom every Kentuckian regarded as "the great renegade, the white savage."[45]

On Christmas Day, Clark reported that three Indians showed up at the encampment and told him, ". . . all the nations were going to war against the Ozous [Osage?]."[46] On March 21, Clark wrote, "I returned to Camp at Wood River down the Missouri from St. Charles in a Boat . . . Cap. Lewis & my self Mr. Choteau & Gratiot & went to stop 110 [?] Kickpo from going to war against the Osages."[47] In explanation of this effort to prevent tribal conflict, Osgood commented, "The St. Louis traders had no intention of allowing this, for it might impair their valuable trade with the tribe."[48]

Wrote Clark, on January 7, "I drew a map for the purpose of Correcting from the information which I may get of the Countrey to the N.W."[49] This entry drew from Osgood an unusually long footnote wherein he emphasized (1) that Lewis, on his arrival in St. Louis, had at once begun seeking additional geographical infor-

[42] *Ibid.*, 3.
[43] *Ibid.*, 4n.
[44] *Ibid.*, 29.
[45] *Ibid.*, 29n.
[46] *Ibid.*, 8.
[47] *Ibid.*, 27.
[48] *Ibid.*, 27n.
[49] *Ibid.*, 16.

mation about the trans-Mississippi West;[50] (2) that he had soon met Antoine Soulard, formerly surveyor general of Upper Louisiana for the Spanish government, who showed him three maps, one of which was "of the Missouri as far north as the Mandans . . . probably made by James Mackay, whom Clark would soon meet at Camp Dubois"; and (3) that William Henry Harrison had sent a map to Clark in November, 1803, and Jefferson, another to Lewis in January, 1804.[51]

Clark would indeed soon meet James Mackay—in fact, just three days after he had sketched his chart of the Northwest. About Mackay, Osgood had this to say: "No one in or around St. Louis could give Clark more accurate and complete information concerning the Missouri than this Scotsman, who had visited the Mandan villages on the Upper Missouri as early as 1787."[52] In all probability Clark *did* receive valuable data from Mackay and, as a result, may well have revised his map. But Clark's only comment on his meeting with Mackay was, "Cap Mackay has Just returned from Surveying of some lands up the Missouri, which has been lately granted he says 'a boutifull Countrey presents it self on the route he went & returned'."[53]

Utilizing cartographic data available to him, Clark devoted much of January 20 to estimating distances from Wood River to the Mandans, the Rockies, and the Pacific, and to calculating times required to reach those destinations. For example, he arrived at a figure of 3,050 miles as the distance to the Pacific and eight months as the approximate time for attaining that objective. Of these estimates, Osgood commented in part:

> For the whole distance from Camp Dubois to the Pacific, Clark's estimate of 3,050 miles was nearly a thousand miles too low; the actual mileage was 3,958 (Thw. VI, 67).

[50] Lewis, of course, had brought maps with him, such as those by cartographers Aaron Arrowsmith, Alexander Mackenzie, and George Vancouver.

[51] Osgood, *Field Notes*, 16n.

[52] *Ibid.*

[53] *Ibid.*, 16. Clark's January map may have been his first. In 1961 Donald Jackson discovered a possible copy of it. He characterized it as "almost certainly the first cartographic product of the Lewis and Clark Expedition." See Jackson, "A New Lewis and Clark Map," Missouri Historical Society *Bulletin*, Vol. XVII, No. 2, Pt. 1 (January, 1961), 117.

It should be noted that in estimating how long it would take to get to the Pacific . . . Clark allowed for no rest periods, nor for the time-consuming councils with the Indians. Out of the 165 days taken to reach the Mandan villages, for instance, 37 days were spent in camp and council with the natives. It is clear . . . that Clark did not intend to winter with the Mandans but push on, and winter (1804–05) far upstream close to the divide. Having reached the ocean in June or July 1805, Clark intended that the party tarry there for only 15 days and then head for home. . . . These estimates reflect the careful thought Clark gave to this problem, with the information he had to go on at the time he made these calculations.[54]

One week later (January 26)—but four months before the explorers evacuated Camp Dubois—Clark wrote, "To Stow away in the Boats Kegs . . . 45 for po[r]k, 50 for flour, 18 Whisky—7 Corn." Thus, at this early date, Clark was again looking ahead, trying to anticipate all contingencies. Commented Osgood, "One of the most important tasks was the collection of supplies and the preparation of them for the journey. This is the first of many entries in the journal which gives lists of provisions to be stowed away in the keelboat and the two pirogues."[55]

Osgood's documentation impresses, as the above examples attest. Clearly, to find statements needing emendation, clarification, or refinement, he had subjected each word, clause, and sentence of Clark's "Field Notes" to close scrutiny. In length, some of his footnotes are Couesian. For example, his commentary on the scrap of paper (Document 1) which begins the "Dubois Journal" exceeds fifteen hundred words. In one respect he differed utterly from Coues. Throughout his annotation of the journal, he employed just one Latin binomial,[56] even though Clark had alluded to quite a number of both plants and animals. But each to his métier; Coues looked at the world through the eyes of the naturalist, Osgood through those of the historian.

[54] Osgood, *Field Notes*, 19–21, 21 n.

[55] *Ibid.*, 24, 24n.

[56] *Ibid.*, 11 n. This binomial was *Nelumbo lutea* (American lotus). In his "Dubois Journal," Clark mentioned ten or more different species of animals. If Coues had been editing this journal, he would have attempted both technical and vernacular names of each.

—8—

As Osgood's editorial labors proceeded, he found Clark's "Field Notes" a unique Pandora's box; not one filled with ills that might plague mankind, but with questions that would persist in tormenting the minds of Lewis and Clark scholars until someone provided acceptable answers. As a result, he devoted many pages of his introduction to grappling with these questions. I propose, in paragraphs immediately ahead, to discuss Osgood's answers to a number of the questions he tackled. The reader will thus be in a position to judge for himself how well Osgood succeeded.

1. Did Lewis and Clark consistently make rough field notes, from which they subsequently prepared fuller and more finished reports? Before Osgood attempted an answer to this query, he compared Clark's "Field Notes" (both the "Dubois" and "River" journals) with the three morocco, gilt-edged volumes at the American Philosophical Society constituting the first part of the "Notebook Journal." Not until then did he conclude that the two captains *had* both made rough field notes, had done so religiously throughout the trip, and had afterward relied on them when writing their finished, more comprehensive accounts. He based his conviction primarily on the conspicuous factual similarity of Clark's "Field Notes" to the "Notebook Journal," the latter being simply an extended, clearer version of the former.[57] Reinforcing his conclusion was his knowledge of another document, namely, Clark's celebrated elkskin-bound journal—then and now in the archives of the Missouri Historical Society—which contained rough field notes covering the period from September 13 through December 31, 1805, and showed every evidence of continued wear and exposure, such as would have occurred if it had been carried daily in pocket in all kinds of weather. This too, Osgood found, bore a close textual similarity to the "Notebook Journal."

These two documents, Clark's "Field Notes" and the elkskin-bound diary, recorded events for fourteen months, just one half of the time required for the entire trip. Thus, if we accept Osgood's premise that both leaders kept similar rough field notes for the duration, we must accept the fact that Clark's for the remaining fourteen months, and Lewis' for the entire twenty-eight, are unaccounted for.

[57] *Ibid.*, xv.

It would make for a more comfortable feeling if we had available more of these rough notes, particularly some by Lewis comparable to those by Clark.

2. Why did Clark retain his "Dubois" and "River" journals after he had written his "Notebook Journal" and, presumably, had finished with them? Osgood answered this question by saying:

> He was carrying out Jefferson's wishes as both he and Lewis understood them. For years the President had seized upon every bit of information about the vast areas that reach westward to the Pacific. ... In preserving these rough notes, Clark was mindful, I believe, of the wishes of his commander-in-chief. The more journals, the less likelihood that any scrap of information would be lost.[58]

As noted in our resumé of the Minneapolis trial, both Metzdorf and counsel for the Hammonds contended that Clark had regarded the "Field Notes" as his personal property. Adding weight to this contention is the circumstance that Clark sent neither the "Field Notes" nor the elkskin-bound journal to Jefferson. We may speculate, therefore—and this is in line with Osgood's reasoning—that Clark held on to his rough notes to have them available in case, at any time, the "Notebook Journals" should be lost.

3. Should Clark's "Field Notes" unearthed in St. Paul be regarded as a "private journal"? Osgood thought not. In no way, he insisted, could the geographic data contained therein, to cite just one example, be considered private. As Lewis had told Jefferson, the "Field Notes" constituted an effective component of the "daily detales" of progress and transactions. But here again Metzdorf's and Stanley's interpretation differed from Osgood's.

4. Did Lewis write a day-to-day diary, like those written by Clark, Ordway, Gass, and Whitehouse, during the months required to ascend the Missouri to Fort Mandan? The only words we have from Lewis himself with a possible bearing on this matter are to be found in his April 7, 1805, letter to Jefferson: "I shall dispatch a canoe . . . from the extreme navigable point of the Missouri . . . [and] by the return of this canoe, I shall send you my journal."[59] Regarding this statement by Lewis as indecisive, Osgood wrote, "I do not think

---

[58] *Ibid.*, xvii.
[59] Thwaites, *Original Journals*, VII, 319.

there is enough available evidence to support a conclusion that Lewis was keeping a journal on the first leg of the journey."[60]

5. Precisely which journals did Lewis and Clark transmit to Jefferson from Fort Mandan in the spring of 1805? In his attempt to answer this question—a most difficult one for him—Osgood relied mainly on passages from two letters sent to the president from Fort Mandan, one by Lewis and the other by Clark. The passage from Lewis' reads, "You will also receive *herewith inclosed* a part of Capt. Clark's *private journal*. The other part you will find inclosed in a separate tin box. This journal (*is in it's original state*, and of course incorrect, but it) will serve to give you the daily detales of our progress, and transactions."[61]

Osgood chose this passage—which it seems necessary here to repeat—to call attention to Lewis' use of the words "private journal," and to his assertion that it was being sent in two parts "in its original state." When first appraising the passage, Osgood thought the two parts referred to by Lewis must be the "Dubois" and "River" journals. But further reflection convinced him this could not be the case, since Clark was sending the former to his brother Jonathan. Osgood then declared:

> Evidence, weighty though not conclusive, will be presented shortly to show that the Dubois Journal did go to Jonathan Clark as Clark had intended, and the three notebooks containing the official journal were sent to Jefferson at this time. However, these notebooks could not be one of the two parts referred to here, for Lewis specifically mentioned that it was Clark's journal in its original state that was in two parts. This being the case, the journal Lewis referred to . . . must be Clark's River Journal [and that alone].[62]

Further strengthening his position that it was the "River Journal" Lewis sent to Jefferson, Osgood produced two telling pieces of evidence. One was from Clark's letter of April 1 in which he informed the president he was sending for his perusal "the notes which I have taken in the form of a journal in their original state."[63] To Osgood, the key words here, as in Lewis' letter, were "original state," for, in

[60] Osgood, *Field Notes*, xvii. Osgood's opinion is in line with that of this writer, earlier expressed. See *ante* pp. 9–10.

[61] Thwaites, *Original Journals*, VII, 318. Author's italics.

[62] Osgood, *Field Notes*, xx.

[63] Thwaites, *Original Journals*, VII, 313.

his opinion, they could have referred only to the "River Journal."[64] His second piece of evidence was the following discovery:

> At the head of each document on which the River Journal is written there is a notation giving the dates of the entries that were put down on that particular document. Since the journal is on loose sheets of paper, this was obviously done to facilitate their arrangement in chronological order. . . . These date headings [which are absent from sheets of the "Dubois Journal"] are in neither Clark's nor Lewis's handwriting.

Osgood then went on to say that he had compared this writing with dates written at the heads of letters by Jefferson and Biddle and, as a result, concluded that Biddle had been responsible.[65]

But how explain the "two parts" in their "original state" alluded to by Lewis? As further evidence of Osgood's continued painstaking examination of the "Field Notes," he discovered that the "River Journal" actually consisted of two parts: (1) a portion from May 14 to September 23, 1804, characterized by rough, hastily written entries, and (2) the remainder (September 23, 1804, through April 2, 1805), a clean, carefully written draft, presumably made by Clark during the winter months at Fort Mandan. Both parts carried the dates Osgood had ascribed to Biddle. Declared Osgood, "That the clean copy is dated in sequence with the rough notes is the basis for my conclusion that it is the second of the two parts of Clark's River Journal."[66]

Though Osgood felt himself on safe ground with these conclusions, he admitted his inability to explain how the "Dubois" and "River" journals later managed to get together (as they were in General Hammond's desk) and, also, why Lewis in his April 7 letter failed to say anything to Jefferson about his forwarding to him, additionally and simultaneously, the three volumes of the official record now reposing in vaults of the American Philosophical Society. Of course, Metzdorf had argued that when Lewis informed the president he was shipping Clark's "private journal," he was referring not to the "Field Notes" at all, but rather to the three-vol-

---

[64] Osgood, *Field Notes*, xx.

[65] *Ibid.*, xxi. However, Osgood told the author that John Bakeless thought the dates were in Jefferson's handwriting.

[66] *Ibid.*

ume official record. Obviously, this position left unexplained Osgood's outstanding discovery, apparently unknown to Metzdorf, of the dates appended to the loose sheets comprising the "River Journal."

After winnowing the above evidence, Osgood finally answered the question raised at the beginning of this section. He believed the journals Lewis and Clark transmitted to Jefferson from Fort Mandan to have been the "River Journal" and the "Notebook Journal" of three volumes.

6. Did Clark's "Dubois Journal" reach its intended destination, namely, Jonathan Clark, then residing at the Clark estate, "Mulberry Hill," near Louisville, Kentucky? Osgood answered this question in the affirmative, basing his opinion on a story printed June 18, 1805, in the *Kentucky Gazette*, Lexington. The *Gazette* stated, "A gentleman from *Jefferson* county has obligingly favored the Editor of the *Kentucky Gazette* with the following account."[67] As printed, this account gave a resumé of events during Lewis and Clark's ascent of the Missouri to Fort Mandan, and a much-compressed description of the terrain, Indian tribes, and animal life along the river.[68]

Osgood had little doubt that the gentleman from Kentucky was Jonathan Clark, and that Jonathan's source of information had been Clark's "Dubois Journal." Strengthening his belief was the scrap of paper (Document 56), on the verso of which Clark had written, "To the Care of Genl. Jona. Clark near Louisville Ky To be opened by Capt. W. Clark or Capt. Meriwether Lewis."[69] and also on the verso, "I must Seal up all those scripts & draw from my Journal at some other time."[70]

About Document 56, which was the final one of the first portion of the "River Journal," Osgood made three points in particular: (1) Clark had used it as a wrapper for Documents 1–55, for, as he said, "The folds of the document, the position of the inscription, the location of the seal, and the tear in the upper left-hand corner leave no doubt in my mind that the packet of notes was made on or about

[67] Thwaites, *Original Journals*, VII, 324.
[68] Osgood, *Field Notes*, xxvi. The only known existing copy of this account appeared in the Boston *Centinel* of July 13, 1805, presumably reprinted from the *Gazette* of June 18.
[69] *Ibid.*, 302.
[70] *Ibid.*, 301.

Sept. 23"; (2) Lewis and Clark had hopes of meeting a boat headed for St. Louis to which they might entrust this packet; and (3) Clark's words, "draw from my journal at some other time," indicated that he was "here referring to his Notebook Journal, and that he will draw from it whatever information he might need of the journey up to this point."[71]

7. Did the three volumes of the "Notebook Journal" shipped from Fort Mandan reach Jefferson? Osgood based his answer to this question on a letter from Jefferson to Dr. Barton. Dated December 22, 1805, it read in part as follows:

> Under another cover I send you drawings & specimens of the seed, cotton, & leaf of the cotton tree of the Western country. . . . it appears from the journals of Lewis & Clarke that the boughs of this tree are the sole food of the horses up the Missouri during winter. Their horses having on a particular occasion gone through extraordinary fatigue, bran of the mais [maize] was ordered for them, which they refused, preferring their ordinary food the boughs of this tree, a few of which are chopped off . . . every evening & thrown into their pen.[72]

As Osgood proved, Jefferson could have obtained this information only from the "Notebook Journal," specifically from Lewis' entry of February 12, 1805, which read, "Drewyer arrived with the horses about the same time, the horses appeared much fatieged I directed some meal brands [bran] given to them . . . but to my astonishment found that they would not eat it but preferred the bark of the cottonwood which forms the principal article of food usually given them by their Indian masters in the winter season. . . ."[73]

Osgood raised other questions in his introduction, and he supplied answers to all except one. Neither he nor anyone else, as of this writing, has been able to explain how General Hammond obtained Clark's "Field Notes." Of course, as Indian agent for Louisiana, Clark accumulated many papers. Following his death, the Indian office in St. Louis was moved, first to St. Joseph, Missouri, then to

---

[71] *Ibid.*, 144, 144n., 302.

[72] Jackson, *Letters*, 272.

[73] Thwaites, *Original Journals*, I, 258. In his "River Journal," Clark made two references to horses and cottonwood, but neither reference alluded to bran, or to the horses' preference for cottonwood bark.

Atchison, Kansas, and finally (in 1869) to Lawrence, Kansas. It is possible that some of Clark's personal papers, even the "Field Notes," may have made the same moves, so that the "Field Notes" were in Lawrence when General Hammond, on orders from the federal government, arrived there in 1878 to close down that Indian office. With the discovery in St. Paul of Clark's "Field Notes" among Hammond's papers, it was only natural that some persons immediately suggested that the general had acquired them while closing down the Lawrence office.[74]

Any way we look at Osgood's introduction, it is a distinguished contribution to Lewis and Clark history. Osgood's rational answers to so many difficult and vexing questions make the introduction of more value to scholars of the Expedition than his annotation, and in saying that we do not mean to depreciate the latter.

—9—

The final chapter in the story of Clark's "Field Notes" (until or unless other developments intrude) ended in 1964, with their publication by Yale University Press. *The Field Notes of Captain William Clark, 1803–1805*, when it came from the press, proved to be a handsomely turned-out quarto volume of 335 pages, with almost half of the pages devoted to photographic reproductions of the 67 original loose sheets.

Reviewers praised Osgood for his role in preparing the "Field Notes" for publication. One wrote:

> Editor Osgood has done his work with thoroughness and with meticulous care. . . . [His] notes, set in smaller type than the text, appear to be much more copious than Clark's and are correspondingly more informative in the sense that they bring to bear at appropriate places not only on the editor's findings but also on a distillation of all important scholarship that has to be done on the Lewis and Clark Expedition.[75]

Said another reviewer, "Mr. Osgood has done admirably, leaving little that is undeciphered or unintelligible in his present text. . . .

[74] So far as this writer knows, at the time of Clark's death all manuscript material then in his possession relating to the Expedition passed to his heirs.

[75] American Academy *Annals*, 358:250 (March, 1965).

All told, the amount of fresh data on the expedition during the first leg of the immense traverse is modest, but every scrap is precious. . . . One thirsts for every new detail."[76]

* * *

As this is written, during the summer of 1972, fifty-eight years have elapsed since Osgood, in 1914, first followed the Lewis and Clark trail up the Missouri to Montana and Helena, and first saw the "innumerable mountains that rise and rise." It seems highly appropriate, as we conclude this chapter, to report that Dr. Osgood this summer is once again at his cabin on Alice Creek, within walking distance of Lewis and Clark Pass, and that on August 9 in Helena, at an age most remote from infancy, he addressed the Lewis and Clark Trail Heritage Foundation at its annual meeting.

The West, to Dr. Osgood, is a perennial lure and joy. Writing recently, he said, "As I drive westward [each summer], the words of the prophet Isaiah come to me, 'For ye shall go out with joy, and be led forth with peace; the mountains and the hills shall break forth before you into singing and all the trees of the field shall clap their hands'."[77]

[76] London *Times Literary Supplement*, July 8, 1965, 583.
[77] Osgood, "I Discover Western History," *loc. cit.*, 251.

CHAPTER X
Donald Jackson

Americans of late have been rediscovering Lewis and Clark. During the first half of this century, the upswing in interest may be likened in some respects to the increased attention accorded the art of George Catlin and the prose of Herman Melville. And within the decade of 1960 to 1970 the resurgence was near explosive. In this brief ten-year span, we witnessed the birth of Lewis and Clark societies,[1] the creation of national and state Lewis and Clark Trail commissions, the designation of Lewis and Clark National Historical Landmarks,[2] the erecting of numerous trail markers, the institution by an internationally known travel agency of Lewis and Clark tours,[3] and the publication of an unprecedented amount of Lewis and Clark writings in the form of magazine articles and books.

Among the books one volume stands out above the others: *Letters of the Lewis and Clark Expedition with Related Documents, 1783–1854*, edited by Donald Jackson. Published in 1962 by the Univer-

[1] The Lewis and Clark Society of America, Inc., 781 Purvis Drive, Wood River, Illinois, 62095, and the Lewis and Clark Trail Heritage Foundation, Inc., 3025 North Vancouver Avenue, Portland, Oregon, 97227.
[2] Pompey's Pillar, on the Yellowstone River near Billings, Montana, and Camp Disappointment, on Cut Bank Creek close to the town of Cut Bank, Montana, have both been denominated National Historic Landmarks.
[3] Four Winds Travel, Inc., 175 Fifth Avenue, New York, N.Y., 10010.

sity of Illinois Press, it stands fair to be the most important contribution to Lewis and Clark literature of the twentieth century excepting the *Original Journals.*

At considerably earlier dates, a smattering of letters and other papers casting light on various aspects of the Expedition had appeared in newspapers,[4] in periodicals like the Philadelphia *Port Folio,*[5] and in such books as Frederic L. Billon's *Annals of St. Louis* (1886)[6] and Coues's 1893 reissue of Biddle.[7] The first serious attempt by anyone to compile existing letters and documents of Lewis and Clark was made by Thwaites, who published them in the *Original Journals* under the heading, "Appendix to the Original Journals."[8] Jackson's *Letters,* which followed Thwaites's "Appendix" by some sixty years, was a far more elaborate and sophisticated package. Indeed, some historians already regard it as the prime stimulus to the flood of published Lewis and Clark material in the 1960's.

—2—

Donald Dean Jackson (1919–) is a product of the Middle West, having been born on a farm in the environs of Glenwood, Iowa, a small town in Mills County situated only three or four miles from the Missouri River and the mouth of the Platte. By virtue of his proximity to those streams, and to places made historically prominent by Lewis and Clark, he learned about them early.

[4] Perhaps the first letter to be printed was that of Clark to William Henry Harrison from Fort Mandan. It was dated April 2, 1805, and appeared in the Baltimore *Telegraphe and Daily Advertiser* of July 25, 1805 (Jackson, *Letters,* 227–30).

[5] *Port Folio* of May, 1812 (Vol. VII, No. 5, 448–49) ran Lewis and Clark's letter of October 31, 1804, to Charles Chaboillez, then in charge of the Department of the Assiniboine for the North West Company (Thwaites, *Original Journals,* VII, 307; Jackson, *Letters,* 213–14).

[6] Billon reproduced a letter from Lewis to Auguste Chouteau. See Jackson, *Letters,* 161–63.

[7] Coues, in his "Memoirs" of Lewis and Clark, printed about one dozen letters in full or in part, the majority from Clark to Biddle (Coues, *History,* I, lxxx-lccxiv and xciii–xciv).

[8] Thwaites, *Original Journals,* VII, 193–423.

Our foremost explorers, as young Jackson soon found out, had arrived at the mouth of the Platte on July 21, 1804, and the next day had established a camp—"Camp White Catfish"—some ten miles above its confluence with the Missouri. Here they halted five days in anticipation of a meeting with Oto and Pawnee Indians and, as Clark wrote, "to let them know of the Change of Government the wishes of our government to Cultivate friendship with them, the objects of our journy and to present them with a flag and Some Small presents."[9] Here, too, Clark drew a map of the Lower Missouri and Lewis prepared papers, with a view to sending them downstream to Jefferson.

It would make a good story if young Jackson had been irresistibly drawn again and again to the banks of the Missouri and to Camp White Catfish as a result of a deep interest early formed in Lewis and Clark. But, if asked, he will tell you that that absorption came later. He did make many visits as a boy to the Missouri, though these were incidental to farm life. In some seasons western Iowa suffered from severe droughts, with the result that Jackson's father rented islands in the river to which he drove his cattle so that they might have ready access to water and the forage provided by willow leaves. On such missions the youthful Jackson went along as a helper.

Like all boys who grow up on a farm, Jackson became familiar with the care of livestock, the use of farm machinery, and the yearly planting, cultivation, and harvesting of crops. He remembers well even today that the proper time to plant corn is when oak leaves are the size of squirrels' ears. Most enjoyable to him were rambles across fields and through woodlands searching for arrowheads and noting the presence of animals and plants. From some progenitor he had inherited a love of nature.

With high school behind him, Jackson entered Iowa State College (now University) at Ames, having acquired the means to do so by winning a Sears, Roebuck and Company scholarship of $150, adequate to pay his tuition for one year. His ambition at the time of enrollment was to study forestry, and during his freshman year he took courses required by that curriculum, such as biology and silviculture. However, that aspiration was short-lived. He soon shifted

[9] *Ibid.*, I, 88.

to journalism, with the result that his B.S. degree, obtained at Iowa State in 1942, was in that subject. At Ames, also, he renewed his friendship with the editor of the Iowa State Press, Harold Ingle, whom he had first known and admired at the age of twelve when Ingle had served for a time as 4-H agent in Mills County.

After a period with the navy in the South Pacific during World War II, Jackson began graduate studies at the University of Iowa, Iowa City. He went with a goal clearly, unalterably fixed. He would become editor of a university press as Harold Ingle had. To that end, he worked out the course of study which thereafter he meticulously followed. How far did he succeed in achieving his goal? Even before the date in 1948 when he received his Ph.D. from the university, he had in his pocket a contract from the University of Illinois Press, Urbana, to join its top editorial staff—and this at the age of twenty-nine.

When the University of Illinois Press later chose Jackson as its editor, it could not have been materially influenced by his literary output. To date he had published only a bit of short fiction and one book, *Archer Pilgrim*, a novel about Iowa farm life.[10] His editorial experience had been limited to that gained as an undergraduate and graduate student, working on student magazines and newspapers. Clearly, the press had chosen him on the basis of his realized preparation for just such a post, the excellence of his record, and strong recommendations from men acquainted with that record. Doubtless, too, it liked the cut of his jib.

—3—

It has been said that nothing is more congenial to an editor than the wholesale dissection of someone else's point of view. Not invariably true, of course, but in months and years ahead as manuscripts demanding attention piled up on Jackson's desk, there were times when he would have preferred the blade of the scalpel to the blue mark of his pencil. In the early fifties, perhaps as a foil to

[10] *Archer Pilgrim* was published in 1942 by Dodd, Mead & Co., New York, when Jackson was just twenty-three. For it the publisher credited him with "Honorable Mention, Intercollegiate Literary Fellowship."

routine, Jackson began to utilize spare time for studies on the early history of the Upper Mississippi Valley. As a consequence, he soon edited and published *Black Hawk, an Autobiography* (1955) and followed it with articles on such topics as "William Ewing, Agricultural Agent to the Indians" (1957) and "Old Fort Madison, 1808–1813" (1958).[11]

At some point while engaged in these studies, Jackson became aware of the seeds of interest in Lewis and Clark that soon germinated and grew prodigiously. As concrete evidence of the enthusiasm attending this new-fledged pursuit, he produced in rapid succession the following articles: "Some Books Carried by Lewis and Clark" (1959), "Lewis and Clark Among the Oto" (1960), "A New Lewis and Clark Map" (1961), and "The Race to Publish Lewis and Clark" (1961).[12] And then, in 1962, as a fitting climax to these articles, Jackson published the aforementioned *Letters of the Lewis and Clark Expedition with Related Documents, 1783–1854.*[13] Beginning in 1958, he had devoted four years to it and, as he told me, had written every word and line of it in spare time—week ends, evenings, and holidays—and without benefit of staff, not even secretarial aid. The final typed draft of the 728-page manuscript was the product of his own personal labor and of his alone.

—4—

In appraising Jackson's *Letters*, we may appropriately begin by comparing it with Thwaites's "Appendix." A few random statistics attest immediately to the greater scope and worth of the former.

[11] *Black Hawk* (Urbana, University of Illinois Press); "William Ewing," *Agricultural History*, XXXI (April); "Old Fort Madison," *Palimpsest*, XXXIX (January). Old Fort Madison, built in 1808 and destroyed by fire in 1813, stood near the mouth of the Des Moines River, Iowa, where the city of Fort Madison has since arisen. Nathaniel Pryor, sergeant with Lewis and Clark but by 1808 a lieutenant, was second in command at old Fort Madison.

[12] The articles appeared, respectively, in the Missouri Historical Society *Bulletin*, Vol. XVI, No. 1 (October); *Nebraska History*, Vol. XLI (September); Missouri Historical Society *Bulletin*, Vol. XVII, No. 2, Pt. 1 (January); *Pennsylvania Magazine of History and Biography*, Vol. LXXXV, No. 2 (April).

[13] See p. 281 for full bibliographical data.

Thwaites	*Jackson*
86 items all told	428 items
About 70 letters	About 370 letters
About 20 documents (as opposed to letters)	About 60 documents
12 letters by William Clark	33 letters by Clark
22 letters by Meriwether Lewis	53 letters by Lewis
22 letters by Thomas Jefferson	81 letters by Jefferson

Thwaites obtained his letters and documents from approximately twenty sources, but almost two-thirds from just three: (1) "Bureau of Rolls, Department of the Interior—Jefferson Papers," (2) the collection of Mrs. Julia Clark Voorhis and Eleanor Glasgow Voorhis, and (3) Jefferson's autobiography in Paul Leicester Ford's *Writings of Jefferson* (New York, 1892–99).

Jackson's 428 items, by contrast, came from some forty sources and, like Thwaites's, about two-thirds from three: (1) Library of Congress, (2) Missouri Historical Society, and (3) National Archives.

Obviously, yet surprisingly, Thwaites's and Jackson's primary sources differed completely, though the explanation is a simple one. Since 1904–05, when Thwaites compiled his "Appendix," the majority of the Lewis and Clark papers had been moved to new lodging places. The large collection of Jefferson's papers credited by Thwaites to the Department of Interior is now in the Library of Congress, and the Voorhis collection, as earlier stated, is in the Missouri Historical Society. Also, "Documents Relating to the Equipment of the Expedition," which Thwaites thought were at the Schuylkill Arsenal in Philadelphia, are today housed at the National Archives in Washington.[14] Additionally, it is worth noting, other items of special interest or significance have also changed hands. As an illustration, Lewis' letter of March 31, 1805, to his mother from Fort Mandan, the letter which Thwaites later located at Ivy Depot, Virginia, in the possession of C. Harper Anderson, "oldest living

[14] Wrote Thwaites in 1905, "Government expeditions were, a century ago, outfitted by the 'purveyor of public supplies' at Philadelphia. Such of the records as now remain, concerning the Lewis and Clark equipment—so far as our knowledge goes—are kept at the Schuylkill Arsenal" (*Original Journals*, VII, 231 n.).

representative of Meriwether Lewis's family,"[15] has since been presented to the Missouri Historical Society.[16]

Of course we should not overlook other sources of Lewis and Clark material important to Jackson, in particular the American Philosophical Society, whose vaults, as we know, contain most of the original manuscript journals as well as much other valuable related matter. In fact, Jackson discovered grist for his mill from Boston Public Library in the East to Bancroft and Huntington libraries in the Far West, and from Vancouver Public Library, British Columbia, of the North to the Mississippi State Department Archives and History of the Deep South. In short, as he determined, Lewis and Clark letters, manuscripts, portraits, specimens, relics, and memoranda are scattered throughout the nation and may be found in practically every one of the fifty states.

In his *Letters* Jackson wrote prefatorially, ". . . of the 428 items in the volume, more than half have not appeared in print. The rest have been published in scattered sources, some difficult to obtain, and they have not always been correctly transcribed or adequately annotated."[17] Of the items, some are patently more provocative than others—some, but which ones? At my request, Jackson graciously provided a list of his favorites—and further obliged by placing an asterisk before three of them, the discovery of which gave him the greatest personal satisfaction:

Item 5—December 12, 1802. George Rogers Clark to Jefferson. Clark recommends his brother William for "any post of Honor and profit, in this Countrey. . . ."[18]

Item 14—February 28, 1803. Lewis' British Passport. A copy in French, found in the Archivo General de Indias, Seville.[19]

Item 15—March 1, 1803. Lewis' French Passport, from a Library of Congress transcript. The original is in the Department of Foreign Affairs, French Archives.[20]

Item 24—April 13, 1803. Albert Gallatin to Jefferson. Gallatin

[15] *Ibid.*, 309n.
[16] Jackson, *Letters*, 225n.
[17] *Ibid.*, vi.
[18] *Ibid.*, 7–8.
[19] *Ibid.*, 19–20.
[20] *Ibid.*, 20.

comments upon a draft of Lewis' instructions, and reveals a broad interest in the West which he will maintain until the end of his life in 1849.[21]

Items 53–57—Lewis' financial records for the outfitting of the Expedition, compiled and annotated by Jackson from documents in the National Archives.[22]

Item 93—November 13, 1803. William Henry Harrison to Clark. This letter provided information which enabled Jackson to identify a famous map carried by Lewis and Clark, the so-called "Indian Office Map," as being a copy of one by James Mackay.[23]

Item 100—December 28, 1803. Lewis to Jefferson. Lewis reports on the situation as he found it in St. Louis, and on the present state of his plans.[24]

* Item 122—May 18, 1804. Lewis to Jefferson. A letter which through the years became separated into three parts, one lodging in the Library of Congress and two in the Massachusetts Historical Society. By recognizing these fragments as parts of a single document, Jackson was not only able to publish the whole letter but was also enabled by its contents to identify a most important map, sent to Jefferson, which was the first cartographic product of the Lewis and Clark Expedition. It is in still another repository, the National Archives.[25]

* Item 209—September 24, 1806. Lewis' draft of Clark's letter to "his brother," either George Rogers or Jonathan Clark. Realizing that Clark's letter would reach the hands of newspaper editors before his own, Lewis drafted it—probably in recognition of the fact that he was a better journalist and certainly a better speller. Jackson was the first to recognize the relationship between this letter and Clark's final draft (of September 23, 1806), which received widespread publication. They are in separate repositories.[26]

* Item 326—[ca. April, 1810]. The Nicholas Biddle Notes. Notes in Biddle's hand, made during a visit by Biddle to Fincastle, Virginia, where he met Clark. Written into two notebooks, they were

[21] *Ibid.*, 32–34.
[22] *Ibid.*, 69–99.
[23] *Ibid.*, 135–36.
[24] *Ibid.*, 148–57.
[25] *Ibid.*, 192–95.
[26] *Ibid.*, 330–35.

overlooked by scholars until discovered and published by Jackson.[27]

In his compilation Jackson did not include every letter and document available to him. He omitted, for example, a number previously published by Thwaites. But the final result is so complete that here and there one finds a series that, when conjoined, succeeds in telling a spirited, well-rounded story. There is, for instance, a sequence about the live magpie and prairie dog shipped by Lewis to Jefferson that survived the difficult trip from Fort Mandan to Philadelphia by way of St. Louis, New Orleans, Baltimore, and Washington and, in the course of this remarkable odyssey, passed through the solicitous hands of such distinguished men (in addition to Lewis) as Jean Pierre Chouteau, prominent early citizen of St. Louis; William Claiborne, governor of Orleans; Henry Dearborn, secretary of war; Thomas Jefferson, third president of the United States; Charles Willson Peale, eminent artist and curator of the Philadelphia (Peale's) Museum; and Alexander Wilson, outstanding contemporary artist-naturalist.[28]

By uniting components from other letters and/or documents, it is possible to fashion (and some writers have) entertaining stories on additional topics, such as Lewis' 1803 stay in Philadelphia equipping the Expedition,[29] the Clark-Biddle problems of publishing the original account,[30] the fate of specimens returned by the two captains, and the role of Frederick Pursh in describing and perpetuating the Lewis and Clark Herbarium.

—5—

The end result of a scholarly book such as Jackson's *Letters* is a collage of many inseparable, interlocking elements, among them bibliography (always first with Jackson), transcription, compilation,

[27] *Ibid.*, 497–545.

[28] At least two articles about the travels of these two live animals have appeared to date: Paul R. Cutright, "The Odyssey of the Magpie and the Prairie Dog," Missouri Historical Society *Bulletin*, Vol. XXIII, No. 3 (April, 1967), 215–28, and Ernest S. Osgood, "A Prairie Dog for Mr. Jefferson," *Montana, the Magazine of Western History*, Vol. XIX, No. 2 (April, 1969), 54–56.

[29] See Paul R. Cutright, "Meriwether Lewis Prepares for a Trip West," Missouri Historical Society *Bulletin*, Vol. XXIII, No. 1 (October, 1966), 3–20.

[30] See Jackson, "The Race to Publish Lewis and Clark," *Pennsylvania Magazine of History and Biography*, Vol. LXXXV, No. 2 (April, 1961), 163–77.

collation, annotation, indexing—though not necessarily in that order. Each requires labor, persistence, and skills beyond the ken of most individuals. Only those who have experienced and suffered through the ups and downs, the euphoria and malaise, preliminary to publication of a lengthy, learned manuscript may speak authoritatively to the subject.

Jackson successfully surmounted the difficulties inherent in each major step. Did he excel in one more than another? Yes, definitely, as I see it—in the province of annotation; for he knew, as an earlier writer once said, "Scholars push undocumented books into limbo and keep the others alive indefinitely."[31]

All told, Jackson's footnotes number close to a thousand, thus averaging approximately two per item. However, that does not begin to tell the complete story, because many are lengthy. Consider, for example, Jefferson's letter of February 11, 1806, to Constantin F. C. Volney (1757–1820), French scholar and writer. The letter itself contains only about two hundred words, but it evoked from Jackson an accompanying seven-page footnote with more than thirty-five hundred words.[32]

Inevitably, Jackson's documentation invites comparison with that of Elliott Coues, both exemplars in that art. Two differences strike me at once. Jackson possessed a subtler appreciation of the fact that the potency of knowledge depends on how and when it is used if full value is to be gained from it. Attesting to this awareness, he writes in lower key, more objectively, and without undue verbiage or positiveness of assertion. The hyperkinetic Coues, in making a point, as we know full well by now, was rarely low key, often went beyond the prescribed limit on words, and frequently tied them together with manifest self-assurance.

The other difference is something of a revelation to me. Jackson, in seeking substance for his notes, exhibits no qualms or reluctance about exploring fields foreign to his training and experience. By and large, Coues stuck closely to areas of prime familiarity, notably zoology, ethnology, and geography.

[31] Joseph Ewan, "Book Reviews: Scientific Americana," *Science*, Vol. CXXXIX (February 8, 1963), 478.
[32] Jackson, *Letters*, pp. 291–98.

By way of illustrating Jackson's predisposition to seek provender in unfamiliar fields, I would call attention again to Jefferson's letter to Volney. Herein the president told him that Lewis had sent

> specimens or information of the following animals not before known to the Northern continent of America. 1. The horns of what is perhaps a species of the Ovis Ammon. 2. A new variety of the deer having a black tail. 3. An antelope. 4. The badger, not before known out of Europe. 5. A new species of Marmotte. 6. A white weasel. 7. The magpie. 8. The Prairie hen, said to resemble the Guinea-hen (Peintade). 9. A prickly Lizard.[33]

As stated above, Jackson's comment on this letter ran to seven pages—and here begins the revelation. Jackson started off by saying, "It is difficult to know exactly what species of birds and [other] animals Lewis and Clark may be credited with discovering." He then introduced George Ord, who, by contributing the zoological section for the 1815 edition of William Guthrie's *A New Geographical, Historical, and Commercial Grammar* and alluding therein to a number of animals collected by Lewis and Clark, had proved himself to be one of the naturalists then best qualified to describe technically those new to science.[34]

Jackson then turned to Elliott Coues, the "next serious student of the zoology of the expedition," who, in an article written in 1876, had devoted space to birds and mammals encountered by the two captains and in 1893, with his reissue of Biddle, had contributed an even lengthier commentary.[35]

As to this commentary, Jackson regretted only that it did not "set forth plainly and in one list the mammals and birds which he [Coues] considered attributable to Lewis and Clark." He therefore

[33] *Ibid.*, 291. Those previously unidentified: (1) bighorn (*Ovis canadensis*); (2) mule deer (*Dama hemionus*); (5) prairie dog (*Cynomys ludovicianus*); (6) long-tailed weasel (*Mustela frenata longicauda*); (8) prairie sharp-tailed grouse (*Pedioecetes phasianellus campestris*).

[34] In Guthrie, Ord alluded to sixteen mammals and six birds, appearing to attribute them to Lewis and Clark (Jackson, *Letters*, 292).

[35] Elliott Coues, "An Account of the Various Publications Relating to the Travels of Lewis and Clarke [*sic*], with a Commentary on the Zoological Results of the Expedition," United States Geological and Geographical Survey of the Territories, *Bulletin*, No. 6, Ser. 2 (1876), 417–44.

resolved to try with aid from Coues and others to remedy the situation by devising "trial" lists of birds and mammals of his own.[36] This effort resulted in twenty-five mammals and seventeen birds and, more importantly, brief to lengthy comment on each.[37] If Coues, an experienced naturalist, had essayed such lists, it would have proved a formidable task, even for him. For Jackson, relatively untutored, it was far more difficult. Consider, for instance, his comment (briefer than most) about one of the most celebrated birds discovered by Lewis and Clark:

CLARK'S NUTCRACKER. *Nucifraga columbiana* (Wilson). A.O.U. 491. WILSON named this bird in Clark's honor and pictured it as plate 29 in the first edition of his work. The first description is in Lewis's journal entry for 22 Aug. 1805: "I saw today a speceis of woodpecker, which fed on the seeds of the pine. It's beak and tail were white, it's wings were black, and every other part of a dark brown. It was about the size of a robin." Lewis presents a much fuller description in his entry for 28 May 1806.

Note that Jackson, in this note alone, (1) supplied the full scientific name (*i.e.*, genus, species, and name of original describer, in this case Alexander Wilson), (2) included, surprisingly, the valuable check-list number of the American Ornithologists' Union, (3) revealed through his reference to plate 29 that he was conversant with Wilson's *American Ornithology*, (4) made it plain that he had familiarized himself with most of the pertinent data about this bird in the *Original Journals*, and (5) had become aware of the fact that this avian is not a woodpecker, as stated by Lewis, but a nutcracker, a corvine species intermediate between a crow and a jay. Quite a feat in itself, for one lacking formal training in ornithology; but there is more to come.

[36] Other sources credited by Jackson with aiding his taxonomy include Gerrit S. Miller, Jr., and Remington Kellogg, *List of North American Recent Mammals* (Washington, Smithsonian Institution, 1955); E. Raymond Hall and Keith R. Kelson, *The Mammals of North America* (New York, Ronald Press, 1859); Elijah H. Criswell, *Lewis and Clark: Linguistic Pioneers*; and American Ornithologists' Union, *Check-List of North American Birds* (5th ed., 1957).

[37] Cutright, *Lewis and Clark: Pioneering Naturalists*, extended Jackson's lists of birds and mammals and added others on reptiles, amphibia, and fishes. (See his Appendix B, 424–47.) He contributed, too, a list of plants, the first of its kind to be attempted (Appendix A, 399–423).

Early in his pursuit of zoological data, Jackson learned that contemporary naturalists had refrained from technically describing Lewis and Clark species unknown to science, having been advised of the impropriety of poaching on Lewis' preserves. However, hard on the heels of Lewis' death in 1809, with all barriers down, they at once fell to work. Jackson's notes reveal a remarkable knowledge of these men, particularly Ord, Wilson, Thomas Say, and Constantine Rafinesque, who initially led the taxonomic assault.[38] Concurrently with his inquiries into biographical data, he became conversant, too, with books and periodicals of that day in which appeared the first descriptions and illustrations of the Lewis and Clark species. Among these were Wilson's *American Ornithology* (earlier mentioned), Richard Harlan's *Fauna Americana* (1825), J. and T. Doughty's *The Cabinet of Natural History and American Rural Sports* (1830–32), Barton's *Philadelphia Physical and Medical Journal*, Samuel Mitchill's *Medical Repository*, and *Proceedings* of the Academy of Natural Sciences of Philadelphia.[39] Also, Jackson did not overlook the artists whom Lewis engaged to make sketches of animals, plants, and Indians that would illustrate his projected history of the Expedition, notably Charles Willson Peale, Wilson, and St. Mémin.

Jackson did not attempt a list of plants discovered by Lewis and Clark similar to those of animals, and has said that he does not know why. His botanical notes, however, are numerous and illumine many pages. For example, he devoted many of them to Frederick Pursh, and to *Flora Americae Septentrionalis* (London, 1814), Pursh's classic on the plants of North America, in which he technically described 124 species discovered by Lewis and Clark and reproduced sketches of 13 of them.

To this writer, who expounded on topics biological to college

[38] Jackson's notes reveal that he was equally well acquainted with other naturalists of the day, among them William Bartram, John Bachman, John Bradbury, Henry Muhlenberg, Thomas Nuttall, Titian Peale, and, of course, Benjamin Smith Barton. The list may easily be extended, particularly if we include contemporary gardeners, such as Bernard McMahon and William Hamilton, each a recipient of western seeds from Lewis.

[39] Jackson even dug into venerable prenineteenth-century technical literature. For example, we find him quoting from Francisco Hernandez, *Nova Plantarum, Animalium et Mineralum Mexicanorum Historia* . . . (Rome, 1651), Albertus Seba, *Locupletissimi Rerum Naturalium Thesauri* . . . (Amsterdam, 1734–65), and Miguel Vanegas, *Natural and Civil History of California* (London, 1759).

students for forty years, Jackson's wide-ranging excursions into zoology and botany represent the most amazing—and at the same time one of the most commendable—features of his *magnum opus*. In conversation with this writer, Jackson tried to minimize this adventure into biology, saying that from early age he had possessed a deep-seated interest in natural history, that he had sat through an introductory course in college biology, and that he had improved his knowledge of science while editing technical books. Nonetheless, we continue to be impressed.

—6—

In some respects, Jackson's inquiries into the cartography of the Expedition were as impressive as those into the biology, for he not only greatly extended his personal knowledge of that subject but also made contributions to it. Initially, he made himself familiar with the great names associated with map making in years preceding Lewis and Clark, in particular those responsible for charts of the known—and sometimes unknown—parts of North America to the west of the Mississippi. Among these names were, as Jackson revealed: Andrew Ellicott and Nicholas King of the United States; Aaron Arrowsmith, John Mitchell, John Cook, Alexander Mackenzie, and George Vancouver, all British; and Frenchmen Jean Baptiste d'Anville and Guillaume Delisle.

As an important detail in preparing for the tour of discovery, Jefferson and Lewis collected and scanned all available maps that might be of value to them. Jackson pursued closely this phase of the groundwork. His first cartographical footnote related to a letter of March 6, 1803, from Andrew Ellicott to Jefferson, in which the former alluded to a map by Arrowsmith.[40] The footnote reads, "Jefferson ordered a copy of this map 17 June 1803, and Lewis probably carried one with him to the Pacific."[41]

Next, in point of time, Jackson unearthed a consequential, previously unpublished letter dated March 14, 1803. From Albert Gallatin to Jefferson, it reads in part:

I have requested Mr. [Nicholas] King to project a blank map . . . which will give us the whole course of the Mississippi and the whole

[40] Jackson, *Letters*, 23–25.
[41] *Ibid.*, 25n.

coast of the Pacific ocean within the same latitudes. . . . In this I intend to insert the course of the Mississippi as high up as the Ohio from Ellicot's [map], the coast of the Pacific from Cook & Vancouver, the north bend of the Missouri & such other of its waters as are there delineated from the three maps of Arrowsmith & from that of Mackenzie, and the Rio Norte and other parts of the Missoury from Danville & Delisle.[42]

Lewis may have originated the idea of this map, for on May 29 of that year while in Philadelphia, he wrote Jefferson:

You will receive herewith inclosed some sketches taken from Vancouver's survey of the Western Coast of North America; they were taken in a haisty manner, but I believe they will be found sufficiently accurate as to be of service in composing the map, *which Mr. Gallatin was so good as to promise he would have projected and completed for me* will you be so obliging, Sir, as to mention to Mr. Gallatin, that I have not been able to procure Danvill's map.[43]

Jackson's footnotes to this letter identified King, D'Anville, and Delisle, and characterized Delisle's map of 1718 as "a pioneering rendering of the American West."[44] However, he failed to discover anything about the future of the Gallatin-King map and, unhappily, no one else has, to our knowledge. If King did complete it, then Lewis may have started west with an extraordinary composite, a cartographical triumph combining salient topographic features lifted from the charts of at least seven well-known map makers: Ellicott, Arrowsmith, Cook, Vancouver, Mackenzie, D'Anville, and Delisle. Whether Lewis did or did not, the journals of the Expedition supply proof that he carried charts by Arrowsmith, Cook, Vancouver, Mackenzie, and others.

After Lewis and Clark had established winter quarters on the

[42] *Ibid.*, 27–28. The Delisle map of 1718 was a pioneer rendering of the American West. The Rio Norte, in the confusion existing then about rivers of the Southwest, could have been either the Rio Grande or the Colorado. In his instructions to Lewis and Clark, Jefferson said, "the North river or Rio Bravo which runs into the gulph of Mexico, and the North river, or Rio colorado, which runs into the gulph of California, are understood to be the principal streams heading opposite to the waters of the Missouri, and running Southwardly" (Thwaites, *Original Journals*, VII, 249).
[43] *Ibid.*, 225. Author's italics.
[44] Jackson, *Letters*, 28n.

Mississippi near St. Louis, they continued their search for maps and succeeded in obtaining several, each a source of information about the country to the west they would soon traverse. For example, on November 13, William Henry Harrison, then governor of Indiana Territory, sent them a chart.[45] In late December, Lewis reported to Jefferson that he had been given three maps: one of the Osage River, one of Upper Louisiana, and a third of the Missouri from its mouth to the Mandan Nation.[46] On January 13, 1804, Jefferson wrote Lewis, "I now enclose you a map of the Missouri as far as the Mandans."[47]

We call attention to these maps because of their obvious importance to Lewis and Clark, especially those providing topographical data as far up the Missouri as the Mandan villages; also, because of Jackson's voluminous notes relative to each, and to present-century authorities cited, such as Herman R. Friis, Aubrey Diller, and Carl I. Wheat.[48]

Jackson's cardinal cartographic accomplishments involved a then unidentified map and two related documents by Lewis. The story is long and complicated, and may be said to have had its origin in St. Louis in 1804 as a result of a delegation of Osage Indians Lewis was sending to Washington in the custody of Jean Pierre Chouteau, a fur trader, Indian agent, and respected citizen of St. Louis who had befriended Lewis since his arrival there. With Chouteau, Lewis sent the above-mentioned map and two documents, one a piece by Lewis entitled "Notes on Salines and Proposed Districts,"[49] and the other a letter from Lewis to Jefferson listing specimens and maps he was forwarding to him by Chouteau. The Indians and documents presumably reached Jefferson July 11, 1804.[50]

The story is continued in 1904–05 when Thwaites, in his "Appendix," printed the latter of the two documents under the heading "Articles forwarded to Jefferson." Included among the articles were

[45] Ibid., 135.

[46] Ibid., 155.

[47] Thwaites, Original Journals, VII, 291.

[48] For published works of these men, see Bibliography.

[49] Jackson, Letters, 180–82.

[50] Jackson, "A New Lewis and Clark Map," Missouri Historical Society Bulletin, Vol. XVII, No. 2, Pt. 1 (January, 1961), 122, 122n.

samples of silver and lead ore, rock crystal, a hair ball,[51] a "horned Lizzard,"[52] and a chart of the Mississippi from the mouth of the Missouri to New Orleans. This document, now in the Library of Congress, was incomplete, as we shall soon see. The "Saline" item remained unpublished until Jackson unearthed it about 1959 at the Missouri Historical Society. These two documents are essential to the identification of the map.

The map itself was originally filed with the War Department records, and is now in the cartographic files of the National Archives. Unfortunately, it is not the original, but a copy made by a professional draftsman on instructions of the War Department.[53] It is a chart of the Lower Missouri, the central Mississippi, and lands lying west of St. Louis, measuring 31½ by 47½ inches and drawn in pencil except for some lines in red and larger rivers in blue.

The final installment of the story centers on a visit by Jackson in the spring of 1959 to the Massachusetts Historical Society in Boston. Events thereafter proved to be both exciting and dramatic, so much so that it is best to have them described by Jackson himself:

> In leafing through the Jefferson collection [at the Massachusetts Historical Society] I came upon an item endorsed "A list of Articles forwarded by Mr. Peter Chouteau." It appeared at first to be a complete document, as it was one full-sized sheet, with writing on both sides, signed by Lewis. The entire document was in William Clark's hand, except the last paragraph, the endorsement, and the signature, in Lewis's. In reading through it, I recognized two things immediately: that it was *not* a list of articles forwarded by Chouteau, but must bear some relationship to that incomplete list which I knew to be in the Library of Congress. Also, that it was not actually a

[51] A concretion of hair, often entangling undigested food particles in stomachs of mammals, particularly ruminants, addicted to swallowing hair. Also called a bezoar, it was formerly thought to be medicinal, especially counteractive to poisons.

[52] The horned toad, *Phrynosoma cornutum*. Whether alive or preserved is unknown. The next year, after another batch of specimens reached Jefferson, he wrote the American Philosophical Society that he was forwarding "a horned or rather thorny lizard, living." See Jackson, "A New Lewis and Clark Map," *loc. cit.*, 119n.

[53] A sentence in Jackson, "A New Lewis and Clark Map," *loc. cit.*, 122, states, "An entry in the report books of the War Department accountant, William Simmons, of July 19, 1804 reads: 'I certify that there is due Seth Pease, the sum of Ten Dollars, being the amount of his Account for a Map of the Territory of the Osage Indians in Upper Louisiana, furnished by the Secy. of War'."

complete document, as it bore no heading; at the top of the first page was the word "Continued." I entered in my notebook a notation that I must order a photostat, and later compare it with the fragment in the Library of Congress.

At the very end of the Jefferson Collection at the Massachusetts Historical Society is a collection of miscellaneous items—undated notes, memoranda, financial vouchers, etc. Since I have been rewarded frequently by searching such miscellany carefully, I inspected all of this material. As a result, I came upon a small fragment which I recognized at once to be in Clark's hand. . . . On the reverse side was the description of a map drawn by Antoine Soulard [surveyor general of Louisiana], and the notation "Presented by Mr. [Auguste] Chouteau." I quickly returned to the larger fragment I had found earlier, and determined that the pieces were related in format. What I had in the smaller fragment was a piece that had become detached from the fragment in the Library of Congress, and I now knew for sure that the three fragments had once been a single, complete document.

In my excitement at having re-united the pieces of this very important Lewis and Clark document, I had neglected to study thoroughly the contents of the larger Boston fragment. When the photostats arrived in Urbana, and I read the larger one with its description of a "Map of a part of Upper Louisiana compiled from the best information that Capt. Clark and myself could collect," I knew that I had verified Herman Friis' suspicions about the War Department copy in the National Archives. I found further verification in another document [the "Salines" one] which Lewis apparently sent to Jefferson, which seemingly was meant to accompany the map and which referred to symbols indicating "the villages of the Snake Lizard and Squirel" on the map. And here, of course, Lewis was referring to prairie dog villages, which were in those days believed also to be inhabited by rattlesnakes and horned toads.[54]

Thus a letter reassembled from three fragments in two repositories enabled me to identify a map in a third repository (National Archives)[55] and to make fuller use of a document in a fourth repository (Missouri Historical Society).[56]

[54] Lewis and Clark later determined to their satisfaction that this age-old story of rattlers living on congenial terms with prairie dogs and other animals was a myth. On September 7, 1804, Clark wrote, "It is said that a kind of Lizard also a Snake reside with those animals (*did not find this correct*)" (Thwaites, *Original Journals,* I, 142).

We have already noted that Jackson regarded the map as probably the first cartographic product of the Expedition, and the sum of these discoveries as one of three that gave him the greatest satisfaction during his years devoted to tracing down unpublished Lewis and Clark documents. By now we should be in complete agreement with him; this discovery is just another example, generally unforeseen, of the rewards that attend the diligent pursuits of the researcher, whether historian, scientist, or votary of some other field.

—7—

Once the fabric is woven, it may be embellished at will. Over the years many controversies related to the Lewis and Clark Expedition have been "woven" and thereafter stretched and colored at will—sometimes *ad nauseam*. One of the features of Jackson's *Letters* attracting attention is his commentary letting it be known where he stands in respect to each of the major controversies.

One that has come to the forefront seems to have originated primarily from the pen of Elliott Coues. Writing in 1893, he declared, ". . . the most serious defect in the organization of the Expedition was the lack of some trained scientist."[57] His quarrel, of course, was with Jefferson, who had often expressed confidence in Lewis' ability to identify and describe plants and animals unfamiliar to him that he would encounter en route to the Pacific. Since 1893 other writers, some at least taking their cue from Coues, have spoken out similarly. The well-known historian Walter Prescott Webb, for one, had this to say:

> Why a man of Jefferson's philosophical and scientific turn of mind should have been unable to select more capable men for the enterprise, keen observers with trained minds, is hard to understand. It was probably because in his capacity of private secretary Lewis had led the President to overestimate his ability. Throughout the journal there is a lack of specific detail, a vagueness, an absence of names of

---

[55] Reproduced in Jackson, "A New Lewis and Clark Map," *loc. cit.*, Pt. 1.

[56] Jackson most obligingly described this event at my request. His pages bear the date July 9, 1970.

[57] Coues, *History*, I, xx. Rafinesque may have been the first to criticize. In 1804 he wondered why the government did not send botanists with expeditions to the West (Jackson, *Letters*, 218).

persons and places in connection with episodes related. The records fail to reveal in their authors much knowledge of geology, physical geography, botany, zoology, or anthropology. . . .[58]

To these and other critics, Jackson forthrightly replied:

> Jefferson made the right decision in not sending a trained botanist with Lewis and Clark. If a botanist, why not also a zoologist and perhaps a geologist? Later the government could send out such specialists; now the problem was to get a few men to the Pacific and back, encumbered no more than necessary by equipment, and intelligent enough to recognize and collect . . . the natural resources of the region. This distinction has not always been appreciated, even by modern observers."[59]

Parenthetically, another distinction not always appreciated is that *trained* naturalists in those days did not exist—trained, that is, in the sense that they had pursued courses in college or university preparing them for that specialization. The majority of those recognized as "trained naturalists"—men such as Barton, Caspar Wistar, Henry Muhlenberg, and Jefferson—had been formally educated, but as physicians, clergymen, and lawyers. Their preoccupation with fauna and flora had been purely avocational. Others, though professional men, had experienced no academic training in any area. For example, Wilson was a weaver by trade, Nuttall a printer, Rafinesque a merchant, Ord a ship's chandler, and John Bartram a farmer. If any of these enjoyed a biological edge over Lewis, it came not through any formal training, but from added years of experience afield and a greater command of Linnaean nomenclature.

Another continuing wrangle involves Dr. Antoine François Saugrain, a French doctor, chemist, and mineralogist who, after a

[58] *The Great Plains* (New York, Ginn & Co., 1931), 143–44. Like so many other critics, Webb obviously had not read the *Original Journals*.

[59] *Letters*, 218n. Another forthright statement, this one by Herman Friis, adequately refutes Webb's charge regarding geography: "It may be said in fairness that no member of the Lewis and Clark expedition was a professionally trained scientist. . . . However, a reading of the Lewis and Clark journals and an examination of their maps reveal that these men quickly learned the fundamentals of observation and description sufficiently well to give us a remarkably clear view of the geographical landscape as well as a reasonably accurate knowledge of where they were in terms of cartographic presentation." ("Cartographic and Geographic Activities of the Lewis and Clark Expedition," Washington Academy of Sciences *Journal*, Vol. XLIV, No. 11, 1954), 343–44.)

number of voyages to the United States, finally settled in St. Louis. Did he provide Lewis and Clark with thermometers and sulphur matches? One version of the story, by now a familiar one, reads this way:

> [Dr. Saugrain] knew the formula for making sulphur matches; so while all the rest of the world was using flint and steel, Lewis and Clark were able to strike matches far out on the Columbia River! Keeping supplies on hand for experimentation was difficult, but he was resourceful, even scraping the mercury off the back of Madame Saugrain's pier glass (a fine mirror brought from France) in order to finish in time the thermometers and barometers he made for those two great explorers to take when they started on their long and perilous journey through unknown prairies, forests, mountains, and rivers to the Western Sea.[60]

The story, essentially as above, has been repeated and accepted at face value by other writers of today, while one at least disparages the mercury part of it and sanctions the sulphur.[61] To Jackson, however, the legend, in its entirety, is "purely family lore."[62]

A somewhat thornier dispute concerns the time and place of Sacagawea's death. Its beginning seems to coincide with the publication in 1933 by Grace Raymond Hebard of *Sacajawea, a Guide and Interpreter of the Lewis and Clark Expedition.*[63] Herein the author produced evidence, incontrovertible to her, that the Shoshoni girl lived to an advanced age and died late in the nineteenth century in the Wind River country of Wyoming.

Unavailable to Mrs. Hebard in 1933 were two bits of information, published later, that throw doubt on her claim. One is a statement written December 20, 1812, by a trader, John Luttig, who at that time was ascending the Missouri. The statement reads, "This evening the wife of Charbonneau a Snake Squaw, died of putrid fever ... aged abt 25 years."[64] The other is a document, actually Clark's

---

[60] William Clark Kennerly, *Persimmon Hill, a Narrative of Old St. Louis and the Far West* (Norman, University of Oklahoma Press, 1948), 141.

[61] Dillon, *Meriwether Lewis*, 41.

[62] Jackson, "A New Lewis and Clark Map," *loc. cit.*, 120n. See also Jackson, *Letters*, 70, 75n.

[63] Glendale, California, The Arthur H. Clark Co.

[64] John C. Luttig, *Journal of a Fur-trading Expedition on the Upper Missouri, 1812–13*, ed. by Stella M. Drum (New York, Argosy-Antiquarian, Ltd., 1964), 106.

cash book and journal for 1825–28. On the front page of this Clark listed the names of the members of the Expedition, and then provided, in terse statements of just two or three words, the latest information he had on each. He reported, for instance, "R. Frazier on Gasconade," "G. Shannon Lexington Ky.," and, most importantly to this discussion, "Se car ja we au Dead."[65] Indicating the direction of Jackson's thinking—as a result of Clark's datum—he wrote, "It is difficult to believe that he could have been wrong about Sacagawea's death."[66]

In Lewis and Clark literature no misstatement occurs more often than Sacagawea guided the explorers unerringly to the Pacific and back. One writer, completely carried away, has insisted that she "piloted them with the sureness of a homing pigeon."[67] Not even at Three Forks, where Sacagawea was on familiar ground, did she direct them. From information obtained earlier from the Hidatsas at Fort Mandan, Lewis and Clark knew that they should take the more westerly of the three streams uniting here, namely, the Jefferson, rather than the Madison or Gallatin. Annotatively, Jackson said, "Of Sacagawea's valor and stolid determination there can be no doubt, but her contribution to the expedition is often magnified by her biographers. For a detached appraisal of her usefulness as a guide to Lewis and Clark, see KINGSTON."[68] This writer, almost in the first sentence, sums up Jackson's position, and that of all other historians thoroughly conversant with the text of the *Original Journals*. Sacagawea, he wrote, "did nothing to determine the course or direction of the expedition on the way to the Pacific or (with one exception) on the return trip."[69]

Of course, as we know well, no controversy about the Expedition has so beguiled readers of Lewis and Clark, and created such sharp divergences of opinion, as the cause of Lewis' death. Did he fall victim to the bullets of a felon intent on robbing him, or did he commit suicide? Such authorities as Elliott Coues, Olin D. Wheeler, and

[65] Jackson, *Letters*, 638.

[66] *Ibid.*, 639n.

[67] Howard R. Driggs, *The Old West Speaks* (New York, Bonanza Books, 1956), 27.

[68] Jackson, *Letters*, 317n.

[69] C. S. Kingston, "Sacajawea as a Guide, the Evaluation of a Legend," *Pacific Northwest Quarterly*, Vol. XXXV (January, 1944), 3.

Richard Dillon have leaned toward the former explanation; Thomas Jefferson, Ernest S. Osgood, Dawson Phelps,[70] and Donald Jackson toward the latter. Jackson put himself on record when he asserted, "I am inclined to believe that he died by his own hand."[71] In taking this stand he was measurably influenced by his discovery of Major Gilbert Russell's statements. To this writer, perfectly visible guiding threads lead directly to suicide as the answer.

—8—

We have stressed only a few highlights of Jackson's editorial competence as revealed by his *Letters of the Lewis and Clark Expedition*. Immediately following its publication, reviewers emphasized others. Joseph Ewan, professor of biology, Tulane University, and author of works on such early naturalists in America as John Banister and William Bartram, declared, "Jackson's book is in no way simply another edition of the journals but, in the best sense, a long detailed commentary on them. Those readers who browse contentedly in footnotes and, as Peattie remarked, do not consider them interruptions on the bridal night, will find the letters a fascination."[72] John C. Ewers, Smithsonian historian and ethnologist, and author of such books as *Artists of the Old West* and *The Blackfeet: Raiders on the Northwestern Plains*, wrote:

> Donald Jackson has performed a great service to scholars in ferreting out these scattered documents and publishing them within the covers of a single volume. His judicious and scholarly annotations greatly aid the reviewer in evaluating the documents. . . . For future students of American exploration and for students of the Indians of the Upper Missouri and the Northwest, this book will be a standard reference.[73]

And A. P. Nasatir, author of *Before Lewis and Clark*, observed, "[The documents] place the expedition in full context . . . original

[70] Dawson A. Phelps, "The Tragic Death of Meriwether Lewis," *William and Mary Quarterly*, Vol. XIII, Ser. 3 (July, 1956), 305–18.
[71] Jackson, *Letters*, 575n.
[72] Ewan, "Book Reviews: Scientific Americana," *Science*, Vol. CXXXIX (February 8, 1963), 478.
[73] *American Anthropologist*, Vol. LXV, 489 (April, 1963).

sources are always the best, and this volume has the compelling interest of actuality."[74]

Recognition more distinguished followed. In 1965 Jackson received the Western Heritage Award and became the first recipient of the Missouri Historical Society Award, and in 1966 the American Association for State and Local History honored him with its Award of Merit.

—9—

In 1968 Jackson resigned his post with the University of Illinois Press to become editor of *The Papers of George Washington*, a project being started at the University of Virginia, Charlottesville. A statement he made soon afterward leaves the impression that he had moments of uncertainty as to its wisdom: "How a western historian ever got himself into this situation I don't know; but I start work this fall and am already inundated with Washingtoniana."[75]

Before Jackson left Urbana for Charlottesville, he had completed or had in progress other works unmentioned so far in this chapter. He had published *Custer's Gold: the U.S. Cavalry Expedition of 1874* and had completed the difficult task of editing *The Journals of Zebulon Montgomery Pike* (2 vols.).[76] Also, he had made substantial headway with an even more difficult literary venture, that of editing, with Mary L. Spence, *The Expeditions of John Charles Frémont* (3 vols.),[77] and had become involved—at his own request —in yet another Lewis and Clark project (see Appendix A).

In his recently published book, *The Fatal Impact*, Alan Moorehead had this to say about Captain James Cook:

> He has a practical workmanlike style [of writing] . . . is interested in everything . . . is simply concerned to cover all the facts and to get them right, and when occasionally he does speculate about his discoveries he always prefaces his remarks by saying that he may be

[74] *American History Review*, Vol. LXVIII, 148 (October, 1962).

[75] Donald Jackson to author in letter of June 3, 1968.

[76] New Haven, Yale University Press, 1966; Norman, University of Oklahoma Press, 1966.

[77] Urbana, University of Illinois Press, 1970.

wrong. But he is not often wrong, nor does much escape the dragnet of that steady commonsense.[78]

With equal justice, these same words may be applied to Donald Jackson—and, come to think of it, to two other notable reporters of the passing scene, namely, Meriwether Lewis and William Clark.

[78] New York, Harper & Row, 1966, 9.

CHAPTER XI

What the Mountain Brought Forth

Lewis and Clark literature falls conveniently into two categories, one consisting of the books, letters, and other documents *written by* Lewis and Clark, and the other made up of like material *written about* Lewis and Clark. In preceding chapters, we have, for obvious reasons, restricted content largely to literature of the first category. It seems advisable that we now give consideration to the large mass of manuscript material in the second division, namely, that which has been *written about* the two leaders of the Expedition. This consists of many items, with each owing its existence, in part at least, to the industry of one or more of the men given prominence in earlier chapters, primarily Jefferson, M'Keehan, Biddle, Coues, Thwaites, Quaife, Jackson, and Osgood. The great majority of the items, however, owe their existence to the *Original Journals* compiled and edited by Thwaites, for this multivolumed work contains practically every word written by the two captains during their transit of the North American continent.

The immediate and long-range effects of the *Original Journals* on scholarship, once they had been published, exceeded by far anything anticipated by Thwaites or anyone else. They proved to be a mountain, but unlike the one in fable that labored and brought forth only a mouse, this one has already produced progeny in the hundreds, and shows no signs of diminishing fecundity. Such a quantity testifies eloquently to the inherent worth of the *Journals* as a nearly inexhaustible source of information heretofore denied the historian. Also worthy of remark is the fact that the number of significant items *written about* Lewis and Clark prior to the appearance of the *Journals* may be counted on the fingers of the two hands.[1]

—2—

A completely new era in the annals of Lewis and Clark literature had its inception with the publication of the *Original Journals* in 1904–05, an era with greatly extended dimensions. Scholars, having in hand for the first time this comprehensive work so replete with heretofore unpublished data, at once began plumbing its depths. Some explored its geography and cartography, others its botany and zoology. Still others appraised the talents of the two leaders as ethnologists, as keen observers of the geopolitical scene, and as experts in Indian diplomacy. A few examined the medical aspects of the Expedition. Whatever the phase attracting the scholar, he found the *Original Journals* to be a rewarding reservoir of salient facts, a storehouse far exceeding the combined riches of Gass, Biddle, and Coues. As a consequence, from 1905 until the present, historians have witnessed not only an accelerated interest in Lewis and Clark, but also a near phenomenal increase in the quantity—and quality—of published material about the Expedition.

Of course, we must not lose sight of the publication since 1905 of *The Journals of Captain Meriwether Lewis and Sergeant John Ordway* (1916), edited by Quaife; *Letters of the Lewis and Clark Expedition with Related Documents, 1783–1854* (1962), compiled and

---

[1] Among the more important were Jefferson's 1806 *Message* and his "Memoir of Meriwether Lewis" published in the 1814 edition of Biddle; Jacob's life of Gass (1859); Coues's 1876 bibliographical-zoological article, "An Account of the Various Publications Relating to the Travels of Lewis and Clarke, with a Commentary on the Zoological Results of the Expedition," United States Geological and Geographical Survey of the Territories *Bulletin*, No. 6, Ser. 2 (February 8, 1876); Nellie F. Kingsley's *The Story of Captain Meriwether Lewis and Captain William Clark* (1900); Noah Brooks's *First Across the Continent* (1901); William R. Lighton's *Lewis and Clark: Meriwether Lewis and William Clark* (1901); Eva Emery Dye's *The Conquest: The True Story of Lewis and Clark* (1902); Thwaites's *A Brief History of Rocky Mountain Exploration, with Especial Reference to the Expedition of Lewis and Clark* (1904); and Wheeler's *The Trail of Lewis and Clark, 1804–1806* (1904).

edited by Donald Jackson, and *The Field Notes of Captain William Clark, 1803–1805* (1964), transcribed and edited by Ernest Osgood. Each of these, by contributing additional unpublished material, has functioned as a high-intensity, intellectual wallop to increase further the general interest in the Expedition.

In ensuing pages, we undertake the task of bringing a semblance of order to the books and articles *written about* Lewis and Clark since the *Original Journals* came from the press and, at the same time, of interjecting commentary that will in some measure serve the purpose of winnowing the chaff from the grain. It is a formidable task, primarily because of the sheer bulk of the material. Titles known to us exceed two hundred,[2] and that number would be considerably larger if we had capitulated to the law of diminishing returns by attempting to find each and every title listed in all periodical guides. Even though our list is admittedly incomplete, we believe it includes those items of most importance, for significant literature, like rich cream, tends to surface, and thus to expose itself.

Before going further, we should like to provide figures which support an earlier stated claim, namely, that publication of Lewis and Clark material has markedly increased during recent years. Of the more than two hundred titles, approximately 60 per cent came from the press during the fifty-seven-year-long period preceding the publication of Jackson's *Letters*, that is, from 1905 through 1961, and 40 per cent in the much shorter period since. But, more to the point, titles per annum during the earlier span averaged just 2.3, while those of the latter averaged 7.2. Thus since 1962 the output of books and magazine articles per annum has more than tripled. Someone has insisted that statistics are like alienists; they will testify for either side. But hardly so in this instance. They clearly demonstrate the late upsurge of interest in Lewis and Clark.

Can we denominate the primary factors responsible for triggering this increase? As we view them, three stand uppermost: (1) the discovery in 1953 of Clark's "Field Notes" and the extensive news coverage which followed; (2) the celebration in 1956 of the sesquicentennial of the Expedition; and (3) the publication in 1962 of Jackson's *Letters*. Of the three—again in our opinion—the last-mentioned has exerted the greatest influence.

2 For complete listing, see Bibliography.

—3—

Literature written about Lewis and Clark falls logically into four main groups: (1) adult nonfictional books, (2) adult fiction, (3) juvenile accounts, and (4) periodical literature. We will now take a look at each—and in the order given.

Adult Nonfictional Books

Today, more so than ever before, the appearance of a new book about Lewis and Clark is something of an "occasion," and, if it measures up to anticipations substantively, it will be eagerly read by numerous enthusiasts, whether they be run-of-the-mill amateurs or scholarly professionals.

Since 1904–05, when the minds of Lewis and Clark students were first quickened by the largess of heretofore unpublished data provided by the *Original Journals*, more than three dozen adult nonfictional books about the Expedition have come from the press. Of these, about one third are retellings of the story; another third, biographies of members of the party; and the remaining third, thematic studies—on such topics as natural history, linguistics, and the present state of the Lewis and Clark route as seen through the lens of a camera.

As to the retellings, they of course vary greatly in quality. A few have no valid reason for being, since they contribute nothing new, lack documentation, bibliography, indexes, and other evidences of scholarship, and, moreover, suffer from errors. Happily, that is true of only an occasional one. A number of today's students of the Expedition, like this writer, may owe their initial glow of enthusiasm for our national epic of exploration to John Bakeless' *Lewis and Clark: Partners in Discovery*. Published in 1947, it is still the most popular retelling of the historic journey and appears regularly on "further reading" lists, even though Bakeless would have it that it is "a biography of the two explorers, not merely the story of their exploration."[3]

That Bakeless' book has thus far withstood tests of time has been due to a number of factors. It is sound factually, well researched,

[3] Bakeless, *Lewis and Clark*, vii.

and consequently includes much useful heretofore unpublished information. Furthermore, Bakeless has few peers when it comes to presenting history accurately and palatably. It would seem that *Lewis and Clark: Partners in Discovery* will be read for a long time to come. We may add a fact not generally known, that this book was the first to carry Clark's now much-quoted words purportedly uttered by him immediately after learning of Lewis' death: "I fear O! I fear the weight of his mind has overcome him."[4]

A recent retelling, *In the Footsteps of Lewis and Clark* by Gerald S. Snyder, cuts an entirely different kind of furrow. Published in 1970, it is the story as told by Snyder, of the National Geographic Society, of travel by automobile, horse, and boat along the historic route from the Mississippi to the Pacific. In a foreword by Donald Jackson we read, "The narrative that Gerald S. Snyder has written, based on research and a personal retracing of the route with his family, is a fine combination of techniques."[5] These techniques, as we learn by reading the book, unite an interesting narrative style with numerous illustrations: black and white drawings; reproductions in full color of paintings by such foremost artists as Charles Willson Peale, Bodmer, Catlin, and Russell; and photographs, also in color. The result is a volume delighting the eye and other senses, the sort of publication that we have come to expect of the National Geographic Society. However, such shortcomings as lack of documentation and a failure to increase existing knowledge may well reduce its life expectancy.

Since 1905 several biographies (other than juvenile) have been published about various members of the Expedition. Known to us at this writing are two of Lewis, two of Sacagawea, three of John Colter, one of George Drouillard, and one (incomplete and unpublished) of Clark.

Charles Morrow Wilson, in 1934, wrote the first of the biographies about Lewis.[6] Today's students will likely ignore this in favor of Richard Dillon's, published in 1965, since the latter contains much information about Lewis' life not found in the other, and the text is more readable and generally free of flagrant error.[7] How-

4 *Ibid.,* 429.
5 Snyder, *In the Footsteps of Lewis and Clark,* 5.
6 *Meriwether Lewis of Lewis and Clark.*
7 *Meriwether Lewis: a Biography.*

ever, reviewers have wished that Dillon had provided more documentation, and that he had given more attention to events of the return journey (condensed by him into the space of just thirty-nine pages). Many readers will, of course, disagree with his verdict that Lewis did not take his own life, but was murdered instead.[8]

Grace Raymond Hebard (1933) and Harold P. Howard (1972) have contributed the biographies of Sacagawea.[9] Mrs. Hebard's *Sacajawea, a Guide and Interpreter of the Lewis and Clark Expedition* has attracted more attention, due in part at least to the author's questionable conviction expressed therein that Sacagawea lived to an advanced age and died in the Wind River country of Wyoming. Testifying to the popularity of this book, it was reissued in 1967. Since several fictional and juvenile biographies of Sacagawea have been published, as well as many magazine articles, I will postpone comment on the written matter about her until later.

Following the return of the Expedition, no member of the party lived a life so full of discovery and dramatic adventure as John Colter. The high point, of course, was his discovery of that region of geysers, mud pots, and waterfalls known today as Yellowstone National Park. This explains why three authors, Stallo Vinton, Ethel Hueston, and Burton Harris, have written full-length biographies about Colter.[10] Readers may take their pick, but should bear in mind that each of these biographies is of more value to historians of Yellowstone than to those of Lewis and Clark.

In their respective journals, Lewis and Clark made it abundantly clear that George Drouillard, interpreter and hunter, was of more worth to them than any other man of the party. By reading their words, and between lines, we must conclude that he was an extraordinary individual. Students of the Expedition, therefore, have been eager to know more about his life in years before and after his service with Lewis and Clark and, on learning that a biography of him by M. O. Skarsten was in the offing, looked forward to its appearance with keen anticipation. However, when published, it disap-

[8] For more about Lewis' life, students will want, of course, to consult Bakeless' *Lewis and Clark.*

[9] Dye's *The Conquest* was a biography of Sacagawea. Published in 1902, it was the first about this Shoshoni Indian girl.

[10] Vinton, *John Colter, Discoverer of Yellowstone* (1926); Hueston, *The Man of the Storm* (1936); Harris, *John Colter, His Years in the Rockies* (1952).

pointed, since it was largely another retelling of the "big traverse."[11] Skarsten himself must have suffered chagrin that he had been unable to add appreciably to what was already known about Drouillard.

In some respects the most valuable biographical study to date about any member of the Corps of Discovery is John Louis Loos's "A Biography of William Clark, 1770–1813," which is an unpublished (though available) Ph.D. dissertation presented in 1953 by Loos to satisfy graduation requirements at Washington University, St. Louis. As seen from the title, this study, by describing events of Clark's life only through 1813, fell short of completion by twenty-five years, since Clark did not die until 1838. From time to time I have heard reports that Loos was hard at work completing his biography. That it has yet to come from the press is a matter of regret. His dissertation, incomplete though it is, affords abundant evidence of sound scholarship in his successful unearthing of hitherto unknown facts about Clark's earlier years, especially those which saw him fighting Indians in the Ohio wilderness in company with Lewis. Historians of the Expedition cannot well ignore this study.

As earlier indicated, other books attack a variety of topics. For instance, Vardis Fisher's *Suicide or Murder? The Strange Death of Governor Meriwether Lewis* (1962) presents a crowded mass of facts, hearsay, and improbabilities all tied together in one package calculated to prove that Lewis was struck down, on that tragic night at Grinder's Inn, by bullets from an assassin. Those who lean to that viewpoint will give it credence.

A monograph of unique design and function is Elijah H. Criswell's *Lewis and Clark: Linguistic Pioneers* (1940). Singularly enough, this work, in spite of its close adherence to linguistics, is valuable—at least it has been to this writer—as a source of much natural history data. For example, it contains a lengthy "zoological index" and a similar botanical one, both of which supply technical and vernacular names of the animals and plants encountered by Lewis and Clark. In another list useful to us, Criswell brought together the botanical terms, close to two hundred, that Lewis had employed in describing western plants. In our opinion, Criswell's monograph deserves inclusion on any list of the ten or twelve most valuable books yet published about Lewis and Clark.

[11] Skarsten, *George Drouillard, Hunter and Interpreter for Lewis and Clark and Fur Trader* (1964).

Raymond Darwin Burroughs' *The Natural History of the Lewis and Clark Expedition* (1961) was the first study to appear whose text was limited exclusively to the biology of the Expedition. This volume (which might more properly have been titled *The Zoology of the Lewis and Clark Expedition*, since it includes nothing botanical) is the product of Burroughs' industry in extracting from the *Original Journals* the exact words Lewis and Clark (and occasionally Ordway, Gass, and Whitehouse) used in describing mammals, birds, reptiles, amphibians, and fishes. Though today's student may feel indebted to Burroughs for bringing together in one place practically everything that Lewis and the other journalists recorded about grizzly bear, western tanager, prairie rattler, or any one of scores of other vertebrate animals, he should actually admit an even greater measure of gratitude for Burroughs' personal observations and for those he culled from such early nineteenth-century naturalists as Maximilian, John Bradbury, Alexander Wilson, Constantine Rafinesque, John Townsend, and George Ord. Some reviewers have expressed regret that Burroughs did not extend his work to include, for example, a listing of animals discovered by Lewis and Clark, or commentary on the fate of animal specimens they brought back with them.

The only other work published to date which deals exclusively with biological aspects of the Expedition is Cutright's *Lewis and Clark: Pioneering Naturalists* (1969). His reasons for writing it? Biddle had excluded from his paraphrase practically all technical matter about plants and animals. Only a few persons have read the entire text of the *Original Journals*, which contain that technical matter. Most Americans continue to think of Lewis and Clark only as courageous explorers, skilled woodsmen, and exemplary military leaders. That being so, Cutright's primary aim was to produce evidence—from the journals of the men themselves—that Lewis and Clark (Lewis in particular) were naturalists of outstanding competence.

Remaining thematic studies include Albert and Jane Salisbury's *Two Captains West* (1950) and Ingvar Henry Eide's *American Odyssey* (1969). Evaluations of these works, both largely photographic, will best be postponed until a following chapter, which takes a look at illustrations and illustrators of Lewis and Clark literature.

In concluding this section about adult nonfictional books, we should call attention to a number of other volumes devoting only portions of their text, perhaps no more than a chapter, to Lewis and Clark. These works often include information of much value. Two that come to mind at once are Carl I. Wheat's *Mapping the Trans-mississippi West* and Susan Delano McKelvey's *Botanical Exploration of the Trans-Mississippi West*.

Adult Fiction

Generally speaking, historians look down their noses at historical novels. They deplore contrived dialogue and, even more so, highly dramatized versions of events which suffer much too often from hyperbole, distortion, and plain unmitigated untruth. Fictional accounts of the Lewis and Clark Expedition published to date have tended to reinforce the historians' stance, for they contain in good measure all the ill-considered ingredients mentioned above. In one of them, for instance, the author (Vardis Fisher) utilizes sixty pages, or one seventh of his entire text, in storifying the meeting of Lewis and Clark with the Teton Sioux which occurred in late September, 1804, near present-day Pierre, South Dakota. And, in so doing, he provides his readers with an amazing assortment of exaggerated, lurid, and specious detail which, if true, would entitle Clark (whose account ran to just eight pages) to go down in history as one of the world's worst reporters and to be adjudged guilty of a cardinal reportorial crime, namely, that of suppressing highlights of a feature story.[12]

Three or four other writers have published adult historical novels about the Expedition, two of whom at least have made themselves quite well known to American readers: Emerson Hough[13] and Donald Culross Peattie.[14] Hough wrote *The Magnificent Adventure* (1916), which centers attention on a particularly amorous affair

[12] Vardis Fisher, *Tale of Valor: a Novel of the Lewis and Clark Expedition* (1958).

[13] Emerson Hough (1857–1923) was born in Newton, Iowa, and wrote such widely read books as *The Story of the Cowboy*, *54-40 or Fight*, and *The Covered Wagon*.

[14] Donald Culross Peattie (1898–1964), author and naturalist, was born in Chicago and graduated from Harvard (1922). Among his best-known books are *Almanac for Moderns*, *Singing in the Wilderness*, and *Green Laurels*.

(fictional) between Lewis and Theodosia Burr Alston, married daughter of Aaron Burr. Peattie produced *Forward the Nation* (1942), the best of the lot in this writer's opinion, for he displays throughout an educated reverence for and knowledge of nature that strikes us most agreeably, and adheres closer to truth than either Fisher or Hough.[15]

Juvenile Accounts

Books for boys and girls about the Expedition—if textual details have been verified and objectively reported—have a genuine reason for being. Among world explorers, Lewis and Clark stand tall and emancipated, like Everest and Aconcagua among mountain pinnacles, and their exploits and achievements should be indelibly engraved on the minds of young Americans.

More than a score of juvenile accounts about this national epic have been published, about one half of them retellings and the remainder biographies—of Lewis, Clark, Sacagawea, and Shannon, and even one about Lewis' Newfoundland dog.

One of the newer volumes to come from the press is Ralph K. Andrist's *To the Pacific with Lewis and Clark* (1967). Another retelling, this contains just about all the elements sufficient to pique the imaginative mind of most any boy or girl: interesting narrative style, abundant action and excitement, and numerous illustrations, half or more in full color. Furthermore, Andrist sticks to facts as reported in the *Original Journals*. He thereby not only avoids over-dramatizing events, such as those in the life of Sacagawea, but also, through his perceptive treatment of facts, provides reason for hope that more and more writers about the Expedition are gradually coming of age in their objectivity.

---

[15] It is regarded today as something of a status symbol when a hardback later appears in paperback. In that department, Lewis and Clark have fared well. Among the works that have, at one time or another, been published in paperback are Peattie's *Forward the Nation* (Armed Services edition); Bakeless' *Lewis and Clark: Partners in Discovery* (Apollo); Fisher's *Tale of Valor* (Pocket Books); Coues (ed.), *History of the Expedition Under the Command of Lewis and Clark* (Dover); DeVoto's *The Journals of Lewis and Clark*, an abridged edition of the *Original Journals* (Sentry); and Bakeless' similar edition of the same work (Mentor).

Periodical Literature

Since publication of the *Original Journals*, almost two hundred articles about Lewis and Clark have appeared in popular magazine or learned journal. To simplify consideration of such a large number, I have divided them into six groups as follows: medical, botanical, zoological, ethnological, geographic-cartographic, and miscellaneous. It is right and proper that five of my divisions are technical, for the preponderance of articles measurably extending knowledge of the Expedition have been scientific in character and content.

Medical—I have knowledge of seven articles dealing exclusively with medical aspects of the Expedition. Their authors, in alphabetical order, are J. Howard Beard, E. G. Chuinard, Paul R. Cutright, Olof Larsell, Doane Robinson, L. L. Stanley, and Drake W. Will.[16] Future medical historians interested in Lewis and Clark will doubtless wish to examine all of these papers. Most of them begin by taking notice of the drugs Lewis obtained in Philadelphia to take with him, these including such commonly used remedies of the day as Peruvian bark [source of quinine], Rush's Pills, saltpeter, and Glauber's Salts.[17] The articles generally include, too, "Rules of Health," which was a set of remarkable instructions that Dr. Benjamin Rush, foremost physician of the time, compiled for Lewis' benefit. One of the more remarkable reads, "Molasses or sugar & water with a few drops of the acid of vitriol [sulphuric acid] will make a pleasant & wholesome drink with your meals."[18]

Most of the space in these medical articles is, as would be expected, given over to Lewis' methods of treating the several disorders, wounds, and infections that periodically afflicted his men during the course of the journey—everything from snake bite, heat stroke, and bullet wound to abscesses, dysentery, and the "pox" [*i.e.*, the great pox, or syphilis].

Now and then Jefferson has been criticized for not sending a trained physician with the Expedition. I am already on record as

---

[16] See Bibliography for titles and bibliographical detail about articles referred to in remainder of chapter.

[17] Lewis spent a total of $90.69 for drugs, lancets, forceps, syringes, and other medical supplies (Jackson, *Letters*, 80–81).

[18] *Ibid.*, 54–55.

contending that Jefferson made no mistake in entrusting the health of the party to Lewis.[19] Considering the primitive state of medicine in the world at that time, who can conscientiously insist that a licensed practitioner could have done a better job of purging, sweating, and blood-letting—the treatments then most commonly in vogue—than Lewis did?

Botanical—Articles written about the plants Lewis and Clark encountered west of the Mississippi number about one dozen. One of the earliest to appear was "Some Neglected Botanical Results of the Lewis and Clark Expedition" by Rodney H. True of the Academy of Natural Sciences of Philadelphia. Therein True discusses successes of Philadelphia gardeners William Hamilton and Bernard McMahon in raising seeds and roots entrusted to them by Lewis on his return from the West and long-range results of this initial attempt to introduce trans-Mississippi plants into the East.

Later botanists such as Joseph Ewan, Velva E. Rudd, Paul R. Cutright, Raymond D. Burroughs, and R. G. Beidleman have centered their attention particularly on the Lewis and Clark Herbarium, namely, the collection of pressed plants brought back by Lewis which is today a most valuable holding of the Academy of Natural Sciences of Philadelphia. Ewan, for example, disclosed the role, hitherto unknown, of botanist Edward Tuckerman in returning to the United States plant specimens collected by Lewis that Pursh had covertly taken to London. Rudd described the herbarium as she found it in 1954 and quoted from Lewis' journal to prove that Lewis provided an excellent running commentary on western plants as he encountered them and, also, a commendable account of agriculture as practiced by the Arikara and Mandan Indians. Cutright reported on the size (216 specimen sheets) and condition of the herbarium in 1966. Additionally, he emphasized Lewis' unusual observational powers, his knowledge of botanical terms, his accurate and detailed descriptions of a surprisingly large number of plants, and his overall competence as a botanist.

Zoological—Once Lewis and Clark reached the High Plains, they encountered an abundance of animals of different species such as

---

[19] Cutright, "I gave him barks and saltpeter," *American Heritage*, Vol. XV, No. 1 (December, 1963), 101.

they had never before seen or imagined to exist, and several of the species were entirely new to them and the scientific world—the coyote, prairie dog, mule deer, and pronghorn antelope, to name just a few. We think it singular, therefore, that such a small number of articles have been written about the zoology of the Expedition (only seven to our knowledge). One of the first, "Relics of Peale's Museum," was written by Walter Faxon, Harvard zoologist who, incidentally, once numbered Theodore Roosevelt among his students. In this paper, Faxon listed birds in Harvard's Museum of Comparative Zoology that once occupied space in Peale's Museum, and one of these was a Lewis' woodpecker. The likelihood is good that this woodpecker was one collected by Lewis on May 27, 1806, while the party was encamped on the Clearwater River, Idaho. If so, then Lewis undoubtedly brought it back with him to Philadelphia, where both Peale and Alexander Wilson painted it. Also, to our knowledge, it is the only animal still surviving of all those returned by Lewis and Clark.[20]

A second article, by Russell Reid and Clell C. Gannon, relates to those birds and mammals that Lewis and Clark observed in North Dakota. The authors copied the several passages in the *Original Journals* pertaining to these animals and, more importantly, attempted identification of each species.

"The Odyssey of the Magpie and the Prairie Dog" by Cutright and "A Prairie Dog for Mr. Jefferson" by Osgood recount Lewis' incredible success in shipping live animals from Fort Mandan to Washington by way of St. Louis, New Orleans, and Baltimore, a distance in excess of four thousand miles. "Meriwether Lewis: Zoologist," also by Cutright, characterizes Lewis as an outstanding observer and reporter of western fauna; the author backs up his claim with numerous quotations from Lewis' own writings.

Still another article, "Zoological Contributions of the Lewis and

[20] Witmer Stone, former curator of birds at the Academy of Natural Sciences of Philadelphia, is on record as saying that this specimen is "without much doubt the original specimen [collected by Lewis]." (See Maynard-Stone correspondence, Manuscript Collection, No. 450, Library of Academy of Natural Sciences.) The only other existing Lewis and Clark zoological material I have been able to locate are elk and moose antlers at Monticello and a single mountain goat horn in the Filson Club, Louisville, Kentucky.

Clark Expedition," is by Henry W. Setzer, Smithsonian zoologist. Setzer, we believe, had no familiarity with the *Original Journals* (he cited only Coues and Faxon). Otherwise, would he have disparagingly characterized Lewis and Clark as "engineers," and belittled their zoological contributions by saying that they were "remarkably slight"?

Ethnological—Here again we find a surprising poverty of articles, considering the deluge of words Lewis and Clark penned about Sioux, Arikaras, Mandans, Hidatsas, Shoshonis, Nez Percés, Chinooks, and many other Indians. Each, however, merits attention. In 1905 Charles C. Willoughby published "A Few Ethnological Specimens Collected by Lewis and Clark." This named and described Indian artifacts that the two captains had presented to Peale's Museum but that later, through twists of good fortune, were acquired by the Peabody Museum of Archaeology and Ethnology at Harvard University, where they may be seen today. Among them are a buffalo robe decorated with quill work, an elk antler bow, a Sioux raven bustle, and a Chinook fiber shirt.

In ensuing years Lewis and Clark students were exposed to other ethnologically oriented papers, such as "Arikara Glassworking" by Matthew W. Stirling, "Plains Indians Reactions to Lewis and Clark" by John C. Ewers, "Lower Chinook Ethnographic Notes" by Verne F. Ray, and "The Contributions of Lewis and Clark to Ethnography" by Verne F. Ray and Nancy O. Lurie. The last-mentioned, in this writer's opinion, deserves particular note. The authors initially stress their conviction that Lewis and Clark were "unappreciated forerunners in a tradition of field research that led to the recognition of the superiority of American field work and the establishment of a sound science of ethnology," and go on from there to bolster this viewpoint with an abundance of evidence taken directly from the *Original Journals*.

Geographic-Cartographic—A dozen or more articles have been published relative to maps and topographic matters of the Expedition. Some have announced the discovery of previously unknown maps. Others have reported on the route as it is today, some one hundred and seventy years later. Still others have described their successes in determining locations of heretofore unknown camp sites. And at least one individual has made a thorough appraisal of Lewis and Clark's contributions to geography and cartography of the West.

Annie Heloise Abel and Donald Jackson have written papers announcing "new" Lewis and Clark maps. Roy E. Appleman has published "Lewis and Clark: the Route 160 Years After." Helen B. West, in "Meriwether Lewis in Blackfeet Country," has reported on the brilliant aerial-ground reconnaissance which resulted in the discovery of the site on Two Medicine River, Montana, where Lewis and party, on the morning of July 27, 1806, contended with Piegan Blackfeet who attempted to steal their horses. This incident, which resulted in the deaths of two of the Indians, was possibly the most dramatic of the entire journey.

Ralph S. Space, Elers Koch, and John J. Peebles, in other papers, have reported on their studies to clarify the exact routes taken by Lewis and Clark through the Bitterroot Mountains and to determine camp sites along the Lolo Trail. Herman R. Friis's "Cartographic and Geographic Activities of the Lewis and Clark Expedition" may be held up as a prize example of objective reporting based on sound, comprehensive research. The content falls logically into three major parts: (1) Jefferson's broad knowledge of maps, geography, and navigational instruments and his imparting of that knowledge to Lewis; (2) Lewis and Clark's industry throughout the journey in making astronomic observations at all strategic points and their attempts, beyond Fort Mandan, to reconcile their own topographic observations with the geography as laid down on charts of Mackenzie and other contemporary map makers; and (3) specific contributions of Lewis and Clark to geography and map making, including their unqualified success in accomplishing the basic goal of exploring and surveying a route from the Mississippi to the Pacific, recognizing and describing for the first time "broad general physiographic regions through which the party passed," and transferring abundant topographic data to maps, such as Clark's large, final one, which was "a major contribution to the geographic knowledge of Western North America."

Miscellaneous—I note that my Bibliography includes approximately one hundred and twenty-five titles under this heading. Such a mass of literature deals, of course, with a wide spectrum of subjects, these ranging from books, guns, Indian peace medals, and biographical sketches (a dozen about Sacagawea alone) to retracings of the route and financial accounts. Of those familiar to me—probably no one has read all, or needs to—I have found the following to be particularly useful:

Bakeless, John, "Lewis and Clark's Background for Exploration."

Cappon, Lester J., "Who Is the Author of *History of the Expedition Under the Command of Captains Lewis and Clark (1814)*?"

Chatters, Roy Milton, "The Enigmatic Lewis and Clark Expedition Air Gun."

Craig, Vernon, "Ride the Wide Missouri Historic Waterway."

Duboc, Jessie L., "Yellowstone Adventure."

Jackson, Donald, "On Reading Lewis and Clark: a Bibliography."

———, "The Public Image of Lewis and Clark."

———, "The Race to Publish Lewis and Clark."

———, "Some Advice for the Next Editor of Lewis and Clark."

———, "Some Books Carried by Lewis and Clark."

Kingston, C. S., "Sacajawea as a Guide, the Evaluation of a Legend."

Osgood, E. S., "The Return Journey in 1806: William Clark on the Yellowstone."

Phelps, Dawson A., "The Tragic Death of Meriwether Lewis."

Quaife, Milo M., "Some New-found Records of the Lewis and Clark Expedition."

Thwaites, Reuben Gold, "The Story of Lewis and Clark's Journals."

Tomkins, Calvin, "The Lewis and Clark Case."

West, Helen B., "The Lewis and Clark Expedition: Our National Epic."

Yates, Ted, "Since Lewis and Clark."

Obviously, no two historians would agree on the composition of a list such as the above. Some, if interested in weapons, would doubtless wish to include Ruby Hult's article, "Guns of the Lewis and Clark Expedition," and others, with different bents, might want to include one or two of Cutright's papers, such as "Lewis and Clark: Portraits and Portraitists" and/or "The Journal of Private Joseph Whitehouse."

Donald Jackson has advised Lewis and Clark enthusiasts, "Read everything you can lay your hands on [about the Expedition]. It cannot be dull, and much of it will be rewarding."[21] In general we agree, if for no other reason than to separate the chaff from the grain—or for the dubious satisfaction of pleasing the ego through discovering mistakes. But Jackson did not say, or imply, that *each and every* book or article about the Expedition would reward the reader. Some are utterly unrewarding. With these we have no real concern, for every sizable body of literature, whatever the subject, has its share of trumpery.

We are deeply concerned, however, with the literature responsible for perpetuating errors. Needless to say, a mistake once committed to print may be repeated, and if it is repeated often enough may become fixed in the minds of readers as established fact. In Lewis and Clark literature there are more than a few such examples of reiterated untruth or distorted fact. Whenever opportunity arises, historians of the Expedition equipped to speak authoritatively should expose and correct them. A few most vexatious to this writer follow forthwith:

1. That Private Joseph Field, on July 4, 1804, was bitten by a rattlesnake. Clark's entry for that date stated simply, "Jos. Fields got bit by a Snake, which was quickly doctered with [Peruvian] Bark by Cap Lewis."[22] The other journalists used even fewer words to describe the incident, thereby evidencing their unconcern, and not one of them even intimated that the snake was venomous. They knew rattlers as well as bears and bobcats, and if Fields had been struck by one, it is a foregone conclusion that one or more of them would have said so.

2. The repeated assertion that Private George Shannon was "always getting lost." Actually, he was lost on just two occasions, the second time through no fault of his own, and neither time, it would appear, through a faulty sense of direction. On the first occasion, as

[21] Donald Jackson, "On Reading Lewis and Clark: a Bibliographical Essay," *Montana, the Magazine of Western History*, Vol. XVIII, No. 3 (July, 1968), 6.
[22] Thwaites, *Original Journals*, I, 66.

is well known, he was separated from his companions for a total of seventeen days, and had no one to blame but himself. But blame for the latter separation rested squarely on the head of a hungry beaver that carried away a stick to which Lewis had attached a message to Clark, and to others with him, including Shannon, which provided directions for the correct route.[23]

3. The conclusion drawn by too many writers that the Teton Sioux, if they had tried, could easily have annihilated the party under Lewis and Clark. Admittedly, these Indians outnumbered the explorers (Sergeant Ordway, for example, estimated the number at between two and three hundred). But the proponents of the annihilation idea, basing their theory on numerical superiority, have overlooked two vital facts: one, that the Teton warriors—that is, the able-bodied fighting men—totaled no more than sixty or seventy,[24] and, two, these warriors relied almost entirely on bows and arrows as weapons, whereas the men of Lewis and Clark, forty-three strong, carried the best rifles then obtainable as well as pistols and three small cannon (swivels). Under the circumstances, if the Sioux had attacked, it is inconceivable that they could have massacred the explorers. To believe the reverse is far easier. Moreover, one searches the journals in vain for intimation that Lewis and Clark entertained misgivings, at any time, as to their ability to cope with this situation.

4. That Jefferson blundered when he failed to send a "trained" naturalist with the Expedition. Actually, as earlier remarked, in those days, trained naturalists did not exist—trained, that is, in the sense that they had pursued a course of study in college or university to prepare them for that specialization. Those so called had gained their knowledge of fauna and flora either through their own efforts or from instruction gratuitously provided by other self-taught naturalists. But more to the point, Lewis, as a youth, had familiarized himself with the common plants and animals of Virginia, and later, while secretary to Jefferson, had received tutelage from the latter which appreciably extended his knowledge of the animate world. In

[23] *Ibid.*, II, 308f.

[24] *Ibid.*, I, 167; VII, 63, 65. The majority of the Teton Sioux, and of many other Indian tribes, were women and children. Because of continued intertribal conflict, so many warriors were killed that women actually outnumbered the men by as much as three to one.

fact, the president once wrote of Lewis' "talent for observation, which had led him to an accurate knowledge of the plants and animals of his own country."[25] It may be said, therefore, that any "trained naturalist" of that day who enjoyed a biological edge over Lewis had gained that edge, not through formal education, but through years of added field experience and a greater command of Linnaean nomenclature.

5. That the total cost of the Expedition to the government was just twenty-five hundred dollars. Of course, that was the sum Congress appropriated. But Lewis spent almost three times that amount for supplies and equipment alone, most of it in Philadelphia, before leaving for the West, and his total accounting with the army, excluding expenses for land warrants and awards to the men in the form of double pay, exceeded thirty-eight thousand dollars.

6. That Sacagawea guided Lewis and Clark to the Pacific and back. In preceding pages we have expressed our views about this claim and will not belabor it further, except to say that the claim persists, and regrettably all too often, in publications to which youngsters frequently turn for information, namely, juvenile-oriented encyclopedias and histories. For example, in an updated (1969) edition of *Encyclopedia Americana* we read, "Sacagawea displayed remarkable ability as a guide, threading the way accurately to her country," and in *World Book Encyclopedia* of the same year, "Sacagawea was the principal guide of the expedition to the Pacific Ocean and back again." And then, in a recently published elementary history, this astonishing sentence: "How lost the group would have been without Sacajawea, Charbonneau, and York."[26]

That Sacagawea has caught the public fancy is all too evident, as the quantity of literature about her abundantly testifies. Even Pocahontas, once the most revered of Indian women, has had to take second place in popularity. No one can rationally disagree with the enthusiasm expressed for Sacagawea; she was a girl of rare courage and spirit. But—and this is our final word about Sacagawea—it is unfortunate that so many writers have overemphasized her role as a guide, which was negligible, and have done her an actual disservice

[25] Coues, *History*, I, xviii.
[26] James I. Quiller and Edward Krug, *Living in Our America* (Chicago, 1964), 242.

by failing to stress her aid as an interpreter, which was considerable.

It goes without saying that no author is incapable of erring. However, the mistakes of the true scholar are generally so trivial as to do no real violence to history. Unfortunately, an occasional writer, pretending a knowledge he does not possess, produces a book about Lewis and Clark. One such book, recently published, is at hand.[27] It is replete with error and should never have been written, let alone published. A sampling of these errors should explain why: (1) William Clark's family moved to Kentucky before he was born (William was actually fourteen years old when that move was made); (2) Lewis and Clark hired Charbonneau in St. Louis (they did not set eyes on him until they arrived among the Mandans); (3) Lewis and Clark visited the celebrated red-pipestone quarries of southern Minnesota on their ascent of the Missouri (they did not come within forty or fifty miles of those quarries); (4) Lewis mounted animal specimens for Jefferson (he preserved specimens, but no record exists to support the claim that he mounted any of them); (5) Lewis and Clark found the Marias River to be wider than the Missouri (actually, according to their own measurements, the Missouri was 372 yards wide and the Marias 200); (6) the two captains were probably unfamiliar with mules until they encountered them among the Shoshoni Indians (pretty ridiculous, of course, since both had spent their boyhood years on Virginia farms); (7) the Lemhi River emptied into the Clearwater (if true, Idahoans would have to revise maps of their state); (8) George Drewyer is "Georges Drewer" throughout, Dorion is "Dorian," and Sergeant Charles Floyd is "Sergeant John Floyd." As we said, this is just a sampling.

In this same book errors of omission disturb us almost as much as those of commission. For instance, the author has allowed just four pages (of one hundred and ninety-one) to the long, hazardous, three-month leg of the journey from Lemhi Pass at the Continental Divide to the Pacific (with, incredibly, no mention whatever of the Lolo Trail *per se*), and a mere nine pages to the nine-month return trip from the Pacific to St. Louis.

Most deplorable of all is the fact that the above and other errors elsewhere constitute false history, and there is no more reason why

[27] Donald Barr Chidsey, *Lewis and Clark, the Great Adventure.*

readers should be exposed to false Lewis and Clark history than to false physical geography, false medical practice, or false anything else. As to our feelings about the perpetrators of such, we can do no better than repeat words Orlando addressed to Jacques in *As You Like It*: "I do desire that we may be better strangers."

—4—

As early as 1905, at a time when the quantity of literature *written about* the Expedition was inchoate and unimpressive, a writer reviewed the first volumes of *Original Journals of the Lewis and Clark Expedition* to come from the press. In a concluding paragraph he posed this question: "Are we getting too much of Lewis and Clark?" He then went on to say, "The Germans are said to have complained because the Goethe admirers have edited the very shaving-papers of their idol and even the contents of his waste-baskets. Is there no danger that in a similar way Lewis and Clark will be 'written to the dregs'?"

The reviewer did not think so. As he declared, "From no achievement of our history have flowed consequences more important; no exploit has been put through with more manful efficiency, or better deserves to be set forth with all fullness of detail."[28]

But what is the answer to that question today, almost three-quarters of a century and well over two hundred published books and articles later? Have Lewis and Clark admirers edited the very "shaving-papers" of their idols? Assuredly not. As all scholars intimately conversant with the history and published writings of the Expedition know, there is genuine need for further studies in several areas. A definitive biography of William Clark is long overdue. Lewis and Clark ethnology is an area wide upen and begging for additional illumination, especially in the collateral subdivisions of ethnobotany and ethnozoology. Much the same may be said for geography.[29] Of paramount importance, the *Original Journals*, be-

---

[28] *Nation*, Vol. LXXIX (September 15, 1904), 216.

[29] We have just been advised (July 12, 1973) by Donald Jackson that the University of Illinois Press will shortly publish John L. Allen, *Passage Through the Garden: Lewis and Clark and the Image of the American Northwest*, a work that deals almost entirely with Lewis and Clark cartography.

cause of the mountain of new and weighty material unearthed since 1905, need re-editing. As one specialist has said, ". . . we return always to the journals for the real essence of the expedition."[30]

[30] Donald Jackson, "The Public Image of Lewis and Clark," *Pacific Northwest Quarterly*, Vol. LVII, No. 1 (January, 1966), 7.

CHAPTER XII

They Illustrated Lewis and Clark

Without illustrative material, the pages of Lewis and Clark, for most of us, would be wanting in charm and color, somewhat like the firmament if deprived of stars, planets, and the occasional fugitive meteorite. I know that my own studies of Lewis and Clark have profited, and that I have gained new perspectives, from the presence of such pictures as Karl Bodmer's bullboats riding the Missouri, Charles St. Mémin's portrait of Lewis dressed in Shoshoni garb, Alexander Wilson's drawings of Clark's nutcracker and Lewis' woodpecker, and George Catlin's paintings of Mandan and Hidatsa villages; and my pleasure of working in the field has been augmented by these and many other depictions of men, animals, and scenes intimately and permanently a part of Lewis and Clark history.

More importantly, many of these illustrations extend and illumine history—add form and flesh to its vertebral bones—for they depict the West in its pristine state, when the prairies were still green and unscored, when bison and antelope and other animals blackened plains and valleys in undiminished numbers, and when aboriginal tribesmen continued to pursue their ancient customs relatively unchanged by alien intruders—scenes difficult for us to conceive without graphic aid. We are ever grateful for them.

—2—

To simplify our description of Lewis and Clark illustrations, we divide them at once into two classes: nineteenth century and twentieth century. Those of the former class include: (1) the counterfeits, (2) the Gass-Carey engravings, (3) the Clark maps, and (4) the Coues-Biddle facsimiles. Since we have described these in foregoing pages, we need to provide here only enough information to recall them to mind.

The counterfeits are, of course, those fanciful illustrations associated with the several apocryphal editions of Lewis and Clark. Prominent among them are the engravings of Omaha, Sioux, and other Indian chiefs and "queens." They initially appeared in 1809, and by virtue of that date bear the dubious distinction of being the very first illustrations to decorate printed matter purportedly Lewis and Clark. They include, too, the "likenesses" of Lewis and Clark found only on frontispieces of the 1812 Fisher (Baltimore and Philadelphia) and 1840 Ells (Dayton, Ohio) editions.

Once properly introduced to the delightfully bizarre, preposterous engravings with which Mathew Carey adorned pages of his three reprints of Sergeant Gass's *Journal*, no one is likely to forget them. Indeed, they have been reproduced so often in recent literature that some readers may wish they had been forgotten.

The six Clark maps were the first *authentic* illustrations to grace Lewis and Clark literature, Biddle employing them in 1814. Unlike the counterfeits and Gass-Carey engravings, these originated on western terrain and were executed by a cartographer, namely, William Clark, who had his subject matter in view.

The fourth group, the Coues-Biddle facsimiles, appeared in the 1893 Coues-edited reissue of Biddle. Therein we find, for the first time in accounts of the Expedition, reproductions of holographic documents, namely, facsimile letters of both Lewis and Clark. More significantly, this reissue includes Charles Willson Peale's celebrated portraits of Lewis and Clark. No previous account of the Expedition, to our knowledge, had carried them.

The illustrations comprising this group followed a surprisingly long, sterile period, one of seventy-nine years (from 1814 to 1893), in which no consequential innovative graphic material whatever emerged. This period saw only the repeated reuse of that from the Apocrypha, Gass, and Biddle—with one lone exception, a view of

Great Falls titled "Principal Cascade of the Missouri," which appeared in the 1817 Dublin reprint of Biddle, and there alone.

The inspiration for this Dublin picture may have come from Lewis himself. Following his discovery of Great Falls on June 13, 1805, he wrote in part:

> I wished for the pencil of Salvator Rosa or the pen of [James] Thomson that I might be enabled to give to the enlightened world some just idea of this truly magnificent and sublimely grand object . . . but this was fruitless and vain. . . . I therefore with the assistance of my pen only indeavoured to trace some of the stronger features of this seen [scene] by the assistance of which and my recollections aided by some pencil I hope still to give to the world some faint idea of an object which at this moment fills me with much pleasure and astonishment."[1]

These words make it clear that Lewis had in mind, once he had returned to the East, giving his rough sketch of Great Falls to an artist capable of doing justice to this "sublimely grand object." And it would appear that he carried out his intention, for, as we reported in an earlier chapter, Clark found in Philadelphia after Lewis' death an imperfect drawing that had been made of "the falls of the Missouri."[2] It is highly unlikely, however, that there is any connection between the Dublin drawing and the one located by Clark. At least, the former bears scant resemblance to later, on-the-scene drawings and photographs of Great Falls.

—3—

With the advent of the twentieth century, Lewis and Clark illustrative material almost immediately took on a new look. This was due primarily to novel ideas fathered by two men, Olin D. Wheeler[3] and Reuben Gold Thwaites.

Wheeler put his ideas on display in *The Trail of Lewis and Clark*,

---

[1] Thwaites, *Original Journals*, II, 149–50.

[2] Jackson, *Letters*, 490.

[3] Olin D. Wheeler (1852–1925), born in Mansfield, Ohio, was educated at Allegheny College and Cornell University. From 1874 to 1879 he was topographer with Major John Wesley Powell during the latter's survey of the Colorado River. In later years (1893–1906) he wrote, in addition to *The Trail of Lewis and Clark*, the "Wonderland Series" of travel books issued by the Northern Pacific Railway.

his two-volume work published in 1904. This was the first book of consequence *written about* the Expedition, and since it came from the press exactly one century after Lewis and Clark abandoned winter quarters on Wood River, it proved to be a valuable hundred-year-after study of the trail.

Apart from its general worth, however, and strictly from the point of view of graphic history, current students of the Expedition will wish to be familiar with this book, for several reasons:

1. It was the first fully illustrated book about the Expedition, the illustrations numbering approximately two hundred.

2. It was the first to display the portraits of Lewis and Clark by artists St. Mémin and Chester Harding.[4]

3. It was the first to reproduce paintings of Karl Bodmer and to decorate pages with drawings executed by such later artists as Charles M. Russell, E. S. Paxson,[5] and Ralph E. DeCamp.[6]

4. Two of these, one by Russell and the other by Paxson, were reproduced in color, and were the first colored Lewis and Clark illustrations.

5. It even exposed the Gass-Carey engravings.

6. It was also the first work in the field to make extensive use of photographs, illustrating famous landmarks like Great Falls, Celilo Falls, Beacon Rock, and Pompey's Pillar; relics such as Lewis' telescope and branding iron, Shannon's housewife (a pocket container for sewing equipment), and an Indian peace medal; and a wide assortment of other objects, including monuments, pages from the original codices, even a photograph of Sergeant Charles Floyd's skull.

Appearing concurrently with Wheeler's book were the volumes constituting the Thwaites-edited *Original Journals*. Illustrations of this *magnum opus*, apart from reproductions of Peale's portraits of

---

[4] Chester Harding (1792–1866) was born in Massachusetts and subsequently went to St. Louis, where he painted at least four likenesses of William Clark.

[5] Edgar Samuel Paxson (1852–1919) was born in Buffalo, New York, and went to Montana in 1877. He is best known for murals in the state capitol at Helena and in the Missoula County courthouse; also for his painting, "Custer's Last Stand." Apparently Wheeler commissioned Paxson to make the paintings, six in all, which he used in *The Trail of Lewis and Clark*.

[6] Ralph E. DeCamp (1851–1907), born in Attica, New York, later went to Montana, where he became well known for his pastorals of that state.

the two leaders and sample pages from the codices, consisted entirely of maps and sketches done by Lewis and Clark themselves.

The maps number almost one hundred (fifty-four of them constituting Volume VIII) and the sketches approximately seventy-five. Clark, who was not only cartographer to the Expedition but also artist, drew all the former and most of the latter. Considering his complete lack of formal training as a draftsman, a few of his sketches reveal unexpected talent. Particularly noteworthy is his pen-and-ink drawing of the candle fish, *Thaleichthys pacificus* (also called eulachon and smelt), as well as those of the steelhead trout, *Salmo gairdneri* (the "salmon trout" of Lewis and Clark) and the sage grouse, *Centrocercus urophasianus* (called "prairie cock" and "cock of the plains" by Lewis).

Thus Wheeler and Thwaites fashioned a pattern for future illustrations of Lewis and Clark literature. By and large it was a template of seven conjoining pieces: (1) Gass-Carey engravings, (2) portraits of Lewis and Clark, (3) Clark maps, (4) Clark sketches, (5) drawings of plants and animals brought back by the explorers, (6) works of western artists, and (7) photographs of many different objects. Since the day of Wheeler and Thwaites these pieces have undergone inevitable change.

1. *Gass-Carey Engravings*—The trend to expose to view this sextet of implausible yet arresting caricatures has notably increased, especially during the last decade. For instance, in 1916 Milo Quaife exposed just one of the six in *The Journals of Captain Meriwether Lewis and Sergeant John Ordway*, and in 1947 John Bakeless, only two in *Lewis and Clark: Partners in Discovery*. But in 1965 Richard Dillon exhibited the entire package of six in his *Meriwether Lewis*, as did Ralph Andrist two years later in *To the Pacific with Lewis and Clark*. Authors of recent magazine articles have been equally eager to make use of them, not always tempered with discrimination. For instance, as delightful as it may be, we still question the relevance of the one titled "An American having struck a Bear but not killed him, escapes into a Tree" to a recently published article on the medical aspects of the Expedition.

We should mention, too, that authors within late years have been tapping the counterfeit editions for illustrations. As an example, of some two dozen pictures Dillon chose for *Meriwether Lewis*, about one half originally appeared in one or another of those editions.

2. *Portraits of Lewis and Clark*—Practically every *illustrated* piece of literature *written about* the Expedition has utilized space for Peale's portraits of Lewis and Clark, thus showing conclusively the unsurpassed popularity of these over those done by other artists. St. Mémin's matched pair of profiles of the two leaders and his full-length of Lewis in Indian apparel have achieved second place in popular regard. And within the last few years writers have been discovering and displaying paintings of Lewis and Clark by other artists: not only Chester Harding (first brought to view by Wheeler), but also Joel Wesley Jarvis,[7] Joseph Bush,[8] and George Catlin. Additionally, likenesses done by unknown hands, including two silhouettes of Lewis, have been unearthed.[9]

3. *Clark Maps*—Several charts done by Clark have illustrated Lewis and Clark literature, but those used by Biddle in 1814, and again by Coues in 1893, are prime favorites. Over and over again we find "Great Falls of the Missouri," "Great Falls of the Columbia River," "Rapids of the Columbia River," and "Map of Lewis and Clark's Track Across the Western Portion of North America" illuminating pages. These, like so many other charts of bygone vintage, possess unique charm, and doubtless will continue to decorate pages of the story of this national epic as long as it is told.

4. *Clark Drawings*—Of these, the ones most often reproduced are those of the candle fish, steelhead trout, and sage grouse alluded to above, and those illustrative of Indian culture, especially the by now well-known series portraying the art of head flattening as practiced by Chinookan tribes of the Lower Columbia. These, like the archaic maps, have their own inherent appeal to viewers.

5. *Drawings of Plants and Animals Brought Back by Lewis and Clark*—In this category we include those figures made in years immediately following the Expedition by artists such as Peale, Wilson,

[7] John Wesley Jarvis (1781–1839), born in England, came to the United States at the age of five. He made a portrait of Clark, probably while Clark was in Philadelphia in 1810.

[8] Joseph Bush (1794–1865), born in Frankfort, Kentucky, studied under Thomas Sully. He induced Clark to sit for a portrait, possibly while Clark was in Frankfort in 1810 on his way from St. Louis to Philadelphia.

[9] For reproductions of known likenesses of Lewis and Clark, see Cutright's "Lewis and Clark: Portraits and Portraitists," *Montana, the Magazine of Western History*, Vol. XIX, No. 2 (April, 1969), 37–53.

and Pursh previously considered in some detail. Only within recent years, more than a century and a half after they were painted, have Peale's portraits of Lewis' woodpecker and mountain quail and those by Wilson of the western tanager and Clark's nutcracker added beauty and interest to books written about the Expedition. In Jackson's *Letters*, for instance, we find reproductions of Lewis' woodpecker and mountain quail, and in the present writer's *Lewis and Clark: Pioneering Naturalists*, those of the western tanager and Clark's nutcracker.

Portraits of various mammals collected and brought back by Lewis and Clark have also begun to find favor. These were done by such other artists of the same, or slightly later, period as Charles Lesueur,[10] Alexander Rider,[11] and Alexander Lawson.[12] Authors have resurrected them from near-forgotten natural histories dating back to the years 1825–32, among them *American Natural History* by Dr. John D. Godman[13] and *The Cabinet of Natural History and American Rural Sports* by J. and T. Doughty.[14] Rider, for example, made drawings of the prairie dog and bighorn for Godman and one of the pronghorn antelope for the Doughtys, while Lesueur sketched the grizzly bear, western badger, coyote, and mountain goat for the Doughty work. Lawson produced beautifully engraved portraits of bighorn, antelope, and wood rat (*Neotoma floridana*), the last named being the very first animal new to science discovered by Lewis and Clark.[15]

[10] Charles A. Lesueur (1778–1846) was a French artist who came to the United States in 1816. He wrote widely on various subjects, particularly ichthyology, and furnished many plates which lent distinction to early volumes of the *Journal* of the Academy of Natural Sciences of Philadelphia.

[11] Alexander Rider (17 –1830), miniaturist, came to the United States from Germany in 1811.

[12] Alexander Lawson (1772–1845), born in Scotland, came to the United States in 1792. Making Philadelphia his home, he soon made a reputation for himself as an outstanding engraver of animal portraits.

[13] John D. Godman (1794–1830) was born in Maryland, studied medicine in Baltimore, and practiced in various places, including Philadelphia. For a time he was professor of natural history at Franklin Institute of Philadelphia.

[14] T. Doughty was Thomas Doughty (1793–1856), a Philadelphia artist, sometimes referred to as "a pleasing landscape painter." J. Doughty was his brother.

[15] Thwaites, *Original Journals*, I, 37. These engravings by Lawson were first reproduced in Lewis and Clark literature by Cutright, in his *Lewis and Clark: Pioneering Naturalists*, from originals held by the Academy of Natural Sciences of Philadelphia.

All of the above-mentioned animal portraits, both bird and mammal, have much to recommend them graphically, being attractive and generally well executed; and, of course, they have further appeal because Lewis and Clark originally discovered the subjects portrayed. No doubt these portraits will be seen increasingly in future studies of the Expedition.

For the very first drawings of plants discovered by Lewis and Clark we must turn to Pursh's *Flora Americae Septentrionalis*, an important two-volume botanical work published in 1814. Therein Pursh figured twenty-seven plants, thirteen of which he had sketched from specimens entrusted to him by Lewis early in 1807. We have seen just two of the thirteen reproduced thus far in literature about the Expedition: *Clarkia pulchella* (ragged robin) and *Mimulus lewisii* (Lewis' monkey flower).[16] Unfortunately, Pursh did not sketch *Lewisia rediviva* (bitterroot), probably the most celebrated of all plants discovered by Lewis and Clark. Not only does it bear the Latin generic name, *Lewisia*, but it is also the state flower of Montana and, through its vernacular, is immortalized in the names of such prominent topographic features as the Bitterroot Mountains and Bitterroot River.[17]

6. *Works of Western Artists*—We include under this heading that considerable aggregation of pencil sketches, crayons, watercolors, and oil paintings which, beginning with Wheeler, have contributed so much life and color to Lewis and Clark literature. The artists responsible include both those who early followed the explorers up the Missouri, lingering in the High Plains country usually only a few months, yet in those brief periods transmitting to canvas a priceless collection of impressions of the land and its diverse inhabitants, principally Indians and the vast concourse of game animals exactly as they saw them, and those who visited the West at

[16] The other Lewis and Clark plants figured by Pursh were: *Claytonia lanceolata, Berberis aquifolium, Berberis nervosa, Gaultheria shallon, Tigarea (Purshia) tridentata, Lilium pudica, Helonias (Xerophyllum) tenax, Rubus spectabilis, Gerardia fruticosa, Psoralea esculenta,* and *Lupinus macrocephalus.*

[17] However, even though Pursh failed to figure this plant, present-day botanists are familiar with an attractive drawing that appeared in an early English journal, *Curtis's Botanical Magazine*, Ser. 3, Vol. XIX (1863). Velva E. Rudd reproduced it in "Botanical Contributions of the Lewis and Clark Expedition," Washington Academy of Sciences *Journal*, Vol. XLIV (November, 1954), 351–56.

later dates, in many cases remaining to make it their permanent home, and, calling upon imagination, portrayed events they had never personally witnessed and that were, typically, quite outside the province of their own experience.

In the former group were such imposing masters of the brush as Samuel Seymour, Titian Ramsay Peale, George Catlin, Karl Bodmer, Alfred Jacob Miller, and John James Audubon. Seymour and Peale were members of the Major Stephen H. Long expedition of 1819–20, the former serving as artist and the latter as assistant naturalist (to Thomas Say) and scientific illustrator.[18] More to the point, they were the first artists to visit the great plains country of the West, and as such the first to make drawings in their natural habitats of Indians and animals that had been discovered by Lewis and Clark. Peale, for instance, sketched such animals as the antelope, mule deer, and black-billed magpie, all unknown to science before Lewis and Clark.[19] I have encountered just one of Seymour's paintings in Lewis and Clark literature, a scene of the Rockies with buffalo grazing in the foreground,[20] and only one by Titian Peale, a portrait of two grizzlies.[21]

George Catlin (1796–1872), a Pennsylvanian by birth, was the next man to carry brushes and paint pots up the Missouri. He went with a fixed goal in mind. At an early age he had demonstrated proficiency in drawing (though entirely self-taught) and, after watching a delegation of Plains Indians parade the streets of Philadelphia, had determined, as he said, to devote the remainder of his life to "reaching, ultimately, every tribe of Indians on the Continent of North America, and of bringing home faithful portraits of their

[18] For more about Samuel Seymour (1796–1823), see John Francis McDermott's "Samuel Seymour: Pioneer artist of the Plains and the Rockies," *Smithsonian Institution Report for 1950* (1951), 497–509, and John C. Ewers' *Artists of the Old West* (New York, Doubleday & Co., 1965), 23–37.

[19] Titian Peale (1799–1885) was, of course, a son of Charles Willson Peale. For more about his zoological portraits, see Robert Cushman Murphy's "The Sketches of Titian Ramsay Peale," American Philosophical Society *Transactions* (1957), 523–31.

[20] See Andrist's *To the Pacific with Lewis and Clark*, 65.

[21] This portrait was reproduced by Dillon in his *Meriwether Lewis*. The two grizzlies had been brought to Philadelphia in 1807 by Lieutenant Zebulon M. Pike, not by Lewis and Clark, as some writers have stated.

principal personages, and full notes of their character and history."[22] To that end, he arrived in St. Louis in 1830 carrying a letter of introduction to General William Clark, whose assistance was essential to furthering his project. In the months ahead Clark, who had welcomed him warmly, sat for a portrait,[23] introduced him to chiefs of Osage, Kansas, Omaha, Oto, and other Indian tribes—whose likenesses Catlin put on canvas—and, in the spring of 1832, helped him obtain passage on the Missouri Fur Company steamboat, *Yellowstone*, which carried him to the Mandan villages and on to Fort Union at the mouth of the Yellowstone River.

Catlin returned to St. Louis that fall, but not before he had filled his portfolio with numerous drawings of Sioux, Arikaras, Mandans, Hidatsas, Crows, Assiniboins, and Blackfeet, and of the land they inhabited, and had written a series of letters to the New York *Commercial Advertiser* which later, with added material, was published under the title, *Letters and Notes on the Manners, Customs, and Conditions of the North American Indians* (London, 1841).

Karl Bodmer (1809–93) ascended the Missouri in 1833, one year later than Catlin. Born in Switzerland, Bodmer was the artist chosen by the German naturalist, Alexander Philip Maximilian, prince of Wied-Neuwied, to accompany him on his travels in the United States. Like Catlin, Bodmer and Maximilian rode the *Yellowstone* to Fort Union. However, from that celebrated trading post they went on to Fort McKenzie, almost as celebrated, situated near the mouth of the Marias River. En route they passed through the spectacularly beautiful Missouri Breaks, or White Rocks, region. On the return they stopped again at the Mandan villages, where they spent the winter of 1833–34.

On one score the canvases of Catlin and Bodmer stand alone. They were the first to depict the Upper Missouri terrain with its abundant complement of Indians and wildlife—and at a time before its indigenes had been appreciably altered by civilized man. Of course, the drawings of the Mandans are today recognized as the

---

[22] George Catlin, *Letters and Notes on the Manners, Customs, and Conditions of the North American Indians*, 2 vols. (London, published by the author, 1841), II, 2–3.

[23] This portrait is now the property of Harold McCracken, director of Whitney Gallery of Western Art, Cody, Wyoming.

most valuable of all, for in 1837 smallpox practically annihilated these Indians as a race. Of an estimated twelve hundred and fifty (the figure supplied by Lewis and Clark in 1805), seemingly no more than a score or two survived that disastrous epidemic. Yet, by virtue of the Catlin and Bodmer drawings, they achieved a measure of immortality that otherwise would be wanting.

From the time of Wheeler, Bodmer's beautifully executed pencil sketches and delicate watercolors have appeared in Lewis and Clark literature with more frequency than the drawings of any other artist. Most popular of all is his portrayal of a Mandan village on the Missouri, with bullboats plied by Indian women conspicuous in the foreground. Often reproduced, too, are one or more of the scenes that Bodmer committed to canvas during his transit of the Missouri Breaks, the "seens of visionary enchantment," as Lewis termed them.[24]

Catlin's appeal to illustrators of Lewis and Clark has lagged behind that of Bodmer's. Indeed, I believe that it was not until 1947, almost half a century after Wheeler used Bodmer originally, that Catlin was first displayed—in Bakeless' *Lewis and Clark: Partners in Discovery*.[25] The primary reason why this was so was that Catlin, as earlier stated, went west entirely without formal training in art, and his work was uneven in quality. For many years following his death, artists, historians, and ethnologists alike tended to disparage the value of his canvases. After the turn of the century, however, men in these fields began to look more closely, and sympathetically. Thus, as early as 1906, a pair of scientists concluded that "in matters of actual fact he seems to be as reliable as any other authority,"[26] and another appraiser, writing just recently, declared, "But at his best, as in *Head Chief of the Iowas*, Catlin's agile drawings . . . could not be equalled for directness and compassion."[27] Bodmer, on the other hand, had received thorough training under European

---

[24] Thwaites, *Original Journals*, II, 101.

[25] Bakeless reproduced five of Catlin's drawings of Indians: two Mandan women, one Arikara woman, and two Nez Percé warriors. The majority of Catlin's paintings, more than six hundred, are the property of the Smithsonian Institution.

[26] George F. Will and H. F. Spinden, "The Mandans, a Study of Their Culture, Archaeology and Language," Peabody Museum of Archaeology and Ethnology *Papers*, Harvard University, Vol. III, No. 4 (1906), 87.

[27] *Time*, May 22, 1972, 66.

tutors. Thus his drawings, of more uniform quality, received high acclaim first and last.

John James Audubon (c.1780–1851) followed Catlin and Bodmer upriver to Fort Union a decade later, departing from St. Louis in the spring of 1843 and returning that fall. During this trip he encountered and painted several of the birds and mammals originally discovered by Lewis and Clark, and these portraits later appeared in his *The Birds of America* and *The Quadrupeds of North America*.[28] To my knowledge just one of them has to date appeared in Lewis and Clark literature. This is a colorful study of three prairie dogs in their natural semiarid plains habitat.[29] Future Lewis and Clark writers may find other Audubon animal portraits to be equally relevant. Two come to mind at once: the poor-will (*Phalaenoptilus nuttallii*) and the western meadowlark (*Sturnella neglecta*). Lewis discovered both of these birds, the former near the mouth of Cannonball River, South Dakota, on October 17, 1804,[30] and the latter at Great Falls, Montana, on June 22, 1805.[31] But it was Audubon who first described them technically (1844) and thereby received the credit which by right should have gone to Lewis.

Of the second, modern, group of artists who made sorties into historical painting, depicting events of an earlier day, including those associated with Lewis and Clark, Charles M. Russell (1864–1926) stands foremost. He produced more pictorial reconstructions of Lewis and Clark happenings than any other artist, totaling thirteen oils, watercolors, and pen-and-ink sketches.[32] Born in St. Louis, Russell, when but sixteen, went to Montana. Here for a number of years he made a living and learned about the West as horse wrangler and night herder for some of the big cattle outfits of the state. In spare time, however, he spontaneously yielded to the demands of his natural gift for transmitting to canvas with brush his impressions

---

[28] *The Birds of America* was published in 1843–44 and *The Quadrupeds of North America* (written in collaboration with John Bachman) in 1849–54. For more of Audubon's 1843 trip to Fort Union, see John Francis McDermott (ed.), *Up the Missouri with Audubon: The Journal of Edward Harris* (Norman, University of Oklahoma Press, 1951).

[29] See Andrist's *To the Pacific with Lewis and Clark*, 42.

[30] Thwaites, *Original Journals*, VI, 132.

[31] *Ibid.*, II, 180.

[32] Ewers, *Artists of the Old West*, 230.

of scenes and events he had witnessed in this open and then unspoiled picturesque land of high plains. In 1888, *Harper's Weekly* published one of his paintings, and, with other periodicals soon reproducing others, Russell began receiving favorable national recognition. In 1903 he settled down in a log cabin studio in Great Falls (now a permanent museum), and here, during the remainder of his life, he painted the great majority of hundreds of canvases that brought distinction to a long and colorful career.

Of Russell's several reconstructions of Lewis and Clark history, his depiction of the explorers' meeting on September 4, 1805, with Flathead Indians in Ross's Hole has been most often reproduced in literature about the Expedition. This is a large mural, 25 by 12 feet, that covers an entire wall in the House of Representatives in the Montana state capitol. Of other historical paintings by Russell which brighten accounts of the Expedition, we find three in particular: the interior of a Mandan lodge with the Negro, York, centrally placed; the flash flood at Great Falls that almost swept Clark, Charbonneau, Sacagawea, and her infant to their deaths; and the meeting on the Columbia of Lewis and Clark with Chinookan Indians.

Other artists attracted to Lewis and Clark as a theme for historical paintings make a long list, one which grows with the passing of the years. Among them are E. S. Paxson (earlier alluded to in this chapter), William H. Jackson,[33] Frederic Remington,[34] Olaf C. Seltzer,[35] Frank Schwarz,[36] J. K. Ralston,[37] and John Clymer.[38]

[33] William Henry Jackson (1843–1942), better known as one of the earliest photographers of the West, made a watercolor titled "The Homecoming of Sacajawea, Horse Prairie Creek." This drawing has yet to appear in Lewis and Clark literature, though Howard R. Driggs reproduced it in *The Old West Speaks* (New York, Bonanza Books, 1956), 64.

[34] Frederic Remington (1861–1909) in late life was commissioned by *Collier's Magazine* to do a series of illustrations of great explorers. One of them, "Lewis and Clark on the Columbia," appeared in *Collier's* of May 12, 1906.

[35] Olaf Carl Seltzer (1877–1957) was born in Copenhagen, Denmark, and arrived in Montana in 1892. He is today regarded as one of the top-ranking western artists. Charles G. Clarke reproduced four of Seltzer's paintings in his *The Men of the Lewis and Clark Expedition.*

[36] Frank Henry Schwarz (1894–1951), born in New York City, became a painter of murals. One of these, depicting the Lewis and Clark party at Celilo Falls, decorates the rotunda of Oregon's capitol in Salem.

[37] James Kenneth Ralston (1907–), talented western artist born in Choteau, Montana, portrayed Sacagawea's reunion with her people. See Snyder's *In the Footsteps of Lewis and Clark*, 146–47.

The drawing of a historical painting, like the writing of a historical novel, is attended with hazards, no matter how talented the draftsman or exacting his research. Russell's painting of York in a Mandan lodge is a case in point. It was a difficult undertaking, as he must have realized. He knew nothing of York's appearance and, seemingly, little about Mandan apparel. Consequently, as a well-known Smithsonian scientist has noted, Russell dressed the Mandans shown in his picture in Blackfoot clothing, which bore designs entirely unlike those on specimens of Mandan apparel Lewis and Clark brought back with them from Fort Mandan.[39] Also, he portrayed York as a tall, lean, handsomely muscled man, whereas we have Clark's word for it that his servant was obese. Writing in late August, after he and York and others visited Spirit Mound, South Dakota, Clark said, "My servant nearly exosted with heat thurst and fatigue, he being fat. . . ."[40]

As another example, Remington rather egregiously slighted his research preparatory to what would seem to be his only painting of Lewis and Clark. This shows the two captains splendidly attired in outmoded Revolutionary War uniforms on a sandy beach of the Columbia and, drawn out of the water behind them, three boats which are not dugouts at all, but birch-bark canoes![41]

Not unexpectedly, many of these paintings attempting to reconstruct Lewis and Clark history exaggerate Sacagawea's importance to the Expedition by positioning her center stage in the company of the two commanders, and one or two show her with arm pointing to the west, thus misrepresenting her role as guide. Olaf Seltzer, in one of his drawings, mistakenly places Sacagawea at the Sulphur Spring across the Missouri from the site of the Lewis and Clark camp at the mouth of Portage (Belt) Creek. During the first week at this camp (while the party was engaged in portaging around the falls), Sacagawea lay quite ill. Lewis obtained water from the spring

[38] John F. Clymer (1907–   ) was born in Ellensburg, Washington, though he now resides in Connecticut. He painted "The Ordeal of the Bitterroots," reproduced in Snyder's *In the Footsteps of Lewis and Clark*, 150–51.

[39] Ewers, *Artists of the Old West*, 230–32.

[40] Osgood, *Field Notes*, 119.

[41] Earlier alluded to as one of twelve constituting a popular series titled "Great American Explorers" which ran in *Collier's Magazine* in 1905–06.

for Sacagawea and thought it benefited her, but at no time did the Indian girl visit the spring.[42]

7. *Photographs*—Following the publication in 1904 of Wheeler's *The Trail of Lewis and Clark*, in which products of the camera appeared conspicuously and abundantly, photography played a minor role in illustrating accounts of the Expedition until 1950, almost half a century later. In that year Albert and Jane Salisbury published *Two Captains West*, a first-rate photographic study of the Missouri-Columbia route from Camp Dubois to Cape Disappointment on the Pacific. Between its covers are 160 black and white photographs of key points and explicit directions on how to reach these points. The study is incomplete in two respects. It fails to include pictures of the Lolo Trail (this ancient Indian road across the Bitterroots being more difficult to follow then than now) and of the Medicine River site (the precise location where Lewis in 1806 skirmished with the Blackfeet being unknown in 1950).

Three years later the *National Geographic Magazine* carried an article by Ralph Gray titled "Following the Trail of Lewis and Clark." Apparently this was the first piece of literature about the Expedition to feature colored photographs—some thirty altogether, mostly of scenes along the Missouri, Clearwater, Columbia, and Yellowstone. Since then colored photographs have appeared increasingly in both books and periodicals and, in some instances, have almost completely supplanted those formerly in black and white. Also, there has been a growing tendency to supplement the colored photographs with full-color reproductions of paintings by such artists as Peale, St. Mémin, Wilson, Catlin, Bodmer, and Russell. Two books, both of recent date, have led the way in these respects: Andrist's *To the Pacific with Lewis and Clark* (an American Heritage publication of 1967) and Snyder's *In the Footsteps of Lewis and Clark* (a National Geographic Society book which appeared in 1970).

Photography as a medium for illustrating Lewis and Clark history took giant steps forward in 1969 when Ingvar Henry Eide, a Missoula, Montana, lensman, published *American Odyssey*. Though similar in concept to the Salisburys' *Two Captains West*, it is a more

---

[42] Clarke reproduced this painting by Seltzer in his *The Men of the Lewis and Clark Expedition*, 167.

impressive work, due in part at least, one suspects, to improvements in photographic equipment and techniques since 1950. Eide seems, also, to have given much time and study to each picture, carefully choosing scenes free of man-made stigmata (often a difficult business) and thereby obtaining photographs—all in black and white—of rare excellence and charm. Moreover, all of these photographs (in excess of two hundred and fifty) are faithful to descriptions as recorded by Lewis and Clark, even to time of year and state of weather.

What can we expect from photography in the future? For one thing, we will probably find the camera being used increasingly in picturing objects intimately associated with the Expedition, such as Indian peace medals, plants constituting Lewis' herbarium, ethnological specimens, holographic documents, and a wide variety of relics; indeed, as an examination of Lewis and Clark literature of the last few years attests, a trend in this direction is already observable. Beyond that, it seems an almost foregone conclusion that another cameraman of the Salisbury or Eide stamp will eventually appear who, with the requisite financial backing of an enthusiastic and moneyed publisher, will give us a volume comparable to *American Odyssey*—except that the photographs therein from first to last will be in full, resplendent color.

—4—

The illustrative material decorating the pages of Lewis and Clark literature is colorful, diversified, representative, and at times provocative. In these respects, it surely rivals that of almost any other comparable body of literature. We find fault with it only on those rare occasions when a publisher's predilection for color blinds his eye to relevancy or to the proper way of achieving the dramatic.

Future illustrators of Lewis and Clark may wish to vary their graphic milieu. If so, there are available to them a number of sources heretofore entirely overlooked or only partially utilized, among them Pursh's *Flora Americae Septentrionalis*, Godman's *American Natural History*, the Doughtys' *Cabinet of Natural History and American Rural Sports*, Audubon's *The Birds of America*, and Audubon and Bachman's *The Quadrupeds of North America*. In these works are numerous drawings of plants and animals discovered by Lewis and Clark,[43] many of which have yet to be reproduced in writings about the Expedition. Another relatively untapped source is Isaac I. Stevens' *Report of Explorations and Surveys from the Mississippi River to the Pacific Ocean*,[44] which included beautifully executed engravings by Gustavus Sohon[45] and John M. Stanley[46] of scenes along the Upper Missouri and the Columbia and in the Bitterroot Mountains. For additional landscapes, one may wish to examine Alfred E. Mathews' *Pencil Sketches of Montana*.[47] If the illustrator is ethnologically minded, and eager to find portraits of Plains Indians other than those by Bodmer and/or Catlin, he may be rewarded with those by Charles Bird King.[48] Last but not least, another rich lode: Titian Peale's "Sketch Book," a highly prized possession of the American Philosophical Society.

It is evident by now, surely, that the growing interest in Lewis and Clark literature does not rest solely on the editorial and annotative genius of such men as Nicholas Biddle, Elliott Coues, Reuben Gold Thwaites, Milo M. Quaife, Ernest S. Osgood, and Donald

[43] In this work, when we have alluded to plants and animals "discovered" by Lewis and Clark, it should be understood that we refer to those unknown to science at that time. It goes without saying that they were known to the Indians and, in some instances, to traders and trappers based at Fort Assiniboine, St. Louis, and elsewhere.

[44] Washington, 1853–55.

[45] Gustavus Sohon (1825–1903), German-born artist, came to the United States at the age of seventeen and in the early 1850's took part in Stevens' explorations and surveys of the Northwest to determine the most practicable railway route through the mountains.

[46] John M. Stanley (1814–72) was born in New York State and at the age of twenty moved to Detroit, where he began painting portraits and landscapes. Later, with Sohon, he accompanied Stevens.

[47] Alfred E. Mathews (1831–74), born in England, came to the United States (Ohio) at an early age. He served in the Union Army during the Civil War and, afterward, traveled extensively in the West making pencil sketches. While in Montana, he sketched such scenes as Great Falls, Gates of the Mountains, and Beaverhead Rock, all, of course, originally discovered by Lewis and Clark.

[48] Charles Bird King (1785–1862) was born in Newport, Rhode Island, and later studied art in London under Benjamin West. On his return to the United States in 1812, he lived in Philadelphia for four years and then went to Washington, D.C. In 1821, when a delegation of Plains Indians visited Washington, he was commissioned to paint them. His paintings formed the nucleus of the famous National Indian Portrait Gallery, most of which was destroyed by fire at the Smithsonian in 1865.

Jackson. A sizable portion derives from the inspired brushes of artists like Charles Willson Peale, Charles de St. Mémin, George Catlin, Karl Bodmer, Charles Russell, and J. K. Ralston, and from the dependable cameras of photographers such as Henry Eide and the Salisburys.

Appendix A

A Journal of Private Joseph Whitehouse,
A Soldier with Lewis and Clark

From distant Fort Mandan, on April 7, 1805, Captain Meriwether Lewis wrote to President Thomas Jefferson, "We have encouraged our men to keep journals, and seven of them do so."[1] At an earlier date, in May of the previous year, he had entered a note in his "Orderly Book" stating that he had enjoined each sergeant "to keep a separate journal from day to day of all passing occurrences. . . ."[2]

It is strange indeed that in neither of these statements, nor in any others found in their journals, did Lewis and Clark actually disclose the names of any of the seven journalists.[3] One consequence is the fact that a full century elapsed before historians of the Expedition learned that Private Joseph Whitehouse was one of the seven. The earliest reference to his journal that I have found anywhere is in a letter dated April 13, 1903, from Reuben Gold Thwaites to I. Minis Hays, then secretary of the American Philosophical Society, Phila-

---

[1] Jackson, *Letters*, 232.

[2] Thwaites, *Original Journals*, I, 32.

[3] The names of specific journalists were first revealed in letters and other documents written subsequent to the Expedition. In due course we become apprised of five of the seven: Sergeants John Ordway, Charles Floyd, and Patrick Gass and Privates Robert Frazer and Joseph Whitehouse. Presumably Nathaniel Pryor, whose journal has yet to come to light, was another. The author of the seventh remains a mystery.

delphia. At that time Thwaites was deeply immersed in editing *Original Journals of the Lewis and Clark Expedition, 1804–1806.* In his letter to Hays he said, "You will be pleased to know no doubt that we have at last secured the original Whitehouse Journal and I am expecting it within a few days."[4]

Thwaites had obtained the journal for the publisher of the *Original Journals,* Dodd, Mead and Company, who printed it in Volume VII of that work. As students of the Expedition know, it is incomplete, ending abruptly on November 6, 1805, and containing several hiatuses preceding that date.

In his preface to the *Original Journals,* Thwaites recorded what little he had been able to learn about the provenance of Whitehouse's account and then said, ". . . there have at last been located presumably all the literary records now extant, of that notable enterprise in the cause of civilization."[5] It wasn't the wisest pronouncement of his long, distinguished career as editor; Lewis and Clark historians of today would shy away from a similar declaration like hares from the sudden swoop of a hawk. And they could cite at least three cogent reasons for so doing. (1) Just ten years later, in 1914, Charles and Edward Biddle, grandsons of Nicholas Biddle, rediscovered the long-missing journal of Sergeant John Ordway and, with it, the till then unknown account of Meriwether Lewis' 1803 journey from Pittsburgh to Wood River.[6] (2) In 1953 Lucile M. Kane, curator of manuscripts, Minnesota Historical Society, St. Paul, discovered a collection of notes which was later published as *The Field Notes of Captain William Clark, 1803–1805* (and the existence of this had

---

[4] This letter is the property of the American Philosophical Society, Philadelphia. Thwaites had learned of the existence of Whitehouse's journal when its owner, Mrs. Gertrude Haley, attempted unsuccessfully to sell it to the Library of Congress (Thwaites, *Original Journals,* I, lv–lvi).

[5] *Ibid.*

[6] These two journals, published in 1916 by the State Historical Society of Wisconsin, were edited by Milo M. Quaife, who proceeded to parrot Thwaites by writing: ". . . all the records [of the Expedition] still extant have probably been found." See Quaife, "Some New-found Records of the Lewis and Clark Expedition," *Mississippi Valley Historical Review,* Vol. II, No. 1 (June, 1915), 116. Quaife's assertion that all the records probably had been found was rendered even more unwise by the fact that he himself overlooked, in the notebook containing Lewis' "Ohio Journal," Nicholas Biddle's important notes made when interviewing Clark in Fincastle, Virginia, in 1810.

been entirely unsuspected).[7] (3) In 1966 George W. White, professor of geology at the University of Illinois, Urbana, while visiting a bookstore in Philadelphia, Pennsylvania, was shown a manuscript which proved to be a paraphrastic version of Whitehouse's journal; and this, too, had been unheard of.

—2—

It seems apparent enough to historians that Joseph Whitehouse's only valid claims to renown rest squarely on the circumstances that he served in the army unit commanded by Captains Lewis and Clark which explored the trans-Mississippi route to the Pacific and return, and that he kept a diary of daily events while so serving. Before and after the Expedition he was an obscure individual, about whom we know little, and that would hardly have been the case if he had distinguished himself in any way, as did, for instance, George Shannon and John Colter, two of his fellow privates among this celebrated band of explorers. Shannon became a judge and Colter discovered what is now Yellowstone National Park.

In a sworn testament to Lewis and Clark at the conclusion of the Expedition, Whitehouse declared himself to be a native of Fairfax County, Virginia.[8] Elsewhere we learn that in 1803 he joined Lewis and Clark at Kaskaskia,[9] where he was a private in an infantry company commanded by Captain Russell Bissell.[10] The earliest references to him I have found in any journal of the Expedition occur in Clark's "Field Notes" of the winter at Camp Dubois, Wood River. On December 26, 1803, Clark reported, "Corpl. White house [commenced] sawing with Whip Saws," and again, on April 13, 1804, "Wh[itehouse] wishes to return."[11]

Thus, we learn, if we have interpreted Clark's terse entries correctly, that Whitehouse handled a saw in the construction of quarters on Wood River, but later, becoming dissatisfied with his lot, ex-

[7] Edited by Ernest Staples Osgood and published in 1964 by Yale University Press.

[8] Jackson, *Letters*, 343.

[9] Kaskaskia was on the eastern bank of the Mississippi some fifty miles below St. Louis.

[10] Previously published statements have indicated that Whitehouse joined Lewis and Clark at Fort Massac (Jackson, *Letters*, 176n.). More about this later.

[11] Osgood, *Field Notes*, 8, 31.

pressed a desire to "return," presumably to Kaskaskia. We cannot explain Clark's reference to him as a "Corpl."

Though Whitehouse failed to effect his release from the Corps of Discovery, he proved nevertheless to be a model soldier throughout the continental traverse; at least, his commanding officers reported nothing to the contrary. In fact, they may have demonstrated a measure of respect for him right at the beginning of the journey when, at St. Charles on May 17, they named him as one of five to sit as arbiters in the court-martial of two of the men charged with insubordination.[12]

In journalistic comment thereafter, Whitehouse's name appears infrequently. Just below Great Falls, on July 11, 1805, Whitehouse himself reported, ". . . trod on a verry large rattle Snake. it bit my leggin on my legg I Shot it. it was 4 feet 2 Inches long."[13] One month later, while descending the Big Hole (Wisdom) River in western Montana, he came closer to losing his life. This happened when the dugout in which he was riding overturned and, according to Lewis, "pressed him to the bottom as she passed over him and had the water been 2 inches shallower must inevitably have crushed him to death."[14]

On just one other occasion did Whitehouse figure in anything like an important event. On the return trip, at the mouth of the Sandy (Quicksand) River, just above present-day Portland, Oregon, Lewis and Clark received word from Indians met there of a large stream entering the Columbia from the south, which, it soon became evident, they had missed so far because intervening islands had obscured it from their view. Whitehouse was one of six men whom Clark chose to accompany him to look for this stream (the "Mult- nomah" of the Indians), and thus he became one of the discoverers of the Willamette River.[15]

What happened to Private Whitehouse after the Expedition returned to St. Louis? Again we learn very little. He soon received his discharge, and with it title to a piece of land[16] and army pay (at

[12] Thwaites, *Original Journals*, I, 19.

[13] *Ibid.*, VII, 113.

[14] *Ibid.*, II, 315.

[15] *Ibid.*, IV, 236.

[16] Jackson, *Letters*, 343–44. Which land Whitehouse promptly sold to George Drouillard for $280 (*Ibid.*).

$5.00 per month) amounting to $166.66⅔.[17] At later date White-house re-enlisted in the army, served during the War of 1812, and, in 1817, deserted.[18] And that concludes the information known to this writer about Whitehouse's life—initially valorous, terminally clouded.

—3—

With these introductory paragraphs behind us, we may now give full attention to the document prompting this writing, namely, the manuscript of Whitehouse brought to light by Professor White in a Philadelphia bookstore. As to his role in discovering it, he has generously provided this writer with the following facts. He had traveled from Urbana to Philadelphia for the primary purpose of attending meetings of the Geological Society of America scheduled for February 10 to 12, 1966, and had gone a day or two early in order to satisfy a secondary design, which was to visit bookshops and call on fellow scientists of the city. To the best of his recollection, he went to the bookstore in question on February 9 and was soon in conversation with the manager of the Americana Rare Book Division, who showed him the Whitehouse manuscript. On his return to Urbana he told his friend, Donald Jackson, about it, and Jackson immediately expressed much interest in it.[19]

Donald Jackson was then editor of the University of Illinois Press and, as White knew, had recently edited *Letters of the Lewis and Clark Expedition with Related Documents, 1783–1854.* On receipt of White's intelligence, Jackson at once informed Newberry Library, Chicago, knowing that that repository held the original Whitehouse journal and might therefore wish to acquire the paraphrase of it found by White. Newberry soon afterward did succeed in acquiring the document, and immediately released it to Jackson, who had requested the privilege of editing it for publication.

Jackson's preliminary examination of this unique manuscript re-

---

[17] *Ibid.*, 378.

[18] National Archives, Record Group 94, Muster Rolls, Roll for Co. L (Capt. J. F. Heilman), 1st Batt., Corps of Artillery, for the period 31 Dec. 1816 to 28 Feby. 1817. The roll carries the notation that Whitehouse deserted on February 1, 1817.

[19] George W. White to author, August 5, 1971.

vealed a number of interesting facts. (1) It was a standard blank book of 360 pages bound in boards—leather spine, paper sides—and small folio in size. The front cover carried a hand-lettered label which read: "Journal of Captains Lewis and Clark's Expedition. Written by Joseph Whitehouse. Formerly the property of E. Clarence Lighthall Mustin. A.M. 5851. Presented to George S. Mustin A.D. 1850." (2) It had been written by someone other than Whitehouse himself. (3) It began with a six-page preface written in St. Louis soon after the return of the Expedition. (4) It extended the original Whitehouse version beyond November 6, 1805, through April 2, 1806. (5) It filled a number of hiatuses which had existed in the original. (6) Preceding the entry of March 23, 1806, it contained a heading, "VOLUME 2ND," this indicating the probability that Whitehouse had continued his journal to the end, until the party returned to St. Louis. (7) It provided incontestable proof that Whitehouse, by having his account rewritten, had in mind its publication. (8) It provided evidence that Whitehouse's writer had access to Clark's facts and figures pertaining to such information as latitude and longitude. (9) It underscored a fact, already known, that there had been widespread copying by the journalists of each other's diaries.

I first heard of "a new Lewis and Clark journal" in May, 1966, and from Jackson himself. He confirmed the discovery, alluded to some of the above determinations gleaned from his preliminary examination, and concluded with these words, "Not a very exciting find, really, but any *new* item on Lewis and Clark is, of course, valuable."[20]

Soon afterward Jackson resigned his post with the University of Illinois Press to assume editorship of *The Papers of George Washington* and moved his office to the campus of the University of Virginia, Charlottesville. Here, in ensuing months as time permitted, he resumed his work on the Whitehouse rewrite, transcribing, collating, attempting to further existing knowledge of the life of Whitehouse, and pursuing leads pointing toward the origin and later history of this unusual document. Intermittently I heard from him on progress made and frustrations experienced. Then, in early fall of 1970, he wrote to me in part as follows:

[20] Donald Jackson to author, May 23, 1966.

You will be surprised and no doubt even startled to learn that I
have decided against going ahead with the Whitehouse journal. I
send you this information for . . . you might be inclined someday to
consider taking it on as a project. Here are my reasons:

(1) When you really get into the thing and start looking for
new observations, they are just too scarce. . . .

(2) This lack of originality vitiates the argument that the "new"
Whitehouse gives us several more months of coverage. More months,
yes, but very little new information.

(3) My effort to track down more biographical information on
Whitehouse, and more on the provenance of the journal, has been
very disappointing. . . .[21]

(4) Add all this together, plus the fact that I would still be publishing a fragmentary document, and the project begins to look
rather thin. . . .

Some time later I obtained a copy of the paraphrase from Newberry Library. After reading it and comparing its text with that of
the original Whitehouse, and with those of Lewis, Clark, Floyd,
Gass, and Ordway, there was no escaping the conclusion that, as
Jackson had determined, it contained an obvious scarcity of new
information. However, for a number of reasons, I felt it deserved
a report, if nothing more than an outlining of essential facts. For
one thing, it does contain many items of interest, and a few of in-
trinsic worth. For another, the Lewis and Clark enthusiasts who
have had wind of it (and nothing more) surely merit a report. And
for still another, anything new relevant to the history of the Expedition, even "shaving papers," possesses some value; hence this
brief announcement.

—4—

Hereinafter we perforce deal with the two versions of Whitehouse's journal: the original and the paraphrase. In interests of
brevity and simplicity we will from now on refer to the former as
JW-A and the latter as JW-B.

As earlier mentioned, JW-B emphasized a fact previously known:

---

[21] One disappointment was the failure of the Mustins, now living in Philadelphia,
to throw light on the provenance of the rewrite.

that the journalists copied each other's accounts. For example, during and following the winter at Fort Clatsop, Clark copied Lewis' entries almost verbatim. JW-B (through JW-A) leaned most heavily, in the early months of the trip, on Gass, and thereafter on Ordway. To illustrate the close resemblance between JW-B and Gass, we herewith reproduce their entries for October 21, 1804.

GASS

We had a disagreeable night of sleet and hail. It snowed during the forenoon, but we proceeded early on our voyage, passed bottom on the south side and hills on the north. We also passed a small river on the south side called Chischeet [Heart] river; and encamped on the south side. Two of our hunters, who had gone out in the morning came in, and had killed a buffaloe and an otter.

JW-B

Last night we had rainy disagreeable weather. We set out early this morning. Shortly after we had some Snow. We passed a small River, lying on the South side of the Mesouri, called Chief Charet. We proceeded on till Evening, & encamped on the South Side of the River. Our hunters came to us, having killed a Buffalo, and one Otter which they brought to our Camp.[22]

As may be seen, the two entries (and they have been chosen at random from others that would have served equally well) approach identicality in both length and substance.

Following the evacuation of Fort Mandan on April 7, 1805, and thereafter through April 2, 1806 (a full year), the entries of JW-B demonstrate a remarkable reliance on Ordway. Again at random, we cite those of May 15, 1805.

ORDWAY

cloudy, we delayed to dry the goods. Some men went up the River a hunting   the day unfavorable to dry the goods.   a Small Shower of rain about 11 oClock   continued cloudy all day   towards evening the hunters returned.   had killed one buffaloe seven deer and four beaver.   the party dressed Skins.

JW-B

This morning we had Cloudy weather. We delayed here to dry the Goods, that got wet Yesterday. They were all opened but we

---

[22] Here and hereafter all quotations from JW-B will be italicized.

had to cover them again soon. A Shower of rain coming on, which lasted about One hour, when it cleared off. The Goods were all opened again to dry. Several of our Men went out hunting this morning, and all returned towards Evening. They had killed one Buffaloo 7 deer & 4 Beaver. We staid here this day. Some of the party were employed in dressing Skins &ca.

Once more events—weather, drying of goods, number of animals shot, and the dressing of skins—parallel each other. And the similarity is even greater if we compare Ordway with JW-A, the latter beginning with identical words, "cloudy, we delayed to dry the goods. . . ."[23] JW-B, we may point out here, is almost invariably wordier than JW-A. For example, JW-B for this date runs to ninety-one words, while JW-A limits itself to just sixty-one.

It seems unlikely that anyone will ever determine the identity of Whitehouse's "ghost writer." We do learn a few facts about him, however, simply by paying close attention to the wording of his product. Obviously he had received more schooling than White-house—but considerably less than David M'Keehan, who about this same time was engaged in a similar free rendering of Sergeant Gass's journal. The unknown author's misspellings were almost Clarkian (Missouri always came out "Mesouri" and Meriwether "Merriweather"), he punctuated disturbingly, and he turned out clauses ("The two men that had went back for to hunt") that would give glee to most of today's third-graders. Rarely do we find M'Keehan guilty of similar grammatical lesions.

There seems little doubt, too, that the author of JW-B lived either in St. Louis or its immediate environs, for he provided topographic and historic information about that area unknown to the Virginia-born Whitehouse; certainly it does not appear in JW-A. For example, on May 16, 1804, the day the party arrived at St. Charles, he supplemented JW-A's entry of like date as follows:

Saint Charles is a Village settled by French Inhabitants. It is a handsome situation, laying on the North side of the River contains about 80 Houses, built in the french fashion, and has a small Roman Catholic Chapel. Its Inhabitants are chiefly canadian french; who are chiefly concerned & employed by others Trading with the Indians who reside on the River Mesouri, and other Rivers that empty into it.

[23] Thwaites, *Original Journals,* VII, 83.

Similar ancillary contributions (absent from all other accounts) appear until the party arrived on May 25 at La Charette, a tiny frontier settlement just above St. Charles. Thereafter they cease, the inference being that the writer has no personal knowledge of the region beyond that point.

By reading JW-B we learn also, for what it is worth, that its author was a pious individual. On September 7, 1805, for example, during the party's descent of the Bitterroot River to Traveller's Rest, he felt impelled to write, "*Our party seemed revived at the success that the hunters had met with. However in all the hardship that they had yet undergone they never once complained, trusting to Providence & the Conduct of our Officers in all our difficulties.*"

Lewis and Clark, and the other diarists of the Expedition, may well have entertained similar religious sentiments, though on no occasion, we believe, did they put them in writing.

—5—

Before considering what is new, and consequently most important, in JW-B, we should note ways in which the two versions differ. JW-B is superior to JW-A in some respects, of lesser worth in others. As instances of superiority we cite the following.

1. JW-B is, as earlier indicated, a fuller account, containing not only an introduction and the continuance covering the period of late 1805 and early 1806, but also material filling hiatuses in JW-A.[24]

2. It supplies words that are illegible or totally missing in JW-A. The first instance occurs on May 21, 1805, on which date JW-A (as transcribed by Thwaites) reads in part, ". . . proceeded on in good heart, about [blank space in MS.] miles."[25] JW-B says, ". . . *proceeded up the River about 3 Miles.*" Also, on July 18, 1805, the entry of JW-A reads, ". . . towards evening we passed a Small River on N.S. about 60 yds wide named [blank space in MS.] River."[26] JW-B provides the missing name, ". . . *passed a small River lying*

[24] Existing hiatuses in JW-A are as follows: May 29, 1804; October 16 to 31, 1804; November 4 to 29, 1804; December 3 to 17 and 26 to 30, 1804; January 6 to 8 and 10, 1805; January 21 through April 30, 1805; and, of course, November 7, 1805, through September 23, 1806.

[25] Thwaites, *Original Journals*, VII, 31.

[26] *Ibid.*, 117.

on the North side 60 Yards wide at its mouth which Captain Lewis named Dearbornes River."

3. JW-B occasionally clarifies statements. As a specific illustration, on June 10, 1804, JW-A (also, Clark, Floyd, Ordway, and Gass) failed to make clear the juxtaposition of the two Chariton (Big and Little) Rivers, which discharge their waters into the Missouri from the north in present-day Chariton County, Missouri. But the author of JW-B explained the apposition perfectly when he wrote, *"The big Charotto* [that is, the Big Chariton] *is 100 yards wide at its mouth. The little Charotto empties itself into it, at about 300 Yards distance above it and is 50 Yards wide at its mouth."*[27]

4. Now and then JW-B corrects errors in JW-A. On June 16, 1805, for instance, JW-A had given the height of the largest water-fall at Great Falls, Montana, as fifty feet.[28] JW-B set the matter straight when he wrote, *". . . the highest being 87 feet perpendicular."*

But every coin has its obverse. On occasion JW-B goes wrong, and in places rather preposterously.

1. For no apparent reason the author of JW-B here and there deletes important information. On September 16, 1804, for instance, Whitehouse had written, "I went out a hunting . . . their was a nomber of buffaloe Elk Deer Goats & one magpy killed this day."[29] But the entry in JW-B for that date is foreshortened to read, *"I went with several of our party out a hunting. We saw large numbers of Buffalo, Elk deer & Goats, but they were very shy."* As can be seen, this restatement excludes mention of the magpie (*Pica pica hudsonia*), a bird unknown to this continent until Lewis and Clark's discovery of it on this date.

2. JW-B impersonalizes. Time and again this version omits names of personnel that Whitehouse had consistently included, perhaps

[27] However, in Lewis' "Summary View of Rivers and Creeks" we read, ". . . the two Shariton rivers discharge themselves on the N. side, the smaller falling into the larger on it's lower side at a small distance from the Missouri" (Thwaites, *Original Journals*, VI, 34). This seems to make clear that Lewis was better informed, or expressed himself more capably, than Clark, Ordway, and the other journalists. The statement suggests, too, that the author of JW-B may have had access to Lewis' "Summary View of Rivers and Creeks."

[28] *Ibid.*, VII, 101.

[29] *Ibid.*, 59.

more so than any of the journalists. On August 23, 1804, as a notable example, Whitehouse had written, "Jo. Fields came to the Boat had killed a Buffalow."[30] But JW-B had it, *"One of hands that we had sent out this morning returned, he having shot a Buffalo Bull."* Thus, as is apparent, JW-B not only omits the name of Joseph Fields, but also, in so doing, denies credit belonging to Joseph Fields as the first member of the party to kill a buffalo. Again, on September 15, 1804, the JW-A version states, "Sergt. Gass & R. Fields went up White River Some Distance."[31] But JW-B altered the sentence to read, *"Two of our men were order'd to go up White River."*

3. The author of JW-B occasionally exaggerates. In his entry for June 26, 1805, written as the party portaged around Great Falls, he declared, *"I had an opportunity of seeing the quantity of buffalo . . . and I can without exaggeration say, that I saw more Buffalo feeding [here] at one time, than all the Animals I had ever seen before in my life time put together."* Needless to say, Whitehouse himself made no such claim on this date (or any other), nor did any of the other journalists.

4. JW-B contains prime errors. In the entry of October 31, 1804, we find, *"This* [second Mandan] *Village we supposed contained 1500 Souls,"* and in that of April 7, 1805, *"This* [first Mandan] *Town or Village Contains from the best calculation we could make 2,000 Inhabitants."* Thus, if we credit these figures, the Mandan population at that time approximated thirty-five hundred individuals. But Lewis and Clark, in their "Estimate of the Eastern Indians," give the "probable Number of [Mandan] Souls" in the two villages as just twelve hundred and fifty.[32]

An equally deplorable mistake occurs in JW-B of November 18, 1805: *"Our officers called the Cape Cape Disappointment on account of not finding Vessels there."* It is true that Lewis and Clark expressed disappointment at not finding one or more trading vessels anchored at the mouth of the Columbia, but this northern headland received its name, Cape Disappointment, from Captain John Meares in 1788. And four years later George Vancouver so identified it in his map of this region. Since Lewis and Clark carried a copy of Van-

---

[30] *Ibid.,* 51.
[31] *Ibid.,* 58.
[32] *Ibid.,* VI, 89.

couver's chart, they knew in advance the name of the cape, and in fact we find Clark employing the name immediately on coming in sight of the Pacific.[33]

The above serve as examples of more flagrant errors encountered in JW-B. But for limitations of space, several lesser ones could be cited.

—6—

The over-all worth of JW-B necessarily stands or falls on whether or not the contained matter appreciably extends existing knowledge of the Expedition. That it fails in large measure to do so has already been indicated; however, not entirely, as the following excerpts testify:

> MAY 23, 1804 [below village of La Charette, near modern Marthasville, Warren County, Missouri]: *We . . . proceeded on very well, and passed some Plantations, which is called Boons settlement lying on the north side of the River. This settlement was made by Colonel Daniel Boone, the person who first discover'd Kentucky, & who was residing at this place, with a number of his family and friends.*

Neither in JW-A nor in any of the other journals kept by members of the Expedition do we find any reference to Boone and this settlement.[34]

> JUNE 10–11, 1804 [at or near the mouth of Big Chariton River, Chariton County, Missouri]: *We had great difficulty swimming the horses . . . to the Island & getting them on Board* [the keelboat]. *. . . This morning* [June 11] *we landed the horses on the banks of the River.*

As is well known, Lewis and Clark obtained two horses at St. Charles which they afterward used for hunting and bringing in game. Although the journalists frequently referred to these horses,

[33] *Ibid.*, III, 230.

[34] But in Lewis' "Summary View of Rivers and Creeks" we find, "This part of the country is generally called Boon's settlement, having derived it's name from it's first inhabitant Colo. Daniel Boon, a gentleman well known in the early settlement of the state of Kentucky" (*Ibid.*, VI, 30).

not one of them alluded at any time to their being brought aboard the keelboat in the evenings and taken off the next morning, obviously a safety measure to prevent possible theft by some wandering band of Kickapoos, Osages, or other Indians.

> AUGUST 2, 1804 [about 15 miles above present-day city of Council Bluffs, Iowa]: *We remain'd still at the Camp of Brareowes* [Badgers].[35] *. . . at 7 OClock A.M. the Zoto* [Oto] *Indians arrived at our Camp, which the Captains had alter'd the name of, to that of Council Bluffs. . . . the number of Zoto Indians that arrived were 12. . . . They are a handsome stout well made set of Indians & have good open Countenances, and are of a light brown colour, and have long black hair, which they do wear without cutting; and they all use paint in order to compleat their dress.*

The above provides two bits of intelligence absent from other accounts of this date, one stating that Council Bluffs was initially called Camp of the Badgers, and the other describing in few words the physical appearance of these Indians.

> AUGUST 17–18, 1804 [two days' travel below Sioux City, Iowa]: *La'Beech* [Francois Labiche] *our Interpreter in the Evening came by himself . . . and told our Captains, if any of the Mahaw* [Omaha] *Indians were with us, we should remain still, but if none were then among us, to fire off our Swivel, the Zoto Indians being at Warr with the Mahaws. . . .* [August 18] *. . . We fired off our Cannon as a signal for the Indiana.*

Only in JW-B do we read of this request for the firing of the swivel and of its actual discharge.

> AUGUST 20, 1804 [in southern environs of present-day Sioux City]: *The disease which occasion'd his* [Sergeant Charles Floyd's] *death, was a bilious cholic, which baffled all medical aid, that Captain Lewis could administer.*

Historians have heretofore presumed that Lewis treated Sergeant Floyd (apparently the victim of a ruptured, gangrenous appendix),

---

[35] On August 1, Whitehouse himself had alluded to "Camp of the Brareowes," and, on the next day, to "Our Camp calld. the Council Bluffs, or the Brarareham prarie" (*Ibid.*, VII, 47). The word "Brareowes" is a corruption of *blaireau*, the French word for badger.

but in no other account do we find specific mention of his having done so.

AUGUST 25, 1804 [near Spirit Mound, Clay County, South Dakota]: *Some of our Men caught Nine Cat fish. 5 of them was very large, weighing on an average each 100 lbs.*

Other journalists verified the catching of nine catfish, and Gass said that they "would together weigh three hundred pounds." But only JW-B upped the weight, for just five of them, to five hundred pounds. The large size suggests the great blue cat (*Ictalurus furcatus*).

AUGUST 29, 1804 [near today's city of Yankton, Yankton County, South Dakota]: *In the afternoon Serjeant Pryor & the two men returned, having with them Sixty Indians of the [Yankton] Sioux nation; they appear'd very friendly. They are a handsome well made set of Indians, are about the middle stature, and do not cutt their hair as most the Savages in this part does.*

No other account includes this comment descriptive of the Yankton Sioux.

SEPTEMBER 22, 1804 [at Loisel's Fort just above Big Bend of the Missouri, South Dakota]: *The Situation of this Fort was a handsome one it commanding a most delightful View of the River & the land lying on both sides of it for a considerable distance and had some beautiful Groves of Cedar, and other trees on it; the Island is 1½ Miles in length and the soil is very rich.*

Only JW-B contains this information about the environs of Fort Loisel.

SEPTEMBER 29, 1804 [a short distance above mouth of the Bad River, Stanley County, South Dakota]: *"We proceeded on, and passed an old Indian Village, lying on the South side of the River; where the Rickorees [Arikaras] had lived five Years before; and we were inform'd by one of the frenchmen, that was with us, that they had raised Corn, Beans, pease & Simblins [squashes] at that place.*

JW-B seems to have been in error about the Arikaras raising peas. We have been unable to find evidence, either in Lewis and Clark or other source, that any of the Upper Missouri agricultural tribes cultivated this garden vegetable.

> OCTOBER 1, 1804 [just above mouth of Cheyenne River, Dewey County, South Dakota]: *We encamped on a Sand barr, in the middle of the River, at which place, a french Trader* [Jean Vallé] *came to us from the South shore, and staid with us all night he being One of a party, who was with Louselle* [Loisel] *& had left him.*

Clark identified the trader as "Jon Vallie,"[36] but only JW-B connected him with Regis Loisel.

> DECEMBER 25, 1804 [at Fort Mandan, below mouth of Knife River, McLean County, North Dakota]: *The officers this day named our Fort, Fort Mandan.*

Not one of the other accounts alluded to the naming of the fort on Christmas Day—or, to the best of our knowledge, on any other day. The likelihood of JW-B being correct is enhanced by Gass's entry of December 25, which referred to the hoisting of the American flag on that day and to "its first waving in fort Mandan." And there is the additional fact that the fort was not completed until the day before Christmas.

> DECEMBER 31, 1804 [at Fort Mandan]: *The fort which we built here . . . is situated on the North East Side of the Mesouri River. It was built in a triangular form, with its base fronting the same, had a platform on the No. Side 12 feet high with Pickets on it, six feet, and a Room of 12 feet square, the under part serving as a Storehouse for provisions &ca. The Three sides were 60 feet in length each, & picketted on the front side only, with pickets of 18 feet long & the houses in which we resided in lay on the So. West side & the Smith & Armourer Workshop was at the South point of the Fort.*

The only other account providing details of the construction of Fort Mandan is that by Sergeant Gass, in his entry of November 3, 1804. During the recent reconstruction of the fort, architects compared Gass with JW-B, since the latter contains details missing from the former.[37]

---

[36] *Ibid.*, I, 176.

[37] Donald Jackson, in a letter dated June 21, 1971, informed this writer that he had sent this information to the people in charge of reconstructing Fort Mandan.

APRIL 7, 1805 [the date Lewis and Clark abandoned Fort Man-
dan and began their further ascent of the Missouri]: *At half past
4 o'Clock P.M. we . . . left Fort Mandan, on our way for the
Pacific Ocean . . . encamped, on the North side of the Mesouri
River, opposite to the first* [upper] *Village of the Mandan Nation.
. . . The Land adjoining it is Priaries, which gradually rise from the
River. The soil is very rich, producing Indian corn, pumpkins,
Squashes, & beans in abundance. The Natives have large fields,
which they cultivate and which produces plentifully. They have
likewise Gardens, which they plant & have several kinds of Garden
Vegetables in it, such as lettuce, Mustard &ca. They have likewise
growing in their Gardens, Gooseberrys, which is superior in Size,
to any in the United States & Currants of different kinds.*

An important statement, if altogether true, for it lists Mandan-
cultivated plants—lettuce, mustard, gooseberries, and currants—unmentioned by other journalists of the Expedition. Of course, currants
and gooseberries grew wild along the banks of the Upper Missouri
and the natives may well have introduced them into their gardens.
Also, the possibility exists that they cultivated wild forms of lettuce
and mustard. If Lewis and Clark's stay among the Mandans had
continued into spring and summer, and they could thus have witnessed the Mandan women cultivating their gardens, they unquestionably would have had much more to say about aboriginal agriculture as practiced at the mouth of the Knife River. They did, of
course, report on two plants ignored by JW-B, Indian tobacco and
sunflower, which the Mandans and neighboring tribes grew here.

MAY 8, 1805 [at mouth of Milk River, Valley County, Montana]:
*. . . passed a River which empties itself into the Mesouri lying on
the North side. This River was about 200 Yards wide at its mouth,
and very deep. The mouth of this River is 2,100 Miles distant from
the mouth of the Mesouri River. Our officers gave this River the
name, Scalding Milk River.*[38]

Beyond reasonable doubt, the above entry explains a problem in
geographical nomenclature that has puzzled historians of the Expedition ever since publication of the *Original Journals* and the appearance therein of such statements as, "We think it possible that this

[38] In JW-A we find, "We named this River Scolding or Milk River (Thwaites,
Original Journals, VII, 79).

may be the river called by the Minitares *the river which scoalds at all others*,"[39] and "no stream of any magnitude discharges itself [into the Missouri from the north above the mouth of the Yellowstone] except the scolding river."[40] The words "scoalds" and "scolding" have heretofore admitted of no logical interpretation—made no sense. Donald Jackson, while transcribing JW-B, was the first to note "Scalding Milk River," and we learned of it from him when he wrote, "This could be a reference to the color and temperature of scalded milk, for centuries a standard cooking item."[41] This is an explanation that *does* make some sense, though the changing of "the river which scoalds at all others" to "the river which scalds at all others" may jar reasonableness equally. Even so, we incline to Jackson's thinking, and to the belief that Thwaites, in transcribing Lewis mistook "scalding" for "scolding."[42]

JUNE 21, 1805 [at Great Falls, Cascade County, Montana]: *This Iron boat, or rather frame was made out of wrought Iron, the keel being 32 feet long and had ribbs, Stauncheons & beams of the same, with holes & screws to fit them. It likewise had screws to fasten the hides or skins that covered the bottom & sides, and was in shape like a Ships Yawl.*

This description of Lewis' iron boat frame, even though it includes references to stanchions, length, and shape unmentioned elsewhere, is not so valuable as it may appear at first glance. For over-all dimensions of the frame, Sergeant Gass's figures should be consulted. In his entry of June 23, 1805, Gass reported that the frame was "36 feet long, 4½ wide and 2 feet 2 inches deep."[43]

JULY 14, 1805 [at Canoe Camp above White Bear Islands, Cascade County, Montana]: *The weeds & Grass in this bottom is as*

[39] *Ibid.*, II, 10.

[40] *Ibid.*, VI, 53.

[41] Letter from Jackson to author, June 20, 1971.

[42] The journalists, unpracticed with pen, often wrote near illegibly, thus making transcription doubly difficult. As another example, we find in JW-B's entry of April 21, 1805, mention of "the River called Le Tear Black." It seems certain that Whitehouse, after listening to one or another of his French-speaking companions, misunderstood their *"La Terre Blanc,"* which, properly translated, means White Earth, the name Lewis and Clark applied to the tributary of the Missouri (today's Little Muddy River) emptying from the north at Williston, North Dakota.

[43] Thwaites, *Original Journals*, VII, 122.

high, as a mans knees, but on the high land not more than 3 Inches long, owing to the number of buffalo that feed on them.

An important observation, since it reveals a little-known fact; namely, that overgrazing existed in the West long before the white man arrived with his herds of sheep and cattle.

JULY 27, 1805 [at Three Forks of the Missouri, Broadwater County, Montana]: *The forks that we are present at, is a most delightful situated place, and exceeds any that we have yet seen, it affording a most delightful prospect, the land extreamly rich & fertile; and the bottoms large and well timbered, and to all appearance must be healthy, and may be called the Paradice of the Mesouri River.*

We will never know why Whitehouse's rephraser became so carried away with Three Forks, a place he had never seen, and one in point of beauty that couldn't hold a candle to the Missouri Breaks, or Gates of the Mountains, earlier visited. Of Three Forks, Whitehouse himself said only, "This is a verry pleasant handsome place, fine bottoms of timber &c."[44] However, today's residents of the town of Three Forks will doubtless interpose no demurrer on learning that they live in the "Paradice" of the Missouri River.

AUGUST 7, 1805 [at mouth of Big Hole River,[45] site of present-day town of Twin Bridges, Madison County, Montana]: *He [Lewis] also fired off his air gun several times in order that the Man [George Shannon] that went out a hunting from the party that was with Captain Clarke up the north fork [of the Big Hole River] Yesterday & who we suppose is lost might hear the report, he having as yet not returned.*

As we view it, the portion of the above statement relating to Lewis' firing his air gun in order to attract Shannon should be disregarded. It appears in no other journal and, although Lewis did fire the gun on this date, he provided an entirely different explanation for so doing: "my air gun was out of order and her sights had been removed by some accedent   I put her in shape and regulated her.   she

---

[44] In Lewis' "List of Requirements," we find, "1 Iron frame of Canoe 40 feet Long" (Jackson, *Letters*, 73).
[45] Wisdom River of Lewis and Clark.

shot again as well as she ever did."[46] Another reason for discounting JW-B's statement is that air guns for the most part were practically noiseless (hence their popularity among poachers of that day).[47]

> AUGUST 26, 1805 [just west of Lemhi Pass, Lemhi County, Idaho]: *Our party drank water out of this Spring so that we might all have it in our power to say: that we had drank from out the head Springs or source of both these great Rivers* [that is, the Missouri and the Columbia].

The entry of JW-A on this date reads, ". . . passed a nomber of fine large Springs and drank at the head Spring of the Missourie and crossed a high ridge [Lemhi Pass] only one mile and drank at the head Spring of Columbian River running West."[48] This entry did not go on to say, however, nor did that of any other journalist, anything about the reason for drinking from both head springs—as did JW-B.

> SEPTEMBER 6, 1805 [among Flathead Indians in Ross's Hole, Ravalli County, Montana]: . . . *purchased 3 Colts, that in case we should be without provisions, that we might have something for to subsist on.*

The other accounts report this purchase, but fail to provide the above explanation for so doing.

> NOVEMBER 24, 1805 [Baker's Bay on north side of Columbia estuary, Pacific County, Washington]: *The greater part of our*

---

[46] Thwaites, *Original Journals*, II, 318.

[47] However, there are different models. Dr. R. M. Chatters, until recently head of Radioisotopes and Radiations Laboratory, Washington State University, and an authority on air guns, recently (August 27, 1971) informed the author, "I believe there are several factors which would affect the degree of silence of an air gun of the pneumatic rather than the spring type (such as some of the B.B. guns). First, I believe that the level of pressure in the containment vessel (either under-the-barrel ball type or in-the-stock vessel) would have a marked effect upon the amount of sound produced. As some of the air guns were capable of being pressurized up to 900 psi one could certainly expect noise when that air is suddenly released through a small vent. . . . Also, the bore of the gun would surely have an effect upon the loudness of the sound as well as the quality of that sound. . . . Further, I believe that the amount of detectable sound would be influenced by the surrounding terrain, the presence or absence of trees, and atmospheric conditions at the time of discharge of the weapon."

[48] Thwaites, *Original Journals*, VII, 142.

Men were of opinion; that it would be best, to cross the River . . .
on account of making Salt, which we are nearly out of at this time,
& the want of it in preserving our provisions for the Winter, would
be an object well worth our attention.

The other accounts stress the desirability of obtaining salt (by boiling down salt water), but leave the impression that this commodity would be used primarily for seasoning food, not preserving it. On February 21, 1806, at Fort Clatsop, Lewis wrote, "Sergt. Ordway returned with the party from the salt camp which we have now evacuated. they brought with them the salt and eutensils, our stock of salt is now about 20 Gallons; 12 gallons of which we secured in 2 small iron bound kegs and laid by for our voyage [back to St. Louis]."[49] Needless to say, the small amount remaining (8 gallons) would hardly have sufficed for both seasoning and preserving the flesh of the numerous elk and other animals killed during the days left at Fort Clatsop.

—7—

Unless our collation has been faulty, the only other information in JW-B which extends existing history of the Expedition is to be found in the preface; and this, in our opinion, is of greater value than that in any of the items cited above, with the possible exception of the "Scalding River" one. Actually, there are three prefatorial passages—three in particular—that demand attention. They were written in St. Louis on December 10, 1806, following the return of the party to that city. The first passage reads:

I had been at Kaskaskia Village some time, when I was informed
That His Excellency Thomas Jefferson Esquire, President of the
United States, had appointed Captain Meriweather Lewis, and
Captain William Clark, to take the command of a party of Con-
tinental Troops, and Volunteers; in order to explore the Mesouri
River; and find out its source; and to find (if possible) by that rout
a passage to the Pacific ocean, I was fortunate in being chosen one
of the party . . . by them, which contributed much to quicken the
execution of my favorite project, and of satisfying my own ambition.

[49] *Ibid.,* IV, 92.

The above is important in that it seems to establish beyond question that Lewis and Clark signed on Whitehouse at Kaskaskia, and not in Kentucky (as one of the "the nine young men from Kentucky") or at Fort Massac.

The second of the prefatorial passages reads:

> *In this Voyage I furnished myself with books, and also got from Captains Lewis and Clark, every information that lay in their power, in order to compleat and make my Journal correct; and part of my Journals were kept by one of them* [Clark] *when I was on a fataigue party. This was done by them, in case of any great accident happening to the party, so that if any of them should return to the United States, or their Journals fall into the hands of any civiliz'd Nation, that the grand object of our discovery's might not be defeated.*

This statement stands out significantly for a number of reasons. (1) It indicates, through inclusion of the clause, "I furnished myself with books," that Whitehouse may have been a man of more intellectual curiosity than heretofore suspected, and, so far as we know, the only enlisted member of the party to obtain books to advance his knowledge of the West. (2) It would appear to confirm, by use of the word "compleat," what we have believed all along, that Whitehouse did finish his journal—by recording events from April 3 through September 23, 1806. (3) It underscores what was already known—that the journalists, including Lewis and Clark themselves, not only exchanged information but also, on occasion, actually made entries for each other when requested to do so. (4) It reveals a closer personal relationship between the two commanding officers and their men than heretofore disclosed by any other document.

The third and final passage by Whitehouse to attract our attention signally reads as follows:

> *I cannot in justice to myself omit saying, that the manly, and soldier-like behaviour; and enterprizing abilities; of both Captain Lewis, and Captain Clark, claim my utmost gratitude; and the humanity shown at all times by them, to those under their command, on this perilous and important Voyage of discovery; I hope will ever fill the breasts of Men who were under their command with the same, and make their characters be esteem'd by the American people, and mankind in general, and convince the generous*

Public, that the President of the United States, did not displace his judgment, when he appointed them to the command of this party on discovery, which is of so great a magnitude and utility, to the United States and mankind in general.

With these words—lofty, ingenuous, and flowery—Whitehouse (through his as-told-to writer) has supplied an answer we have long sought. How did the rank and file of the Lewis and Clark party regard their commanding officers? If we can credit the above—and there seems no tangible reason for discrediting it—and if the other subalterns shared Whitehouse's opinion, then they held Lewis and Clark in high esteem, not only for their manliness, soldierly qualities, and unbroken enterprise, but also, and perhaps most significantly, for their "humanity shown at all times." We have found no comparable evaluation in the pages of other accounts.

So, in what better way may we conclude this report than by a scriptorial doff of the hat to Private Joseph Whitehouse? Beyond question he demonstrated great courage, stamina, and commitment throughout the twenty-eight-month-long journey. But, more to the point, with the assistance of his more literary confederate, he gave us new perspectives on the history of the Expedition, and our only on-the-spot appraisal of Meriwether Lewis and William Clark, foremost commissioners of discovery and destiny.

Appendix B

Legal Aspects of *Minnesota Historical Society* v. *United States of America in re Lewis and Clark Expedition Papers*
by
C. A. Peairs, Jr.

Since the day in 1956 when Judge Gunnar H. Nordbye handed down his decision regarding Clark's "Field Notes," various individuals have debated its legality and, at times, with the generation of considerable heat. Plainly, the Hammond heirs, as well as many librarians and collectors of rare books, had no quarrel with it. Conversely, as was to be expected, the coterie of men representing the government expressed sharp disagreement. So did a number of attorneys disrelated to the case, and distinguished historians, particularly those who had favored the government's stance from the beginning. Not all historians evinced dissatisfaction, however, among them Dr. Osgood. As he told Paul Cutright, "I'm glad the case turned out the way it did."

On one score, to *both* plaintiff and defendant, Nordbye's ruling was highly unacceptable. It settled one point only, namely, the government's failure to establish its claim to Clark's "Field Notes." The larger, more important issue, as to who owned a small mountain of other documents seemingly public, had not been settled. In this category were, of course, such manuscripts as the original journals of Lewis and Clark housed at the American Philosophical Society,

Clark's maps in Yale University Library, and numerous other "public" papers scattered from coast to coast in similar depositories. Obviously, present holders of these, so long as this doubt of ownership remains, will perforce live under a shifting cloud of disquietude and uncertainty.

—2—

Litigation involving ownership rights arising out of written documents commonly involves a number of rather nice legal distinctions not essential to the case presented to Judge Nordbye. Usually the right of publication, or some other rights in the information content or particular language contained in the document, is more important than ownership of the physical document itself.

The right to publish, or to prevent others from publishing—copyright—is the prime right in the language—or illustrations such as drawings, or other intellectual content such as formulas—as distinct from the physical piece of paper, the document itself. This copyright, so far as the use of a particular form of statement or presentation is concerned, if original, belongs to the author, and will pass to others only by assignment of copyright, as distinct from the document, or through some contract or equivalent means of altering the normal rule. Copyright is largely a matter of statutory regulation today, but the author's copyright to an unpublished document exists independently of the statutory protection, which largely regulates rights in published documents. In the St. Paul case, insofar as the locus of copyright determined who might be able to authorize the publication enterprise in which Dr. Osgood was concerned, it was of course involved in the case, though the case was directly concerned with document ownership, which, in the particular circumstance of the case, in turn governed the copyright or power to authorize publication.

Document ownership is not always controlling. In the case of a book or article, the author of course initially owns both the document and the copyright; but he may transfer either one without losing the other. If he licenses the book for publication, for example, he may turn the copyright over, or, what amounts to the same thing, by contract permit the publisher to take the statutory copyright in its name rather than his upon publication. This, however, will not affect his ownership of the original manuscript. On the other hand, he may, without publication, give the manuscript to another, without surrendering right to control publication. This situation arises most frequently in the case of letters; the addressee owns the document in such case, and cannot be forced by the writer to return it, but the copyright, the sole right to publish or prevent publication, remains in the writer. But in the instant case there had been no such separation of the two classes of rights by either publication or gift of the document, so far as the history of Clark's "Field Notes" indicate.

Copyright is also limited in what it protects, and may also be affected by contract or relationship under which the writing was done, as well as by the nature of the material. Its protection, for example, is limited to the particular form of phraseology, and does not extend to the essence of the ideas expressed. Darwin's theory of the origin of species, for example, was not so protected, nor would the formula for a new drug or engineering device be. The latter might be, and the former would not be, eligible for protection of the patent laws, properly applied for; but this is quite a different thing from the protection of the language form by copyright; this latter would extend to publication rights in the formulation of Darwin's theory, or in the inventor's description of his new formula or device. But both the information and the language in which it is expressed may be pre-empted or reserved by the contract or relationship of the parties. If the formula was worked out by an employee, on his employer's time, both the formula and the write-up he has made may by that token belong to the employer rather than to the employee; and here hung a part of the government theory in the St. Paul case. Or, secondly, even if the relationship would not produce this result, the parties may agree that the employer, or someone financing research work, will have all these rights; and this contention was also made in the instant case.

Certainly the relationship alone in the case of Lewis and Clark would entitle the government to the information value—what might be analogous to patent value—of anything developed by the Expedition. Information as to location of mineral deposits, or as to fur resources, or information of military value, would automatically belong to the government as sponsor, financer, and in a sense the owner of the Expedition. As to the scientific knowledge, outside the scope of any such ownership value, no exclusive rights would exist, and Lewis and Clark would be free to talk all they chose, and to write all they chose, so far as their service relationship went. But in this case there was more, in the specific injunction in their charter from Jefferson to prepare full journals and to submit them to him. These instructions, accepted by them as the organic document of the Expedition, were equivalent to the kind of special contract which may bind a scientist doing research work for the government, or for a large industrial concern, today; and it was in these special instructions—in this special charter provision—that the central government contention in the St. Paul case lay.

Two or three special comments may be appropriate on the significance of the special Jefferson instructions relied on in this case. In the first place, if the government had prevailed on this basis, it would *not* have followed, as it has been loosely assumed it would, that other original documents scattered in libraries and private collections over the country would be subject to be called in by the National Archives. The papers, diaries, correspondence copies, notes taken by the various presidents, for example, or held by their heirs and successors, would not be within the scope of such a holding, had Judge Nordbye made it, unless there was also in any such case some special contract or equivalent undertaking requiring such papers to be left in government archives or files. Had there been at any time such a law, for example, requiring such action, it would have been equivalent to what Lewis and Clark had for their governance.

This question has been idly raised from time to time, for example, when the huge collection of copies of official documents which had been gathered at government expense during World War II and preceding years was taken to Hyde Park, and again when former Secretary of the Treasury Morgenthau removed papers kept by him in office for the purpose of writing memoirs; but throughout our history, and for most key officials of the government, there has been no such law.

The second point, however, is that even though a favorable decision by Judge Nordbye would not have affected other documents, it might very well have been loosely taken to do so, just as has been done hypothetically; and the event might well have been the assembling into national ownership and under one roof of a great mass of material without determined opposition. The curious psychological reaction which occurred in this case, that it is not much worth while fighting the government, given impetus by such a decision, might have had just the hoped-for effect for the Archives staff, and one may doubt that they would have hesitated to capitalize on it, or that they would have hastened to point out the limited range of the effect of a favorable decision.

But the decision does not deny the government's rights in documents kept or prepared under such special instructions as existed here. It is limited strictly to the interpretation of those instructions as applied to these particular papers. Jefferson could have forbidden Lewis and Clark to keep any private notes; or the informal notes involved here could have been regarded as having been made in compliance with the instructions. In fact, Lewis and Clark were not limited in what they might make or maintain, over and above what might be required for the purposes of the Expedition; and in fact it was believed by the court that Clark did not mean these particular notes to be in compliance with the instructions, but merely as private, preliminary aids to enable him to make the publicly owned journal required of him. The decision, telling us so little of how much the two captains were limited, or of how much they might have been limited—in throwing so little light on what claim might have been made, for example, to the journals of the sergeants—rests on assumptions and not on laws determined to exist on these points. Had it gone the other way, it would have compelled little in favor of the government, in the absence of special instructions like those of Lewis and Clark; going as it did, it compels little in favor of private collectors; but here, as in most military operations, the psychological effect of a won or lost battle may go far beyond its physical accomplishments or necessary consequence.

Bibliography

We limit the scope of this bibliography to titles of books and magazine articles *written about* Lewis and Clark. For literature *written by* Lewis and Clark and other journalists of the Expedition, we refer the reader to "Bibliographical Data" by Victor Hugo Paltsits in *Original Journals of the Lewis and Clark Expedition, 1804–1806* (I, lxi–xciii), edited by Reuben Gold Thwaites, to the bibliography in *Letters of the Lewis and Clark Expedition with Related Documents, 1783–1854*, edited by Donald Jackson, and to the author's notes accompanying the text of this work.

Needless to say, we make no claim to having assembled titles of all books and magazine articles written about Lewis and Clark, a near impossible task. However, we have combed all literary "Guides" easily available to us and have had at hand a complete set of Library of Congress cards for Lewis and Clark literature held by that repository.

BOOKS
Adult Nonfiction

Bakeless, John. *The Adventures of Lewis and Clark*. Boston, Houghton Mifflin Co., 1929.

———. *Lewis and Clark: Partners in Discovery*. New York, William Morrow & Co., 1947.

Bordwell, Constance. *March of the Volunteers: Soldiering with Lewis and Clark*. Portland, Oregon, Beaver Books, 1960.

Brooks, Noah. *First Across the Continent: the Story of the Exploring Expedition of Lewis and Clark in 1803-4-5*. New York, Charles Scribner's Sons, 1901.

Burroughs, Raymond Darwin. *Exploration Unlimited: the Story of the Lewis and Clark Expedition*. Detroit, Wayne University Press, 1953.

———. *The Natural History of the Lewis and Clark Expedition*. East Lansing, Michigan State University Press, 1961.

Chidsey, Donald Barr. *Lewis and Clark, the Great Adventure*. New York, Crown Publishers, 1970.

Clarke, Charles G. *The Men of the Lewis and Clark Expedition*. Glendale, California, The Arthur H. Clark Co., 1970.

Criswell, Elijah Harry. *Lewis and Clark: Linguistic Pioneers*. University of Missouri Studies, 15, No. 2. Columbia, Missouri, University of Missouri Press, 1940.

Cutright, Paul Russell. *Lewis and Clark: Pioneering Naturalists*. Urbana, University of Illinois Press, 1969.

———. *Meriwether Lewis: Naturalist*. Portland, Oregon Historical Society, 1968.

Daugherty, James Henry. *Of Courage Undaunted: Across the Continent with Lewis and Clark*. New York, Viking Press, 1951.

Dillon, Richard. *Meriwether Lewis: a Biography*. New York, Coward-McCann, 1965.

Dye, Eva Emery. *The Conquest: the True Story of Lewis and Clark*. Chicago, A. C. McClurg & Co., 1902.

Eide, Ingvard Henry. *American Odyssey: the Journey of Lewis and Clark*. New York and Chicago, Rand McNally & Co., 1969.

Fisher, Vardis. *Suicide or Murder? The Strange Death of Governor Meriwether Lewis*. Denver, Colorado, Alan Swallow, 1962.

Harris, Burton. *John Colter, His Years in the Rockies*. New York, Charles Scribner's Sons, 1952.

Hawthorne, Hildegarde. *Westward the Course, a Story of the Lewis and Clark Expedition*. New York, Longmans, Green & Co., 1946.

Hebard, Grace Raymond. *Sacajawea, a Guide and Interpreter of the Lewis and Clark Expedition*. Glendale, California, The Arthur H. Clark Co., 1933. Reprinted by Clark in 1967.

Hitchcock, Ripley. *The Lewis and Clark Expedition*. Boston, Ginn & Co., 1905.

Holloway, David. *Lewis and Clark and the Crossing of North America*. The Great Explorers Series. New York, Saturday Review Press, 1974.

Howard, Harold P. *Sacajawea*. Norman, University of Oklahoma Press, 1972.

Hueston, Ethel. *The Man of the Storm, a Romance of John Colter Who Discovered Yellowstone*. Indianapolis, Bobbs-Merrill Co., 1936.

———. *Star of the West: the Romance of the Lewis and Clark Expedition*. Indianapolis, Bobbs-Merrill Co., 1935.

Jackson, Donald, ed. *Letters of the Lewis and Clark Expedition with Related Documents, 1783–1854*. Urbana, University of Illinois Press, 1962.

Jacob, John G. *The Life and Times of Patrick Gass*. Wellsburg, Virginia, Jacob & Smith, 1859.

Lighton, William Rheem. *Lewis and Clark: Meriwether Lewis and William Clark*. Boston, Houghton, Mifflin Co., 1901.

Link, Louis W. *Lewis and Clark Expedition, 1804–1806; from St. Louis, Missouri, to Pacific Ocean and Return, with Particular Reference to the Upper Missouri and Yellowstone Rivers*. Cardwell, Montana, 1962.

McKelvey, Susan Delano. *Botanical Exploration of the Trans-Mississippi West*. Boston, Arnold Arboretum of Harvard University, 1955.

Osborne, Kelsie Ramey. *Peaceful Conquest: Story of the Lewis and Clark Expedition*. Portland, Oregon, 1955.

Salisbury, Albert and Jane. *Two Captains West*. Seattle, Superior Publishing Co., 1950.

Skarsten, M. O. *George Drouillard, Hunter and Interpreter for Lewis and Clark and Fur Trader*. Glendale, California, The Arthur H. Clark Co., 1964.

Smyth, Clifford. *Lewis and Clark, Pioneers in America's Westward Expansion Movement*. New York, Funk & Wagnalls Co., 1931.

Snyder, Gerald S. *In the Footsteps of Lewis and Clark*. Washington, D.C., National Geographic Society, 1970.

Thwaites, Reuben Gold. *A Brief History of Rocky Mountain Exploration, with Especial Reference to the Expedition of Lewis and Clark*. New York, D. Appleton & Co., 1904.

Tomkins, Calvin. *The Lewis and Clark Trail*. New York, Harper & Row, 1965.

U.S. Bureau of Outdoor Recreation. *The Lewis and Clark Trail: a Proposal for Development*. Washington, Government Printing Office, 1965.

Vinton, Stallo. *John Colter, Discoverer of Yellowstone*. New York, Edward Eberstadt, 1926.

Wheat, Carl I. *Mapping the Transmississippi West*. 3 vols. San Francisco, Institute of Historical Cartography, 1958.

Wheeler, Olin D. *The Trail of Lewis and Clark, 1804–1806*. 2 vols. New York, G. P. Putnam's Sons, 1904.

Wilson, Charles Morrow. *Meriwether Lewis of Lewis and Clark.* New York, Thomas Y. Crowell Co., 1934.

Fiction

Fisher, Vardis. *Tale of Valor: a Novel of the Lewis and Clark Expedition.* Garden City, New York, Doubleday, 1958.

Hough, Emerson. *The Magnificent Adventure; This Being the Story of the World's Greatest Exploration, and the Romance of a Very Gallant Gentleman.* New York, D. Appleton & Co., 1916.

Peattie, Donald Culross. *Forward the Nation.* New York, G. P. Putnam's Sons, 1942.

Morrill, Madge. *Lewis and Clark, Explorers to the West.* New York, Abingdon Press, 1959.

Juvenile

Adams, Julia Davis. *No Other White Men.* New York, E. P. Dutton & Co., 1937.

Andrist, Ralph K. *To the Pacific with Lewis and Clark.* New York, American Heritage Publishing Co., 1967.

Bebenroth, Charlotta M. *Meriwether Lewis, Boy Explorer.* Indianapolis, Bobbs-Merrill Co., 1962.

Blassinghame, Wyatt. *Sacagawea, Indian Guide.* Champaign, Illinois, Garrard Publishing Co., 1965.

Bowman, Gerald. *With Lewis and Clark Through the Rockies.* London, F. Muller, 1964.

Chandler, Katherine. *The Bird-woman of the Lewis and Clark Expedition.* New York, Silver Burdett Co., 1905.

Churchill, Claire Werner. *South of the Sunset: an Interpretation of Sacajawea, the Indian Girl that Accompanied Lewis and Clark.* New York, R. R. Wilson Co., 1936.

Curl, Grace Voris. *Young Shannon, Scout with Lewis and Clark.* New York, Harper & Brothers, 1941.

De Kay, Ormonde. *The Adventures of Lewis and Clark.* New York, Random House, 1968.

Eifert, Virginia Louise. *George Shannon, Young Explorer with Lewis and Clark.* New York, Dodd, Mead & Co., 1963.

Emmons, Della G. *Sacajawea of the Shoshones.* Portland, Oregon, Binsfords and Mort, 1943.

Farnsworth, Frances Joyce. *Winged Moccasins, the Story of Sacajawea.* New York, Julian Messner, 1954.

Frazier, Neta. *Sacajawea, the Girl Nobody Knows*. New York, David McKay Co., 1967.

Howard, Bonnie C., and Ruth Higgins. *On the Trail with Lewis and Clark*. New York, Silver Burdett Co., 1939.

Kingsley, Nellie F. *The Story of Captain Meriwether Lewis and Captain William Clark*. Chicago, Werner School Book Co., 1900.

Montgomery, Elizabeth Rider. *World Explorers: Lewis and Clark*. Champaign, Illinois, Garrard Publishing Co., 1966.

Moorehead, Blanche Woods. *New World Builders: Thrilling Days with Lewis and Clark*. Philadelphia, The John C. Winston Co., 1937.

Munves, James. *We Were There with Lewis and Clark*. New York, Grosset & Dunlap, 1959.

Neuberger, Richard Lewis. *The Lewis and Clark Expedition*. New York, Random House, 1951.

Polking, Kirk. *Let's Go with Lewis and Clark*. New York, G. P. Putnam's Sons, 1963.

Sabin, Edwin L. *Opening the West with Lewis and Clark*. Philadelphia, J. B. Lippincott Co., 1917.

Schaare, C. Richard. *The Expedition of Lewis and Clark in Picture and Story*. New York, Cupples and Leon, 1940.

Schultz, James Willard. *Bird Woman (Sacajawea) the Guide of Lewis and Clark*. Boston, Houghton Mifflin Co., 1918.

Seibert, Jerry. *Sacajawea, Guide to Lewis and Clark*. Boston, Houghton Mifflin Co., 1960.

Seymour, Flora Warren. *Meriwether Lewis, Trail-blazer*. New York, D. Appleton-Century Co., 1937.

————. *Sacagawea: Bird Girl*, Indianapolis, Bobbs-Merrill Co., 1959.

Sprague, William Cyrus. *The Boy Pathfinder, a Story of the Oregon Trail*. Boston, Lee and Shepard, 1905.

Stoutenberg, Adrien, and Laura Nelson Baker. *Scannon, Dog with Lewis and Clark*. New York, Charles Scribner's Sons, 1959.

Stratemeyer, Edward. *Pioneer Boys of the Great Northwest: or, with Lewis and Clark Across the Rockies*. New York, Still Publishing Co., 1905.

Voight, Virginia Frances. *Sacajawea*. New York, G. P. Putnam's Sons, 1967.

Wade, Mary Hazelton. *The Trail Blazers: the Story of the Lewis and Clark Expedition*. Boston, Little, Brown & Co., 1924.

Wilkie, Katharine Elliott. *Will Clark, Boy in Buckskins*. Indianapolis, Bobbs-Merrill Co., 1963.

PERIODICAL LITERATURE, ESSAYS, AND MONOGRAPHS

Botany

Beidleman, R. G. "Lewis and Clark: Plant Collectors for a President," *Horticulture*, Vol. XLIV, No. 4 (April, 1966).

Burroughs, Raymond Darwin. "The Lewis and Clark Expedition's Botanical Discoveries," *Natural History*, Vol. LXXV, No. 1 (January, 1966).

Cutright, Paul Russell. "Lewis and Clark and Cottonwood," Missouri Historical Society *Bulletin*, Vol. XXII, No. 1 (October, 1965).

———. "Meriwether Lewis: Botanist," *Oregon Historical Quarterly*, Vol. LXIX, No. 2 (June, 1968).

———. "Well-travelled Plants of Lewis and Clark," *Frontiers*, Vol. XXXI, No. 3 (February, 1967).

Duboc, Jessie L. "Montana's Historic Bitterroot," *Nature Magazine*, Vol. XL (October, 1947).

Ewan, Joseph. "Frederick Pursh, 1774–1820, and His Botanical Associates," American Philosophical Society *Proceedings*, Vol. XCVI (1952).

Pennell, Francis W. "Historic Botanical Collections of the American Philosophical Society and the Academy of Natural Sciences of Philadelphia," American Philosophical Society *Proceedings*, Vol. XCIV (1950).

Rudd, Velva E. "Botanical Contributions of the Lewis and Clark Expedition," Washington Academy of Sciences *Journal*, Vol. XLIV (November, 1954).

True, Rodney Howard. "Some Neglected Botanical Results of the Lewis and Clark Expedition," American Philosophical Society *Proceedings*, Vol. LXVII (1928).

Ethnology

Ewers, John C. "The Indian Trade of the Upper Missouri Before Lewis and Clark: an Interpretation," Missouri Historical Society *Bulletin*, Vol. V, No. 4 (July, 1954).

———. "Plains Indians Reactions to Lewis and Clark," *Montana, the Magazine of Western History*, Vol. XVI, No. 1 (January, 1966).

Jackson, Donald. "Lewis and Clark Among the Oto," *Nebraska History*, Vol. XLI (September, 1960).

Ray, Verne F. "Lower Chinook Ethnographic Notes," *University of Washington Publications in Anthropology*, Vol. VII, No. 2 (May, 1938).

————, and Nancy O. Lurie. "The Contributions of Lewis and Clark to Ethnography," *Washington Academy of Sciences Journal,* Vol. XLIV (November, 1954).

Stirling, Matthew W. "Arikara Glassworking," *Washington Academy of Sciences Journal,* Vol. XXXVII, No. 8 (August, 1947).

Willoughby, Charles C. "A Few Ethnological Specimens Collected by Lewis and Clark," *American Anthropologist,* n.s., 7 (October-December, 1905).

Geography and Cartography

Abel, Annie Heloise. "A New Lewis and Clark Map," *Geographical Review,* Vol. I (May, 1916).

Allen, John L. "Lewis and Clark on the Upper Missouri: Decision at the Marias," *Montana, the Magazine of Western History,* Vol. XXI, No. 3 (Summer, 1971).

Appleman, Roy E. "Lewis and Clark: the Route 160 Years After," *Pacific Northwest Quarterly,* Vol. LVII, No. 1 (January, 1966).

————. "The Lost Site of Camp Wood: the Lewis and Clark Winter Camp, 1803–1804," *Journal of the West,* Vol. VII, No. 2 (1968).

Diller, Aubrey. "Maps of the Missouri River Before Lewis and Clark," *Studies and essays . . . in homage to George Sarton.* New York, 1946.

Douglas, Jesse S. "Lewis Map of 1806," *Military Affairs,* Vol. V (Spring, 1941).

Friis, Herman R. "Cartographic and Geographic Activities of the Lewis and Clark Expedition," *Washington Academy of Sciences Journal,* Vol. XLIV, No. 11 (November, 1954).

Gill, Larry. "The Great Portage," *Great Falls* (Montana) *Tribune,* August 15, 1965.

Jackson, Donald. "A New Lewis and Clark Map," Missouri Historical Society *Bulletin,* Vol. XVII, No. 2, Pt. 1 (January, 1961).

Koch, Elers. *Lewis and Clark Across the Bitterroot Range.* Missoula, Montana, Forest Service, U.S. Department of Agriculture, 1962.

————. "Lewis and Clark Route Retraced Across the Bitterroots," *Oregon Historical Quarterly,* Vol. XLI (June, 1940).

Peebles, John J. "Lewis and Clark in Idaho," *Idaho Historical Series,* 16, December, 1966.

————. "The Return Journey of Lewis and Clark," *Idaho Yesterdays,* Vol. X, No. 2 (Summer, 1966).

————. "Rugged Waters: Trails and Campsites of Lewis and Clark in the Salmon River Country," *Idaho Yesterdays,* Vol. VIII, No. 2 (Summer, 1964).

Space, Ralph S. *Lewis and Clark Through Idaho.* Lewiston, Idaho, Tribune Publishing Co., 1964.

West, Helen B. *Meriwether Lewis in Blackfeet Country.* Browning, Montana, Museum of the Plains Indians, Blackfeet Agency, Bureau of Indian Affairs, U.S. Department of the Interior, 1964.

Medicine

Beard, J. Howard. "Medical Observations and Practices of Lewis and Clark," *Scientific Monthly,* Vol. XX (May, 1925).

Chuinard, E. G. *The Medical Aspects of the Lewis and Clark Expedition.* Corvallis, Friends of the Library, Oregon State University, 1965.

Cutright, Paul Russell. "I gave him barks and saltpeter," *American Heritage,* Vol. XV, No. 1 (December, 1963).

Larsell, Olof. "Medical Aspects of the Lewis and Clark Expedition," *Surgery, Gynecology, and Obstetrics,* Vol. LXXXV (November, 1947).

Robinson, Doane. "The Medical Adventures of Lewis and Clark," *South Dakota Historical Collections,* Vol. XII (1924).

Stanley, L. L. "Medicine and Surgery of the Lewis and Clark Expedition," *Medical Journal and Record,* Vol. CXXVII (1928).

Will, Drake W. "The Medical and Surgical Practices of the Lewis and Clark Expedition," *Journal of the History of Medicine,* Vol. XIV (July, 1959).

Zoology

Cutright, Paul Russell. "Meriwether Lewis: Zoologist," *Oregon Historical Quarterly,* Vol. LXIX, No. 1 (March, 1968).

———. "The Odyssey of the Magpie and the Prairie Dog," *Missouri Historical Society Bulletin,* Vol. XXIII, No. 3 (April, 1967).

Faxon, Walter. "Relics of Peale's Museum," *Museum of Comparative Zoology Proceedings,* Vol. LIX (1915).

Harrison, H. H. "Wildlife Along the Lewis and Clark Trail," *National Wildlife,* Vol. VII (February, 1969).

Osgood, Ernest S. "A Prairie Dog for Mr. Jefferson," *Montana, the Magazine of Western History,* Vol. XIX, No. 2 (April, 1969).

Reid, Russell, and Clell C. Gannon. "Birds and Mammals Observed by Lewis and Clark in North Dakota," *North Dakota Historical Quarterly,* Vol. I (July, 1927).

Setzer, Henry H. "Zoological Contributions of the Lewis and Clark Expedition," *Washington Academy of Sciences Journal,* Vol. XLIV (November, 1954).

Miscellaneous

Adreon, William Clark. *William Clark of the Village of St. Louis, Missouri Territory*. St. Louis, Lewis and Clark Heritage Federation, 1970.

Alexander, D. B. "Tracking Down a Heritage; Reblazing the Wilderness Route of Lewis and Clark," *Parks and Recreation*, Vol. I (March, 1966).

Anderson, Augusta. "A List of Northwest Juveniles: the Lewis and Clark Expedition," *Pacific Northwest Quarterly*, Vol. XXXV (October, 1944).

Anderson, Irving W. "Probing the Riddle of the Bird Woman," *Montana, the Magazine of Western History*, Vol. XXIII, No. 4 (October, 1973).

Anderson, K. N. "Tracing the Trail of Lewis and Clark," *Today's Health*, Vol. XL (September, 1962).

Bahmer, Robert H. "The Case of the Clark Papers," *American Archivist*, Vol. XIX, No. 1 (January, 1956).

Bakeless, John. "Lewis and Clark's Background for Exploration," Washington Academy of Sciences *Journal*, Vol. XLIV (November, 1954).

Barbour, William R. "The Guns of Lewis and Clark," *Gun Digest*, 18th ed., 1964.

Bentley, James R. "Two Letters of Meriwether Lewis to Major William Preston," *Filson Club Historical Quarterly*, Vol. XLIV (April, 1970).

Brown, D. Alexander. "The Lewis and Clark Adventure," *American History Illustrated*, Vol. IV, Nos. 8–9 (December, 1969, and January, 1970).

———. "The Mysterious Death of a Hero," *American History Illustrated*, Vol. V, No. 9 (January, 1971).

Cappon, Lester J. "Who Is Author of *History of the Expedition Under the Command of Captains Lewis and Clark* (1814)?" *William and Mary Quarterly*, Vol. XIX, Pt. 2 (April, 1962).

Caywood, Louis R. "The Exploratory Excavation of Fort Clatsop," *Oregon Historical Quarterly*, Vol. XLIX, No. 3 (September, 1948).

Chatters, Roy Milton. "The Enigmatic Lewis and Clark Expedition Air Gun," *The Record* (Friends of the Library, Washington State University), Vol. XXXIV (1973).

Christophenson, Edmund. "Expedition West," *Montana, the Magazine of Western History*, Vol. V, No. 3 (Summer, 1955).

Clark, Ella E. "Watkuese and Lewis and Clark," *Western Folklore*, Vol. XII (July, 1953).

Clarke, Charles G. "The Roster of the Expedition of Lewis and Clark," *Oregon Historical Quarterly*, Vol. XLV, No. 4 (December, 1944).

Coues, Elliott. "An Account of the Various Publications Relating to the Travels of Lewis and Clarke [*sic*], with a Commentary on the Zoological Results of the Expedition," United States Geological and Geographical Survey of the Territories *Bulletin*, Ser. 2, No. 6 (February 8, 1876).

———. "Description of the Original Journals and Field Notes of Lewis & Clark, on which was based Biddle's History of the Expedition of 1804–1806, and which are now in the possession of the American Philosophical Society of Philadelphia," American Philosophical Society *Proceedings*, Vol. XXXI, No. 140 (1893).

———. "Notes on Mr. Thomas Meehan's Paper on the Plants of Lewis and Clark's Expedition Across the Continent, 1804–1806," *Academy of Natural Sciences of Philadelphia Proceedings*, Pt. 2 (April–September, 1898).

———. "Observations on *Picicorvus columbianus*," *The Ibis*, Vol. II, Ser. 3 (January, 1872).

Craig, Vernon. "Ride the Wide Missouri Historic Waterway," *Montana Wildlife*, November, 1965.

Crawford, Helen. "Sakakawea," *North Dakota Historical Quarterly*, Vol. I (April, 1927).

Crawford, Polly Pearl. "Lewis and Clark's Expedition as a Source of Poe's 'Journal of Julius Rodman'," University of Texas Studies in English, 12, 1932.

Creel, G. "Path of Empire," *Collier's*, Vol. LXXVII (April 17, 1926).

Cutright, Paul Russell. "Jefferson's Instructions to Lewis and Clark," Missouri Historical Society *Bulletin*, Vol. XXII, No. 3 (April, 1966).

———. "The Journal of Private Joseph Whitehouse: A Soldier with Lewis and Clark," Missouri Historical Society *Bulletin*, Vol. XXVII, No. 3 (April, 1972).

———. "Lewis and Clark and Du Pratz," Missouri Historical Society *Bulletin*, Vol. XXI, No. 1 (October, 1964).

———. "Lewis and Clark Begin a Journey," Missouri Historical Society *Bulletin*, Vol. XXIV, No. 1 (October, 1967).

———. "Lewis and Clark Indian Peace Medals," Missouri Historical Society *Bulletin*, Vol. XXIV, No. 2 (January, 1968).

———. "Lewis and Clark: Portraits and Portraitists," *Montana, the Magazine of Western History*, Vol. XIX, No. 2 (Spring, 1969).

———. "Meriwether Lewis on the Marias," *Montana, the Magazine of Western History*, Vol. XVIII, No. 3 (July, 1968).

————. "Meriwether Lewis Prepares for a Trip West," *Missouri Historical Society Bulletin*, Vol. XXIII, No. 1 (October, 1966).

DeVoto, Bernard. "An Inference Regarding the Expedition of Lewis and Clark," *American Philosophical Society Proceedings*, Vol. XCIX, No. 4 (1955).

————. "Passage to India; from Christmas to Christmas with Lewis and Clark," *Saturday Review of Literature*, Vol. XV (December 5, 1936).

————. "Turning Point for Lewis and Clark," *Harper's Magazine*, Vol. CCV (September, 1952).

Drury, Clifford M. "Sacajawea's Death—1812 or 1884?" *Oregon Historical Quarterly*, Vol. LXII, No. 3 (September, 1961).

Duboc, Jessie L. "Yellowstone Adventure," *Montana, the Magazine of Western History*, Vol. V, No. 3 (1955).

Ewan, Joseph. "Book Reviews: Scientific Americana," *Science*, Vol. CXXXIX (February 8, 1963).

Forrest, Earle E. "Patrick Gass, Carpenter of the Lewis and Clark Expedition," *Missouri Historical Society Bulletin*, Vol. IV (July, 1948).

Freeman, D. Curtis. "The Location of Historic Fort Clatsop," *Lewis and Clark Journal* (published to promote Lewis and Clark Exposition in Portland, Oregon) (1905).

Freeman, Lewis R. "Trailing History Down the Big Muddy: in the Homeward Wake of Lewis and Clark," *National Geographic Magazine*, Vol. LIV (July, 1928).

Garver, Frank Harmon. "Lewis and Clark in Beaverhead County [Montana]," *The Dillon* (Montana) *Examiner*, December 10, 1913. Reprint, 1964.

————. "The Story of Sergeant Charles Floyd," *Mississippi Valley Association Proceedings, 1908–1909* (1910).

Gray, Ralph. "Following the Trail of Lewis and Clark," *National Geographic Magazine*, Vol. CIII, No. 6 (June, 1953).

Guinness, Ralph B. "The Purpose of the Lewis and Clark Expedition," *Mississippi Valley Historical Review*, Vol. XX (June, 1933).

Hafen, Ann. *Baptiste Charbonneau*. Denver, Denver Brand Books, 1949.

Holman, Frederick V. "Lewis and Clark Expedition at Fort Clatsop," *Oregon Historical Quarterly*, Vol. XXVII, No. 3 (September, 1948).

Howard, Helen Addison. "The Mystery of Sacagawea's Death," *Pacific Northwest Quartery*, Vol. LVIII, No. 1 (January, 1967).

Hult, Ruby El. "Guns of the Lewis and Clark Expedition," *Pacific*

Northwest Historical Pamphlet, No. 1, Washington State Historical Society (1960).

Hunt, J. C. "Great Portage," *American Forestry*, Vol. LXXI (July, 1965).

Jackson, Donald. "A Footnote to the Lewis and Clark Expedition," *Manuscripts*, Vol. XXIV, No. 1 (Winter, 1972).

————. "On Reading Lewis and Clark: a Bibliographical Essay," *Montana, the Magazine of Western History*, Vol. XVIII, No. 3 (July, 1968).

————. "The Public Image of Lewis and Clark," *Pacific Northwest Quarterly*, Vol. LVII, No. 1 (October, 1967).

————. "The Race to Publish Lewis and Clark," *Pennsylvania Magazine of History and Biographies*, Vol. LXXXV, No. 2 (April, 1961).

————. "Some Advice for the Next Editor of Lewis and Clark," Missouri Historical Society *Bulletin*, Vol. XXIV, No. 1 (October, 1967).

————. "Some Books Carried by Lewis and Clark," Missouri Historical Society *Bulletin*, Vol. XVI, No. 1 (October, 1959).

James, Harry C. "Following the Footsteps of Lewis and Clark," *Westerners Brand Book*, Los Angeles (1949).

Janson, D. "Retracing the Lewis and Clark Trail," *New York Times*, February 26, 1967.

Jensen, Belva. "Trailing Lewis and Clark," *Natural History*, Vol. LXXVIII, No. 1 (August-September, 1969).

Jensen, M. "Pompey's Pillar," *American Forestry*, Vol. LXVII (April, 1961).

Kingston, C. S. "Sacajawea as a Guide, the Evaluation of a Legend," *Pacific Northwest Quarterly*, Vol. XXXV (January, 1944).

Kinkead, Ludie J. "How the Parents of George Roberts Clark Came to Kentucky in 1784–1785," *The History Quarterly*, Vol. III, No. 1 (October, 1928).

Korell, F. F. "American Trail Blazers," *National Republic*, Vol. XIX (October, 1931).

Laut, A. C. "Conquerors of the Northwest," *Travel*, Vol. XLVIII (March, 1927).

Lee, J. T. "Sergeant Ordway's Notebook," *The Nation*, Vol. XCVIII (April 16, 1914).

Lewis, Andrew T. "Meriwether Lewis," *Oregon Historical Quarterly*, Vol. VI, No. 4 (December, 1905).

Lewis, Grace. "Financial Records: Expedition to the Pacific Ocean," Missouri Historical Society *Bulletin*, Vol. X, No. 4, Pt. 1 (July, 1954).

————. "The First Home of Governor Lewis in Louisiana Territory," *Missouri Historical Society Bulletin*, Vol. XIV, No. 4 (July, 1958).

Lincoln, A. "Jefferson and the West," *Pacific Discovery*, Vol. XVII, No. 1 (January–February, 1964).

Loos, John Louis. "They Opened the Door to the West," *The Humble Way*, Vol. III, 364 (1964).

————. "William Clark's Part in the Preparation of the Lewis and Clark Expedition," *Missouri Historical Society Bulletin*, Vol. X, No. 4, Pt. 1 (July, 1954).

McClelland, J. M., Jr. *Lewis and Clark in the Fort Columbia Area.* Ilwaco, Washington, Tribune Publishing Co., 1955.

McDermott, John Francis. "William Clark's Museum Once More," *Missouri Historical Society Bulletin*, Vol. XVI, No. 2 (January, 1960).

————. "William Clark: Pioneer Museum Man," *Washington Academy of Sciences Journal*, Vol. XLIV (1954).

Mattes, Merrill J. "On the Trail of Lewis and Clark with Thomas Hart Benton," *Montana, the Magazine of Western History*, Vol. XVI, No. 3 (July, 1966).

Meany, Edmond S. "Doctor Saugrain Helped Lewis and Clark," *Washington Historical Quarterly*, Vol. XXII (1931).

Meehan, Thomas. "The Plants of the Lewis and Clark Expedition Across the Continent, 1804–1806," *Academy of Natural Sciences of Philadelphia Proceedings*, Pt. 1 (January–March, 1898).

Meriwether, Lee. "Meriwether Lewis—His Work and Place in History," *Virginia Magazine of History*, Vol. XLV (January, 1937).

Neuberger, Richard Lewis. "The Lochsa, Realm of History and Grandeur," *Montana, the Magazine of Western History*, Vol. IV, No. 3 (Summer, 1954).

————. "Our Greatest Exploration," *Reader's Digest*, Vol. XXXVIII (March, 1941).

————. "They're Taming the Lolo Trail," *Saturday Evening Post*, April 10, 1954.

Osgood, Ernest S. "The Return Journey in 1806: William Clark on the Yellowstone," *Montana, the Magazine of Western History*, Vol. XVIII, No. 3 (July, 1968).

Overland, Helen Howard. "Fabled Friendship—Lewis and Clark," *Montana, the Magazine of Western History*, Vol. V, No. 3 (Summer, 1955).

Peattie, Donald Culross. "Nature of Things," *Audubon Magazine*, Vol. XLIV (March, 1942).

Petersen, William J. "The Lewis and Clark Expedition," *Palimpsest*, Vol. XXXV (September, 1954).

Phelps, Dawson A. "The Tragic Death of Meriwether Lewis," *William and Mary Quarterly*, Vol. XIII, Ser. 3 (July, 1956).

Pollard, Lancaster. *Lewis and Clark at Fort Clatsop, 1805–1806.* Astoria, Clatsop County Historical Society, 1962.

———. *Lewis and Clark at Seaside, Oregon.* Seaside, Chamber of Commerce, 1954.

Poole, Edwin A. "Charbono's Squar," *The Pacific Northwesterner*, Vol. VIII, No. 1 (Winter, 1964).

Pringle, L. A. "Sacajawea of the Shoshones," *American Mercury*, Vol. XXXI (July, 1955).

Quaife, Milo M. "Some New-found Records of the Lewis and Clark Expedition," *Mississippi Valley Historical Review*, Vol. II, No. 1 (June, 1915).

Rees, John E. *Madame Charbonneau.* Salmon, Idaho, Lemhi County Historical Society, 1970.

———. "The Shoshoni Contribution to Lewis and Clark," *Idaho Yesterdays*, No. 2, 1958.

Reid, Russell. *Sakakawea, the Bird Woman.* Bismarck, State Historical Society of North Dakota, 1950.

Robinson, Doane, "Lewis and Clark in South Dakota," *South Dakota Historical Collections*, Vol. IX (1918).

Ross, N. W. "Heroine in Buckskin," *Reader's Digest*, Vol. XLIV (February, 1944).

Russell, Carl P. "The Guns of the Lewis and Clark Expedition," *North Dakota History*, Vol. XXVII (Winter, 1960).

Ruth, Kent. "Autograph Albums of the West," *Ford Times*, Vol. LVI, No. 6 (June, 1963).

Sanford, M. C. "Sacajawea, the Bird-woman," *Woman's Home Companion*, Vol. XXXII (June 5, 1905).

Shaul, David L. "The Meaning of the Name Sacajawea," *Annals of Wyoming*, Vol. XLIV (Fall, 1972).

Smith, James and Kathryn. "Sedulous Sergeant, Patrick Gass," *Montana, the Magazine of Western History*, Vol. V, No. 3 (Summer, 1955).

Space, Ralph S. *The Lolo Trail: A History of Events Connected with the Lolo Trail Since Lewis and Clark.* Lewiston, Idaho, Printcraft Printing Co., 1970.

Stearns, Harold G. "Lewis and Clark Trail: Historic Avenue Across

America," *Montana, the Magazine of Western History*, Vol. XIV, No. 1 (January, 1964).

Stuckert, Gilbert F. "Whither the Wide Missouri?" *National Parks Magazine*, August, 1965.

Swain, J. "Natchez Trace: a Journey to the Grave of Meriwether Lewis," *Everybody's*, Vol. XIII (1905).

Taber, Ronald W. "Sacagawea and the Suffragettes—an Interpretation," *Pacific Northwest Quarterly*, Vol. LVIII, No. 1 (January, 1967).

Teggart, Frederick John. "Notes Supplementary to Any Edition of Lewis and Clark," American Historical Association *Annual Report for the Year 1908*, Vol. I (1909).

Thwaites, Reuben Gold. "Lewis and Clark: Discoverers of Empire," *Christendom*, Vol. I, No. 12 (July 4, 1905).

———. "The Story of Lewis and Clark's Journals," American Historical Association *Annual Report for the Year 1903*, 58 Cong., 2 sess., *House Doc. 109*.

———. "William Clark: Soldier, Explorer, Statesman," Missouri Historical Society *Collections*, Vol. II, No. 7 (October, 1906).

Tomkins, Calvin. "The Lewis and Clark Case," *The New Yorker*, October 29, 1966.

U.S. Department of the Interior. *Lewis and Clark, a Brief Account of Their Expedition*. Washington, Government Printing Office, 1962.

———. *The Lewis and Clark Trail: Final Report of the Lewis and Clark Trail Commission*. Washington, Government Printing Office, 1970.

———. *The Lewis and Clark Trail: A Proposal for Development*. Washington, Government Printing Office, 1965.

———. *A Proposed Lewis and Clark National Wilderness Waterway*. Omaha, Mid-west Regional Office, National Park Service, 1962.

U.S. Department of Agriculture. *Lewis and Clark Trail Through the National Forests*. Missoula, Montana, Northern Region, Forest Service, 1965.

Watkins, George T. "Washington State's Lewis and Clark Medal," *The Record* (Washington State University, Friends of the Library), Pullman, 1965.

Weddle, Ferris. "The Lewis and Clark Trail Today," *The Spokesman Review*, March 16, 1969.

West, Helen B. "The Lewis and Clark Expedition: Our National Epic," *Montana, the Magazine of Western History*, Vol. XVI, No. 3 (July, 1966).

Wheeler, Olin D. "Trail of Lewis and Clark," *Sunset*, Vol. XVI (February, 1906).

Wood, R. K. "Lewis and Clark Expedition," *Mentor*, Vol. VII (May 1, 1919).

Yates, Ted. "Since Lewis and Clark," *The American West*, Vol. II, No. 4 (Fall, 1965).

Young, Frederick George. "The Higher Significance in the Lewis and Clark Expedition," *Oregon Historical Quarterly*, Vol. VI, No. 1 (March, 1905).

————. "The Lewis and Clark Expedition in American History," *Oregon Historical Quarterly*, Vol. II, No. 4 (December, 1901).

Zahniser, H. "Towards the West," *Nature Magazine*, Vol. XLVIII (December, 1955).

Zochert, Donald. "This Nation Never Saw a Black Man," *American Heritage*, Vol. XXII, No. 2 (February, 1971).

DISSERTATIONS

Allen, John L. "The Geographical Images of the American Northwest." Unpublished. Clark University, 1969.

Loos, John Louis. "A Biography of William Clark, 1770–1813." Unpublished. Washington University, 1953.

McDonald, Mary Jane. "The Lewis and Clark Expedition: the Return Trip." Unpublished. St. Louis University, 1970.

SHORT TITLES

Biddle edition
Coues, *History*
Gass, *Journal*
Jackson, *Letters*
Osgood, *Field Notes*
Quaife, *Ordway*
Thwaites, *Original Journals*

Index

The following abbreviations are used in this index:

ANS, Academy of Natural Sciences of Philadelphia

APS, American Philosophical Society

L & C, Lewis and Clark

LCE, Lewis and Clark Expedition

ML, Meriwether Lewis

TJ, Thomas Jefferson

WC, William Clark

a Voyage up the Missouri in 1811 by, 98; description of Big White, 113
Bradbury, John: 189n., 209; *Travels in the Interior of America* by, 209
Bradford and Inskeep: 84; agree to publish L&C journals, 62; re copies of L&C printed, 64; letter of Biddle to, 66
Bran: 174 & n.
Branding iron (of ML): 227
Bratton, William: 24
Brooks, Noah: 203n.
Brown, Robert T.: 151
Brown, Stewardson: 111; Thwaites letter to re L&C Herbarium, 110; botanical notes to Thwaites, 112
Brown University: 63
Brownsville, Pa.: 8
Buchanan, James (son of president): Gass builds house for, 23
Buckeye: 139
Buffalo: 77–78, 232, 249, 252, 253, 260; overgrazing by, 260
Buffaloberry: 100
Bullboat: 132, 234
Bureau of American Ethnology: 86, 87
Burr, Aaron: 141
Burroughs, John: re observational ability, 141
Burroughs, Raymond Darwin: *The Natural History of the Lewis and Clark Expedition* by, 209; re botany of LCE, 213
Bush, Joseph (artist): portrait of WC, 229, 229n.
Burton Historical Collection (Detroit Public Library): 144

Cahokia, Ill.: 146; visitors to Camp Dubois from, 165
Cameahwait (Shoshoni chief): presents robe to ML, 45
Camp Chopunnish, Ida.: 134; named by Coues, 99
Camp Disappointment, Mont.: 177n.
Cape Disappointment: 238; named by Capt. John Meares, 253
Camp Dubois: 134, 138, 150, 158, 161,

164, 165, 167, 238, 244; Gass at, 24; original site of, 164; visited by men from St. Louis, 165; arrival of Drouillard at, 166
Camp of Brareowes: *see* Council Bluffs
Camp of the Badgers: *see* Council Bluffs
Camp White Catfish: 179
Candle fish: *see Eulachon*
Cannonball River: 235
Canoe Camp, Ida.: 131
Canoe Camp, Mont.: 259
Cappon, Lester J.: re history of LCE, 217
Carey, Mathew: 225; publishes Gass's journal, 29; engravings for Gass's journal, 30, 31; biographical sketch of, 30
Carlisle, Pa.: 22, 23
Caroline County, Va.: 4
Cartography: L&C articles re, 215–16
Carver, Jonathan: 35
"Cash Book" (of WC): re Ordway's death, 135n.
Catfish Camp (now Washington, Pa.): 22
Catfish, great blue: 142, 256
Catlin, George: 101, 177, 206, 232, 238, 241; biographical sketch of, 133; makes portrait of WC, 229, 233; early years of, 232; drawings of Mandan Indians by, 233–34; *Letters and Notes on the Manners, Customs, and Conditions of the N.A. Indians* by, 233; letters of to N.Y. *Commercial Advertiser*, 233
Caton's Rangers: Gass joins, 22
Cedar: 256
Celilo Falls: 101, 227; portrayed by Schwarz, 236n.
Centrocercus urophasianus: *see* grouse, sage
Century Dictionary: Coues as editor of, 80, 81, 103
Chaboillez, Charles: 178n.
Chambersburg, Pa.: 22
Charbonneau, Baptiste: 236
Charbonneau, Touissant: 24, 197, 220, 221, 236

27, 113, 122, 133, 159, 209, 242n.;
hiatuses in, 9, 115n., 243, 251n.;
purchased by Dodd, Mead, 114; at
N.Y. Historical Society, 114; sold to
Ayer, 115; Newberry Library obtains, 115; discovered by Thwaites,
128; re completion of, 263; L&C
help in writing of, 263
Journals (Whitehouse rewrite): *242–64*
Juniper: 123

Kamiah, Idaho: 99
Kane, Lucile M.: 156n., 243; talks with
Mrs. Vytlacil, 145; visits Mrs. Foster's home, 145–46; re Gen. Hammond's desk, 146; recognizes "Field
Notes" of WC, 146; turns to Osgood,
147; assists Osgood, 151
Kansas Indians: 233
Kaskaskia: 165, 244, 245, 262; L&C
arrive at, 23; Gass stationed at, 23;
L&C find Ordway at, 133; location
of, 244n.
Kaskaskia River: 138
Keelboat: 8
Kentucky: "nine young men from," 263
Kentucky Gazette (Lexington): re account of LCE ascent of Missouri to
Ft. Mandan, 173
Kickapoo Indians: 255; visit WC at
Camp Dubois, 166
Kieran, John: re bird biographies by
Coues, 79; re Coues, 96
King, Charles Bird: 240 & n.
King, Nicholas: and composite map requested by Gallatin, 190–91
Kingsley, Nellie F.: 203n.
Kingston, C. S.: re Sacagawea as guide
to LCE, 198, 217
Knife River: 12, 257, 258
Knistenaux (Cree) Indians: 35
Knowlton, F. H.: 87n.
Koch, Elers: re Lolo Trail, 216

Labiche, François: 255
Labrador: Coues's trip to, 74
La Charette, Mo.: 251, 254
Lady's slipper, mountain: 100

Lafayette, General: 30; letter to WC,
125n.
Lane, William Carr: letter to WC,
125n.
Larsell, Olaf: re medical aspects of LCE,
212
La Terre Blanc River: *see* White Earth
River
Lawrence, Kan.: Indian Office moved to,
175
Lawson, Alexander: 230 & n.
Lawyer's Creek, Ida.: 135n.
Lebanon, Pa.: 36
Ledyard, John: 3
Lee, Guy Carlton: 116
Lemhi River: 221
Lemhi Pass: 261
Lester, Hubbard: publishes apocryphal
L&C, 34
Lesueur, Charles: 47–48 & n., 230 & n.;
zoological contributions of, 48
Lettuce: 258
Lewis and Clark: 178, 268; instructions from TJ, 5; journals of,
11 & n.; shipments of from Ft. Mandan to TJ, 12; re transcription of
journals, 15; apocryphal likenesses
of, 37, 38, 225; authentic portraits
of, 84, 228–29; number of words in
journals of, 132n.; find Ordway at
Kaskaskia, 133; entrust Ordway with
missions, 134; at mouth of Wood
River, 146; site of Camp Dubois predetermined by, 164; societies, trail
commissions, National Historical
Landmarks, and trail markers of,
177; search for maps at Camp Dubois, 190–91; importance of maps to,
192; and Dr. Saugrain, 197; as competent naturalists, 209; drawings of,
229–31; discoverers of wood rat,
230; re sworn testament of Whitehouse, 244; religious sentiments of,
251; re number of Mandan Indians,
253; carry map by Vancouver, 253–
54; obtain horses at St. Charles, 254;
exchanging of information with sub-

his collection, 119; WC's collection of at Yale, 156; of U.S. Geological Survey, 165; of Northwest by WC, 166; sent by TJ to ML, 167, 192; sent by Harrison to WC, 167; of Lower Missouri by WC, 179; first of LCE, 184; carried by LCE, 184; of Indian Office, 184; studied by ML and TJ, 190; requested of King by Gallatin, 190–91; importance of to L&C, 192; drawn by Soulard, 194; final one by WC, 216; of WC as illustrations, 225; of *Original Journals*, 228; of WC, 228–29, 266; of Vancouver, 253

Marietta, Ohio: 140; ML arrives at, 141

Marias River: 221, 233; ML explores, 24

Marmotte: *see* prairie dog

Marshall, Moses: 3

Martha's Vineyard: heath hen last seen on, 142

Massachusetts Historical Society: 184, 193

Matches, sulphur: of Dr. Saugrain, 197

Mathews, Alfred E.: 240n.; *Pencil Sketches of Montana* by, 240

Maumee Indians: visit WC at Camp Dubois, 166

Maximilian, Prince of Wied-Neuweid: 98n., 101, 209; and Karl Bodmer, 233

Meadowlark, western: 235

Meares, John: names Cape Disappointment, 253

Medals, Indian Peace: 217, 239

Medicine: L&C articles re, 212–13

Meehan, Thomas: and L&C herbarium, 110n.

Melville, Herman: 177

Mercersburg, Pa.: 22

Meriwether, William: letter from WC to, 55

Metzdorf, Robert: 156, 157, 160, 170, 172

Michaux, André: 3; TJ's instructions to, 4

Milk River: 258

Miller, Alfred Jacob: 232

Mimulus lewisii: *see* monkey flower, Lewis's

Minnetares: *see* Hidatsa Indians

Minnesota Historical Society: 145, 147, 148, 152, 153, 154, 243; claims ownership of "Field Notes," 152; Osgood major witness for, 157

Minnesota Historical Society *v*. United States of America: 157, 163, 265–69

Mississippi River: 164

Mississippi State Department of Archives: 183

Mississippi Valley Historical Review: 144

Mistletoe: described by ML, 143

Mitchell, James T.: 119

Mitchell, John: 190

Mitchill, Samuel: *Medical Repository* of, 189

Missouri Botanical Garden: 112n.

Missouri breaks: 233, 260; drawings of by Bodmer, 234

Missouri Fur Company: 233

Missouri Historical Society: 126n., 169, 182, 183, 194; repository of L&C journals, 11n.; L&C letters at, 15n., 54; L&C material willed to by Mrs. Voorhis, 125; minutes of, 125n.; and "Saline" article by ML, 193; award of to Jackson, 200

Missouri River: 16ff.

Missouri River Commission: maps of, 99, 136

Monkey flower, Lewis's: 231

Monroe, James: Biddle secretary of, 58; names Biddle bank director, 71; letter of to WC, 125n.

Monticello: 12; and L&C specimens, 44; ML arrives at, 54; moose antlers of L&C at, 214n.

Moorehead, Alan: 200

Moose: antlers of at Monticello, 214n.

Morgan Library: 154, 155

Morgenthau, Henry: 268

Mouse River: 78

Muhlenberg, Henry: 67n., 189n., 196